ADVANCE PRAISE FOR *CUTTING EDGE*

"*Cutting Edge* is an incredibly timely and personal examination of hockey at its cultural crossroads. Daniel Gawthrop honours the beauty of the game while confronting the masculinity, gatekeeping, and institutional hesitation that have shaped it while seamlessly highlighting LGBTQ+ milestones in the sport's history. Gawthrop argues persuasively that queerness is not outside hockey's history and is certainly part of its future. This book is a treasure trove of information. 5 stars."
—Ren Dawe, Education and Programs Director, You Can Play

"Love letter, reminiscence, and critique by a lifelong hockey fan, here's a comprehensive and progressive account of what the sport is—and can become. Impressively, too, Daniel Gawthrop's enthusiasm is infectious enough to keep me—a lifelong hockey nonfan—wholly engrossed."
—Brett Josef Grubisic, author of *The Age of Cities* and *My Two-Faced Luck*

"Can anyone besides white straight bros truly love a game as rife with ugly fights, casual racism, and toxic masculinity as hockey? That screaming you hear from the stands is women, LGBTQ+, and racialized fans shouting 'Of course!' Still, in the National Hockey League's 109-year history, no active player has ever come out as gay. In his exploration of the alternative game, Daniel Gawthrop shows us that it doesn't have to be this way. *Cutting Edge* is a must-read for queer hockey lovers—in all senses of the phrase."
—Carellin Brooks, author of *One Hundred Days of Rain*

CUTTING EDGE

CUTTING EDGE

HOCKEY AS QUEER CULTURE

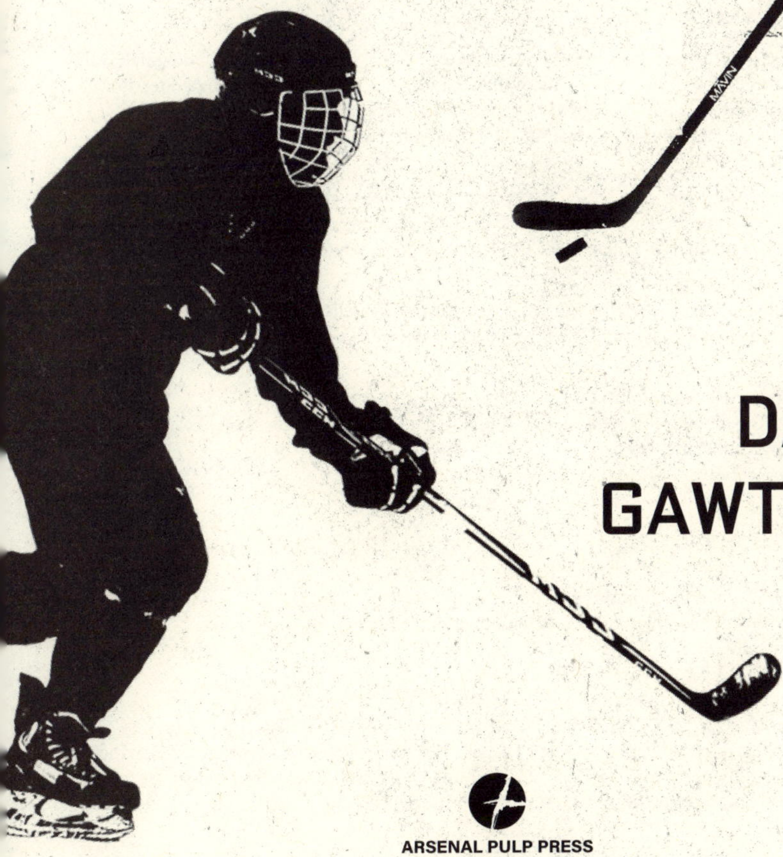

DANIEL GAWTHROP

ARSENAL PULP PRESS
VANCOUVER

CUTTING EDGE

ARSENAL PULP PRESS
Suite 202 – 211 East Georgia St.
Vancouver, BC V6A 1Z6
Canada
arsenalpulp.com

The publisher gratefully acknowledges the support of the Canada Council for the Arts and the British Columbia Arts Council for its publishing program and the Government of Canada and the Government of British Columbia (through the Book Publishing Tax Credit Program) for its publishing activities.

Arsenal Pulp Press acknowledges the xʷməθkʷəy̓əm (Musqueam), Sḵwx̱wú7mesh (Squamish), and səlilwətaɬ (Tsleil-Waututh) Nations, custodians of the traditional, ancestral, and unceded territories where our office is located. We pay respect to their histories, traditions, and continuous living cultures and commit to accountability, respectful relations, and friendship.

Arsenal Pulp Press is committed to reducing the consumption of non-renewable resources in the making of our books wherever possible. We make every effort to use materials that support a sustainable future. This book is printed on paper made with 100 percent sustainable recycled fibre content.

EU Safety Regulations authorized representative: Easy Access System Europe,
Mustamäe tee 50, 10621 Tallinn, Estonia, gpsr.requests@easproject.com.

Cover and text design by Rebecca Poulin
Cover art created by Rebecca Poulin with modified photos by Gerhard Crous / Unsplash
Edited and indexed by Catharine Chen
Proofread by Alison Strobel

Printed and bound in Canada

Library and Archives Canada Cataloguing in Publication:
Title: Cutting edge : hockey as queer culture / Daniel Gawthrop.
Names: Gawthrop, Daniel, author
Description: Includes index.
Identifiers: Canadiana (print) 20260140589 | Canadiana (ebook) 20260140597 |
ISBN 9781834050485 (softcover) | ISBN 9781834050492 (EPUB)
Subjects: LCSH: Sexual minorities and sports. | LCSH: Hockey—Social aspects. | LCSH: Hockey players—Social conditions. | LCSH: Gay athletes. | LCSH: Masculinity in sports.
Classification: LCC GV847 .G39 2026 | DDC 796.962086/6—dc23

To queer hockey players everywhere,
and to Vancouver's LGBTQ+ hockey association, the Cutting Edges,
especially
#33 Kevin Griffin (the Builder)
#16 Trevor MacNeil (Heart & Soul)

CONTENTS

INTRODUCTION

After being dominated for more than a century by straight white males and their unchecked privilege, Canadian hockey culture finally got a day of reckoning with the recent Hockey Canada scandals, including the sexual assault trial of the "London Five." The end of the old boys' network's hold on our national sport began in 2022 with revelations that Hockey Canada used player registration fees to settle sexual misconduct cases. It culminated in 2025 with the acquittal of five members of the national Junior men's team accused of raping a woman while celebrating their 2018 gold medal victory. Media coverage of these events exposed the extent of toxic masculinity's contamination of our Junior hockey system—the prime development source for the National Hockey League—and the hockey world at large. During this time, it seemed the only good news for hockey culture was the birth of the Professional Women's Hockey League. Fan interest in the PWHL was so strong that it was clear Canadians, especially women and queer folk, were starving for a different kind of hockey, a new hockey culture.

Then along came *Heated Rivalry*, the television series whose sensational launch near the end of 2025 changed the conversation completely. Viewers—and readers of the books that inspired the screen version—couldn't get enough of the deepening gay relationship between Shane Hollander and Ilya Rozanov, two major league hockey stars (one Canadian, the other Russian) who play for different teams and find themselves falling hard for each other while keeping their relationship secret for nearly eight years. Crave renewed *Heated Rivalry* for another season after several countries purchased broadcast rights. Hockey as queer culture has been on a rapid upswing ever since, and that's where *Cutting Edge* comes in.

By "queer culture," I am referring primarily to sexual and gender identities that fall outside of the heteronormative. But my definition is a little broader. Despite the more lamentable qualities of Canadian hockey culture—especially its long-time dominance by straight white cisgender men wary of others entering their sacred space—the best qualities of the game have always appealed to those who have been marginalized by it. We know that hockey can be good, so "queerness" in this context also recognizes the women's game, which undermines the orthodox men's game in glorious ways. And it recognizes the courage and contributions of non-white players whose presence makes the game more representative of our society at large.

But hockey can't build on its own queer culture without first exorcising the ghosts of its homophobic and misogynistic past. And that requires a deep dive into the history of orthodox masculinity in the game, dating back to its origins. What is it about our national sport that has enabled so much white hetero male entitlement? Why did the women's game disappear for decades after such a good start? Why did so many gay men of a certain age turn away from hockey during their teens, while others would have nothing to do with it at all? And why has it taken so long for the NHL to get the memo that you shouldn't call another guy a "cocksucker" unless you're complimenting his skills? This book answers these questions and more.

Cutting Edge is not an academic text but pop culture commentary grounded by memoir. It is as much a personal exploration of my own relationship with the sport as an inquiry into the sociopolitical evolution of hockey at its highest levels.

In this, I am proud to declare no skin in the game. That is, I am not an employee of the NHL, Hockey Canada, or any other mainstream hockey organization. (Thus I am not a former player, coach, general manager, or broadcaster whose name on the cover would indicate reputation in the sport.) I was never more than a beer league third liner at best, and now I'm an old-timer whose skills as a forward can best be described as "perpetually intermediate." Nor, as a writer, am I part of the hockey journalism fraternity, still a significant pillar of mainstream straight male hockey culture. As a cis gay intellectual, my relationship with Canada's national sport is complex. There are countless others like me whose love for the game was destroyed at puberty, when locker-room politics put us at odds with the hockey world we presumed to be part of and led us to a gay world that could make no sense of it. Part of my mission is to build on the groundbreaking work of *Heated Rivalry* and its creators, showrunner Jacob Tierney and author Rachel Reid, to reconcile these two worlds.

Cutting Edge is for every queer person who has ever thought of playing hockey and for the many of us who did or still do. It's also for the straight hockey fan who wonders why the game has caused such torment for so many of us. But it's not for everyone. The title alone should turn off the kind of hockey fan who visits his NHL team's Facebook page every Pride Night just to gaslight queer fans as if we're not in the same forum. You know the type: the trolls who ridicule "woke culture" and spread their hate from the cowardice of anonymity. Stupid homophobes are an ongoing problem for the NHL's diversity campaigns, as they represent a major source of revenue. Would the NHL lose fans by banning fighting? Probably. But it would gain so many more, and better ones, by doing so. And that is another purpose of queer culture in hockey: to make the sport better, more appealing, and more welcoming for a broader fan base.

Given the long history of hockey bigotry specifically targeting gay men, there was bound to be more content here on the gay male perspective than on other queer hockey experiences. Although I have dedicated chapters to the women's game and to trans/non-binary perspectives, I encourage readers to look into organizations such as You Can Play, which has done excellent work to combat gender policing and gender discrepancy in hockey and which highlights the importance of minor hockey codes of conduct in helping to foster a healthier youth hockey culture. (These include protocols for better educating coaches and for increasing awareness of how early locker-room culture shapes masculinity—subjects that Rick Westhead probed in his outstanding 2025 book, *We Breed Lions: Confronting Canada's Troubled Hockey Culture*.)

The story of the hockey association that shares this book's title is about much more than the personal pride I take in having co-founded it. Vancouver's Cutting Edges, who hit the ice for their thirty-third season in 2026–27, are just one in a constellation of queer hockey organizations that have cropped up all over North America and even in Australia, further empowering sexual and gender minorities in our relationship to the game while showing the rest of the world how much better hockey can be when sexuality and gender identity/expression are validated instead of vilified, when toxic masculinity is not part of the mix. (All opinions expressed in *Cutting Edge* are mine alone, by the way; that is, I am strictly a player member who neither speaks for the Cutting Edges organization nor holds a position on its board of directors.)

As always, it is in the mainstream hockey world—especially the NHL—that change has been glacial. I offer a hint of this while recalling a brief moment in the early 1990s when, in an article, I declared (stating the obvious) that Vancouver Canucks superstar Pavel Bure was "drop-dead gorgeous." For sharing such an opinion in public while male, I received more national exposure than I later would for any of my published books. I had stepped out of my lane, presuming to speak frankly on matters from which gay men were excluded.

Professional hockey remains a forbidding place for queer men to be completely themselves. To this day, the NHL—the game's ultimate authority—remains the last bastion of homophobia, the final major professional sports league never to have had an openly gay roster player. While You Can Play has done its part to raise awareness, the irony-deficient NHL remains so fiercely protective of its traditionally masculine branding that it doesn't have any clue how to welcome an openly gay player. (The only player under NHL contract ever to come out was Nashville's Luke Prokop in 2021. But, five years later, he's in another team's minor league system and, as I write, has yet to make it to "the Show.")

And so I've supplemented *Cutting Edge* with an appendix that offers NHL clubs a media plan to assist players who might be considering coming out or who are ready to take the plunge. In presuming such assistance to be welcome, I recognize that NHL teams and players alike place the highest value on team dynamics, discouraging publicity that centres the player at the expense of the team. So my plan includes specific ways to avoid becoming a distraction from the business of winning. If the player and his team execute the plan properly, the payoff will be considerable—both for them and for the game itself.

Daniel Gawthrop
New Westminster, BC
April 2026

"Ten men hurtling around a fenced perimeter with glorious speed. Cuts, switches, abrupt stops and misdirections. Hits, bumps, a focused grit and then the sweeping ballet of the open ice, the action funnelling down to a point where it became just the stick, the puck, the pads, the net, the red light and the klaxon sound of the buzzer that sent thousands erupting into glee. It thrilled me."

—RICHARD WAGAMESE, *Indian Horse*

"Watch the puck for dear life. *The puck* is *life ...*

. . . .

But you can take it, you're committed now (it's somehow like being a Red Crosse Knight in the service of Una), as you watch the puck, that has its own life among the players, in the game (that is worth the candle)"

—GEORGE STANLEY, "The Puck"

Hobey Baker in uniform as an airman during the Great War; the myth-making began soon after his death in 1918

PROLOGUE

Hockey's First Gay Superstar

A hundred and ten years ago, a brilliant young American athlete exploded into the hockey world, his star shining brighter than those of most of his contemporaries. A highly gifted playmaker who worked his magic on the ice for Princeton University, he would never see a minute of action in the professional game but would one day be regarded as the best hockey player in history never to have played in the National Hockey League. In 1945, twenty-seven years after his death and the year after the NHL's formation (1917), he became one of the first nine inductees into the Hockey Hall of Fame. In 1980, the National Collegiate Athletic Association honoured his memory by establishing a prestigious annual award to the top American male university hockey player. This athlete's name was Hobart Amory Hare Baker—Hobey Baker.

Hockey historian Michael McKinley has described Baker as "a classically handsome American pilot" who "came from an aristocratic Philadelphia family."[1] Thanks to inherited wealth, Baker could afford to turn down professional offers—including from the Montreal Canadiens—because he didn't need the money. He played for the joy of the game. "Being a privileged American at the turn of the twentieth century," wrote McKinley, "gave Baker a lofty height from which to view the world and, from where he stood, the world was his. Sporting prowess, friends, women, fame, and victory came so easily that he didn't have to think about it—until it was gone."[2]

Okay, let's put aside that "women" part for a moment. Here's the official story on Baker.

According to his authoritative biography, Hobey Baker was America's first hockey superstar.[3] He was so good that, as a fifteen-year-old winger, he led his schoolboy roster to a 4–0 win over a Princeton University team. Naturally gifted at every sport, he first made his mark in football after arriving at Princeton as a student himself. During his freshman year, he once ran the length of the field to score the winning touchdown against archrival Yale. As Princeton's all-American captain, Baker's exploits on the field were so well known that Woodrow Wilson, on the day he was elected US president, was said to have dropped by the Princeton campus to watch him practise. Philadelphia sportswriters dubbed him "the blond Adonis of the gridiron," partly because he played football without a helmet.[4]

But hockey was Baker's real passion. Fans attended his games just to watch him skate rings around the opposition. He was such a fast skater that he could blow past opponents without having to fake them out, and his shot was so hard he could score from centre ice. By 1913, when he was twenty-one, the *Boston Journal* called him "the greatest amateur hockey player ever developed in this country or in Canada."[5] After graduating from Princeton the next year, Baker went to Wall Street but soon grew bored of working for J.P. Morgan. Two years later, with World War I raging, he joined a squadron of American pilots based in France as part of the French Air Service. By spring 1918, the Lafayette Squadron became part of the US Armed Forces. Baker saw his first action in the Great War.

His legend only grew in Europe. Promoted to captain and commander of his unit, he won a French Cross for shooting down an enemy plane over Ypres and set the record for the steepest ascent of an airplane. After the war ended, he wanted to stay in northern France for a while, but his request was denied. On December 21,

1918, Baker was due to board a train to Paris for the trip back home. But first, he decided to take one last flight from the airfield where his squadron was stationed, choosing a plane that had just undergone repairs. Shortly after taking off in heavy rain, he was attempting one of his daring vertical ascents when the engine failed. Not far from the airfield, his plane took a nosedive and crashed, killing him. He was twenty-six.

The mythologizing began two years after Baker's death, when fellow Princetonian F. Scott Fitzgerald published his debut novel, *This Side of Paradise*. A Jazz Age story about carefree American youth, the novel included a character, Allenby, said to be based on Baker. "He was an ideal worthy of everything in my enthusiastic admiration," Fitzgerald once said of him, "yet consummated and expressed in a human being who stood within ten feet of me."[6] Some men who knew Baker and later communicated with his biographer, John Davies, compared his handsomeness to that of a Greek god, and photos from the time indeed reveal a glamorous pretty boy.* One high-quality image from his final days shows a dashing young man in military uniform, a brooding expression on his boyish face. His sparkling eyes and perfectly coiffed hair hint at some self-awareness of his beauty. Or at some secret he's keeping.

In June 2024, ESPN's 30 for 30 series broadcast *Searching for Hobey Baker*, a feature podcast that drew from archival sources to connect the dots around the hockey star's life. Narrated by actor David Duchovny, the podcast debunked Baker's image as a ladies' man, thanks to revelations surrounding his relationship with a flamboyant male socialite ten years his senior. Percy Rivington Pyne II was a financier and philanthropist whose mother was a direct descendant of Richard Stockton, a signer of the Declaration of Independence. A Princeton alum, Pyne was heir to a family sugar and banking fortune. The Wikipedia entry on him notes that he was a "friend and benefactor" to Baker, whom he invited to live with him

---

* Henry Beyer, in a 1960 letter to Davies, wrote of Baker, "I could still visualize that amazing Greek god physique, the finest I believe I have ever seen. It was difficult to take my eyes off that wonderful, beautiful body." (John Casey, "Inside the Undiscovered Queer Life of U.S. Hockey's First Superstar, Hobey Baker," *The Advocate*, June 24, 2024, https://www.advocate.com/sports/hobey-baker-queer-life.)

at his Madison Avenue mansion. Pyne, it adds, "sent Baker gifts and clothing while he was fighting in France."[7]

Princeton classmates quoted from earlier sources did not recall any instances of Baker dating women. On the contrary, there were stories about the lengths to which he'd go to avoid such a possibility. Though he got engaged to a woman while in Europe—she was a friend of Pyne's—Baker broke off the engagement two months later, around the time of the armistice and shortly before his death.* After reviewing letters exchanged between Baker and Pyne, the 30 for 30 investigative team concluded that the pair were in a romantic, loving relationship. The following passage combines sentiments taken from a few letters Baker sent to Pyne:

> Dear Percy, for heaven's sake, don't stop writing me, even if I am here for a year, for I can't tell you what your letters mean to me ... I get horrible homesick and get thinking of the wonderful times we had when we weren't scrapping ... the picture of you came, also. I think the one standing is wonderful. The other, not so good. But that one standing could not be better and I love it. When I feel especially dirty, I shall look at that picture. These photos sort of connect me up again ... I had such a vivid dream about you, last night. And it was so strong, it sort of stayed with me all day. I went somewhere to meet you and was terribly glad to see you.[8]

From these and other details revealed in the podcast, contemporary listeners might recognize in Baker and Pyne's relationship something like that between a kept boy and his older lover; there's more than a hint of the sugar daddy squiring his boy toy trophy lover around town. In the podcast we learn how Pyne and Baker dined and partied at the thirty-five plus private clubs where Pyne had a membership: "On summer weekends, they could be found hunting game or shooting

* Jeanne Marie "Mimi" Scott, another rich socialite, had enlisted as a nurse at a hospital in France. Almost immediately after the breakup with Baker, she began a relationship with an American diplomat in Paris.

trap at the Long Island South Side Sportsmen's Club. Or lounging poolside at Rivington House, Pyne's palatial mansion on Long Island's north shore."[9] And there were plenty of gifts from the adoring Pyne to his hunky young lover. These included a leather toiletry kit and a silver-plated cigarette box engraved with Percy's and Hobey's initials—an item, Duchovny tells us, you can still find today at the Hobey Baker archives at Princeton University. While Baker was in Europe, Pyne's care packages included photos, candy, and cigarettes. And also Brooks Brothers shirts. And underwear.

With the evidence there at Princeton for all to see, why did it take so long to identify Hobey Baker as hockey's first gay icon? Part of the answer is that sexuality in early-twentieth-century American society was not so easily fixed or labelled, especially among the upper classes. Attractive and charismatic young men like Baker, realizing their appeal across the sexes, could be fluid or bisexual. But another explanation might be found in the reluctance of hockey's gatekeepers to acknowledge the presence of homosexuality in their traditionally masculine world for fear of undermining it. Such a defensive reflex extended far beyond the walls of Princeton, reaching throughout the hockey world in North America and most everywhere else the sport was played.

The notion of hockey as queer culture might begin with the Hobey Baker story, but only now are we able to recognize that fact. One hundred and eight years after Baker's death, there is a great deal of work to do in dismantling the powerful narrative of orthodox masculinity that has long dominated—and too often demeaned—the great game of hockey.

But it looks like we're getting there.

PART 1
O CANADA, MOST VIRILE

CHAPTER 1

The Whitest Game You Can Name

"Hockey does more for the racial unity of this country than all the speeches of all the politicians who ever pointed with pride at Ottawa ... It laughs at the supremacy of any racial faction."
—MORLEY CALLAGHAN, "The Game That Makes a Nation"

Deep in the heart of middle-class suburbia, in a leafy stretch of single-family acreages in Nanaimo's Departure Bay, a young boy sits on the floor of his crowded family room in the autumn of 1972, his eyes glued to the screen of an RCA colour TV. Until the 1972–73 regular season, *Hockey Night in Canada* has been a background feature of his Saturday nights. Unlike his father and older brothers, he hasn't fully engaged with it until now. Paying close attention to the on-ice action, he marvels at the crescendos of Danny Gallivan (or Bill Hewitt, or Jim Robson, depending on which team is playing) and how they add drama to the play. For him, their voices carry the same authority as a favourite parish priest—and with equal promise of reward.

The heroic feats of NHL stars awaken him to the magic of Canada's national sport. And there are so many players forcing their way into his consciousness: Yvan Cournoyer, Frank and Pete Mahovlich, Henri Richard, Ken Dryden, Dave Keon, Darryl Sittler, Bobbys Orr and Hull, Phil and Tony Esposito, Johnny Bucyk, Stan

Mikita, Mickey Redmond, Jean Ratelle, and Brad Park, for starters. *Hockey Night* becomes his entry point for what is to become a lifelong relationship with the sport: an on-again, off-again love affair with plenty of hate thrown in. It all began with the thrilling Summit Series, Canada versus the Soviet Union, that ended just a few weeks earlier. By the time this NHL season is over and the Montreal Canadiens have won yet another Stanley Cup, he will be a confirmed hockey junkie.

From the beginning, it was the beauty of hockey's movement—the poetic flow of the game, its invigorating speed—that drew me in. The sight of hockey players gliding and weaving their way through every zone of the ice was mesmerizing. To my young mind, the aspect of blades cutting through a smooth and slippery cold surface elevated hockey to something more graceful, more elegant, than the clunkier physiology of football, soccer, baseball, or basketball, with all that jerky staccato motion of legs stomping around a field or a court. (For the same reason, I was also moved by figure skating, but more on that later.) Hockey's purpose was like soccer's: using passing and finesse to move an object down the playing surface to score in the opposing team's net. But hockey was much faster, and more exciting, than soccer.

This was around the same time a talented young superstar from the Boston Bruins was revolutionizing the game for the better. Bobby Orr was a highly skilled, offensive-minded defender who was so naturally gifted that he often controlled the course of a game at will. Ragging the puck as he chose his openings, retreating to start over if necessary, he skated down the rink in a way that seemed effortless but was always deliberate. Wherever he was on the ice, he showed great artistry in eluding opponents and reaching teammates with perfect passes or in holding on to the puck to go for the shot himself, scoring more often than not. He led the league in scoring twice, won the Norris Trophy as the NHL's best blueliner eight seasons in a row, and, by the time I started watching hockey, had won two Stanley Cups.*

Watching this sport on television, I knew I was witnessing what Stompin' Tom Connors called "the best game you can name" in his anthemic "The Hockey Song."† I was impressed by the seeming ease with which NHL players—even those not in Orr's stratosphere—could reach teammates with hard, accurate passes while in full motion; by the coordinated manner in which they plotted their way around the ice; by the brilliant goals they scored or set up for their linemates; and by the commitment they showed, on defence or in goal, to containing the opposition and keeping the puck out of their own nets. All of this made hockey the "beautiful game" in those first few years I watched and then began playing it. This was a period of innocence during which I remained oblivious to the sport's harsher realities. These included the orthodox masculinity that had governed it and the homogenous culture it had begun to develop from its earliest appearance in Canada less than a decade after Confederation.

If you're a younger fan who has seen your share of live hockey action, try to imagine a game where there's nothing to see but the action on the ice. No advertising on the boards, no league or team logos, no product placement under the ice surface, and no instant replays on a high-tech Jumbotron. Imagine a game where there's no preset pop music or trained-seal inducements to encourage engagement ("Make

---

* Visit YouTube for his career highlights, and you will find a Bobby Orr whose physical presence and charisma were every bit as beautiful as his playmaking, his reputation in youth untainted by unfortunate opinions. Though harder for many Canadians to appreciate after his public endorsement of US president Donald Trump's 2020 re-election bid, Orr's hockey brilliance can never be taken away from him. The same is true of Wayne Gretzky, once known as the Great One, who is also a proud Trump supporter.

† Rheostatics rhythm guitarist Dave Bidini used that phrase for the title of his second hockey book, published by McClelland & Stewart in 2005.

some noooooiiiiiisse!"), no deafening cannon booms or horn blasts to celebrate the home team's goals, no flashy light shows or fog displays announcing the home team's players, no kiss cams to embarrass the shy or adulterous, and no otherwise distracting pyrotechnics. Yes, imagine a game where the only use of lights is to illuminate the playing surface. That was the way things were in the hockey world when I began paying attention in the early 1970s. Simple. Minimalist. Pure.

When I started watching, hockey's Golden Era of the Original Six teams (1942–67) had ended just five years earlier. The league had doubled in size before adding four more teams by the fall of 1972, but the world of hockey hadn't changed all that much. On the ice, there were still no Europeans. Almost all NHL players were Canadian born and raised and, with few exceptions, white. In the stands, there were few women to be seen, as the crowds were predominantly male and, again, mostly white. Just browse through any collection of archival photos of NHL games up to the mid-sixties, let's say, and you'll find no shortage of images reflecting the game's homogenous fan base. Not only are most of the spectators men, but some of those crowds could be mistaken for a Dick Tracy convention. (Yes, trench coats and fedoras really were the thing in men's fashion back in the day. Visit the Hockey Hall of Fame in Toronto and you'll find legendary Habs coach Toe Blake's famous hat on display.)

Back in the 1940s, it was possible for this country's cultural arbiters to see diversity in the public expression of Canadians enjoying their sport. One night, author Morley Callaghan was walking to Maple Leaf Gardens when he spotted a group of boys playing street hockey: "Anglo-Saxon faces and Scandinavian faces and Italian and Slavic faces ... though they were all one, they were just a collection of Canadian kids playing shinny. The game held them all together."[10] Callaghan's take, which went on to say that hockey "laughs at the supremacy of any racial faction,"[11] would not age so well in the multicultural Canada of the 1980s and '90s and beyond, when the sport's mainstream establishment was still making it difficult for Indigenous, Black, Asian, and other racialized players to make it in the big league.

When I first tuned in, hockey was approaching the centenary of its first recorded game in Canada. History records the sport's founding father as lawyer, engineer, and journalist from Halifax James Creighton. After earning his BA in engineering at Dalhousie University and working on the Intercolonial Railway, Creighton moved to Montreal in 1872 to work on the building project for the Lachine Canal. As expected for a man of his status, he made contacts in society that helped him advance. These included joining a rugby club and serving as a figure skating judge at the Victoria Skating Rink, where he also taught the locals his version of hockey on ice. Creighton had imported from his native Nova Scotia, at forty-five cents per dozen, hockey sticks made by Mi'kmaq crafters using wood from the hornbeam tree (later replaced with birch), and he also brought skates. Within a few years, he'd introduced the indoor version of the game, replaced the ball with a puck, and developed the first set of rules to govern play. At this point, ice hockey was still the domain of the moneyed class. But that would change quickly with the sport's growing popularity.

Hockey was grounded in the same colonial assumptions that led to Confederation itself. Even the sport's holy grail, the Stanley Cup, is a product of Canada's colonial origin story. In 1888, Lord Frederick Arthur Stanley arrived in Canada as the country's sixth Governor General. Within a few years he would fall in love with hockey, and in 1892 he donated a silver trophy to be awarded each year as a "challenge cup" to the leading hockey club *in Canada* (emphasis mine). As if to put a fine point on its colonial origins, Stanley also named it the Dominion Hockey Challenge Cup. Intended for amateur teams at that point, the Cup was promoted as a unifying symbol for a country of settlers that had only existed on paper for a quarter century. A team photo of its first winners in 1893, the Montreal Hockey Club, shows a group of white men, all but one sporting identical handlebar moustaches.

Over the next thirty-four years, various teams from different hockey associations in Canada and the US would compete for the Cup as the game expanded across the continent. But in 1926 it became the sole possession of the National Hockey League when the Western Hockey League collapsed and the NHL, founded in 1917, absorbed its remaining assets.

In hockey's first half century there were leagues for women and leagues for Indigenous and Black players. But the women's game collapsed after World War II from lack of funding, and non-white men who played the game were mostly ignored by NHL scouts; up against the same racial barriers they faced in society, they were similarly marginalized in the sport. This meant that hockey's so-called Golden Era, followed by the first decade of expansion, was steeped in a triumphalist culture of white Anglo-Saxon male sameness. This was a culture, informed by neo-colonial assumptions about nationhood and patriotism, that incorporated traditional orthodox masculinity as a core value. Such deep cultural coding began with World War I recruitment posters urging hockey players to be "real men" by fighting overseas—a call many players heeded both then and in World War II, serving with distinction.*

Hockey's first mass media personality—the man who caught the nation's attention with his high-pitched accounts of on-ice action—was both product and promoter of hockey's connection to our national myth. Born and raised in Toronto, Foster Hewitt was a child of privilege who was educated at Upper Canada College before attending the University of Toronto, where he was a member of the Beta Theta Pi fraternity.† As a teenager, he joined his father on a trip to Detroit to attend one of General Electric's first demonstrations of radio technology. In 1925, at age twenty-two, he and his father produced the world's first broadcast of a horse race. Two years later, he was guest announcer for the Detroit Red Wings' first game at Olympia Stadium. And in 1931, he got his big break in broadcasting, the gig that would earn him nationwide fame, induction into the Hockey Hall of Fame, and appointment to the Order of Canada.

* That culture died off in 2019 with the final broadcast of "Coach's Corner," in which Don Cherry blasted immigrants for not wearing poppies on Remembrance Day. Times had changed. Cherry had not. More on this in Chapter 9.

† Father of Bill Hewitt, mentioned earlier, who succeeded him as play-by-play announcer for Leafs games.

In the middle of the Great Depression, Toronto hockey mogul Conn Smythe was determined to build an arena that would turn his Maple Leafs into "Canada's team." After the Eaton's department store chain sold him a piece of land at the corner of Church and Carlton for $350,000 and a stock option, he broke ground for Maple Leaf Gardens. Less than six months later, English Canada had its hockey shrine when the Gardens opened on November 12, 1931. Foster Hewitt was there to participate in the opening ceremonies, calling the game from the broadcast gondola he had helped design.* For the next three and a half decades, Hewitt was the premier hockey broadcaster in English Canada, first on radio and then on television, with General Motors Canada and then Imperial Oil as sponsors of *Hockey Night in Canada*.

His best-known phrase, delivered in a high-pitched squeal—"He shoots, he scores!"—became his trademark, along with the standard greeting "Hello Canada, and hockey fans in the United States and Newfoundland."† In some ways, Hewitt's radio presence was as effective in uniting Canadians as President Franklin Roosevelt's fireside chats were in uniting Americans during the same period. As hockey historian Michael McKinley noted, "The voice also imprinted itself on young boys who dreamed of one day suiting up in the big leagues so people could hear Hewitt rhapsodize about them."[12] These included Bobby Hull, a budding young star from the Chicago Blackhawks. Meeting Hewitt for the first time, said Hull, was like meeting God. Hewitt, for his part, relished his role as a great uniter. He was a man, said McKinley, "who believed his broadcast provided a crucial psychological link in the national drama."[13]

Self-important as that sounds, Hewitt's socio-cultural role was a lofty one indeed and perfectly suited to the new television age. The first full CBC network telecast was on October 11, 1952. That season, Imperial Oil purchased the television rights to advertise on *Hockey Night* for only $7,000, or $100 a game. The following

---

* When the Gardens were built, Conn Smythe granted Foster Hewitt Productions exclusive broadcasting rights to every event under its roof.

† This was before 1949, when Newfoundland joined the Confederation.

season, with the value of television's reach much clearer, they paid $150,000 a year for three years. Thus began the "Esso tradition" of *Hockey Night*—along with the Ford/Mercury tradition, the Molson/Labatt tradition, the Home Hardware / Canadian Tire tradition, and of course the Tim Hortons tradition, the latter combining NHL cred with a favourite Canadian way of huddling against the cold.*

With Hewitt providing the soundtrack to our national game and all the right sponsors on board, *Hockey Night* during the twentieth century's second half became a powerful source of nostalgia for simpler times when "men were men" and things like feminism, multiculturalism, and reconciliation didn't complicate our love for the game. To keep the nostalgia going, some *Hockey Night* traditions would be repeated across generations. The "Hot Stove league," for example, recalled winter nights from the 1930s and '40s when people would gather at the local general store to warm up while listening to Foster Hewitt's play-by-play commentary of Leafs and Canadiens games on wireless radio. By recreating such an atmosphere in the TV studio seventy-five years later—and inviting current players, retirees, coaches, and sportswriters to share their wisdom and gossip on burning hockey issues of the day—*Hockey Night* could help younger generations of viewers feel what it was like to be connected to their fellow Canadians through the simple act of storytelling, inspired by what they heard on the radio. They could be part of the Hot Stove league.†

When I started watching *Hockey Night*, other intermission features aimed at kids in particular included Peter Puck, a puck-shaped cartoon character animated by Hanna-Barbera who explained hockey rules, equipment, and history in nine

---

* Tim Horton was a four-time Stanley Cup champion and Maple Leafs defender who began a successful chain of coffee and doughnut restaurants while still playing in the NHL. He was a member of the Buffalo Sabres—his third stop after the Leafs—when he was killed in a car crash in 1974. More than half a century later, the coffee brand bearing his name is world famous, with outlets as far away from Ontario as Bangkok. It's no longer Canadian, having been sold to the Brazilian–American investment firm 3G Capital.

† As a holdover from radio, "Hot Stove" had mixed results on television, and the format has been reworked several times over the decades. See Craig Baird, host, *Canadian History Ehx*, podcast, "Hockey Night in Canada," Curiouscast, July 30, 2022, https://canadaehx.com/2022/07/30/hockey-night-in-canada/.

slick segments of three minutes each. Another was "Showdown in the NHL," hosted by colour commentator Brian McFarlane, a penalty shot competition involving twenty of the NHL's best players—sixteen shooters and four goaltenders. Taped in advance, the feature showed popular scoring stars bearing down on the hottest goalies, all determined to win the showdown despite the absence of anyone else in the rink and only bragging rights being up for grabs. The feature eventually expanded from penalty shots to various skills competitions.

Although more women could gradually be seen attending NHL games than during the early Golden Era, there were none to be seen on the *Hockey Night* broadcast team, nor in the intermission features—unless a player was being interviewed at home with his wife—and almost none were in the TV ads, which were mostly for cars, tool kits, and beer. Apart from Jim "the Chief" Neilson of the New York Rangers, born to a Cree mother in Big River, Saskatchewan, I don't recall seeing any Black, Indigenous, or people of colour (BIPOC) NHL players when I was a kid. This was the big white world of hockey men I'd witnessed since my earliest days of fandom.

I was too young to appreciate what all this meant in terms of politics and culture, too naive to see what the cult-like environment of the mainstream hockey world had in common with organized religion. Earlier I alluded to play-by-play announcers as reminiscent of certain parish priests, with their dramatic cadences and promise of reward. There were also obvious parallels to the hockey arena as a place of worship, to the fans as devotees of their chosen hockey gods. But in terms of realpolitik, I could not yet see how the game's gatekeepers in the NHL or Hockey Canada functioned like Vatican cardinals and the NHL president (later commissioner) like the pope in wielding power over the institution. The way the game was presented to the faithful and defended from its critics—and the way tradition preserved the game's hegemonic influence in society—only became familiar to this lapsed Roman Catholic with age.

In the meantime, religion in the literal sense sometimes had a role in determining hockey loyalties. According to this equation, fans of the country's two oldest NHL teams could be divided by denomination: fans of the Ontario-based Toronto Maple Leafs were more likely to be Protestant, while fans of the Quebec-based

Montreal Canadiens were more likely Roman Catholic.* My mother, an Ottawa francophone from a large Catholic family, had married the son of a British Catholic convert. Most of her family who weren't in Ottawa lived in Montreal. Although she and my father moved our growing family to the anglophone and less Catholic province of British Columbia, where Dad was born and raised, there was no question where the Gawthrop/Rochon hockey loyalties lay.

Our house was a Habs house, all the way.

Montreal Forum
May 10, 1979
Late in Game 7 of the conference final, the Habs are faltering. After starting the third period down 3–1 to the Bruins, the Canadiens storm back to tie the game, with Guy Lafleur assisting on both goals. But with only a few minutes remaining, my team has fallen behind again. It seems their time is up—their dynasty will end at three consecutive Stanley Cups. Stressed out in front of the TV, my teenage self feels like weeping. But then, with 2:34 left, Boston is called for too many men and receives a bench minor penalty. On the ensuing power play, Lafleur skates out of his zone with the puck and sends a quick pass up to Jacques Lemaire. After entering the Bruins' zone, Lemaire drops a perfect blind pass back to Lafleur, who leans into the puck with a hard slapper and ... scores! Tied game. The Canadiens win in OT, then easily beat the New York Rangers in the final to win that fourth straight Cup.

---

* Of course, that's ridiculous. There are plenty of Roman Catholic Leafs fans, the most famous example being one of their own Stanley Cup–winning players from 1948. A speedy and talented left winger who had also won two Memorial Cups with Toronto's St. Michael's Junior team, Les Costello quit hockey at the peak of his career to become a priest. "I'd rather teach people to live with God than thrill them occasionally on Saturday nights," he famously said. He came back years later to join a group of hockey-playing priests whose games raised money for sick children. The Flying Fathers raised more than $4 million for charity by their fourth decade (Michael McKinley, *Hockey: A People's History*, [McClelland & Stewart, 2006], 172.)

At age fifteen, I have been spoiled by the Habs for years and can't get enough of my favourite player, Lafleur, having his way with the Bruins. That clutch goal of his late in Game 7 will always remind me just how dominant he and the Habs were during my adolescence. But more than a dozen years later, I will drop the Habs as my favourite team, jumping off the Montreal bandwagon without so much as a backward glance. This will have nothing to do with their on-ice performance; Les Canadiens will win the Cup again in 1986 and once more in 1993, though without coming close to their dynastic status of the late 1970s. Nor will it be because I've adopted the Vancouver Canucks as my new favourite team out of regional loyalty. The big reason—which I'll get into later—is about the disillusioning loss of innocence that occurs when you discover that your heroes have feet of clay. And it has to do with the subject of this book.

Perhaps the mystique that has always surrounded the Habs is partly to blame for the letdown. Every young hockey fan who embraces the Montreal Canadiens gets swept up in all the great stories surrounding their legend. From Howie Morenz and Georges Vézina in the early days to Maurice "Rocket" Richard, Jean Béliveau, Doug Harvey, and Jacques Plante during the late-1950s five-year dynasty, the "Flying Frenchmen" were the world's most successful hockey franchise and often the best team in the NHL. I was lucky to witness their final dynasty through its last gasp. This was a Habs team that included Guy Lafleur, Ken Dryden, the "Big Three" defence of Larry Robinson, Serge Savard, and Guy Lapointe, a core leadership group of Yvan Cournoyer, Bob Gainey, Jacques Lemaire, and Steve Shutt, and a supporting cast of Pete Mahovlich, Réjean Houle, Doug Risebrough, Mario Tremblay, Yvon Lambert, Pierre Mondou, and Doug Jarvis. Mark Napier, Pierre Larouche, and Rod Langway came later.

The team's coach, Scotty Bowman, was a master motivator/manipulator who, apart from his five Cups with the Habs, would go on to win four more as head coach (one with the Pittsburgh Penguins and three with the Detroit Red Wings), plus five more in the front office with Pittsburgh, Detroit, and Chicago. The general manager, Sam Pollock, was a shrewd negotiator with a sharp instinct for talent who took full advantage of the stockpile of draft picks at his disposal—and the final years of a farm system that benefited the Canadiens by giving them the right to claim most Québécois players. This allowed the Habs to build for the future from a position of strength. (Pollock also had a great sense of timing: After he retired in 1978, the cupboard was bare, and his replacement, Irving Grundman, had much less to work with.)

As I wrote this section, Ken Dryden died of cancer. Media tributes reminded us that he won six Stanley Cups in a playing career of less than eight full seasons and was the only player in NHL history to have won the Conn Smythe Trophy as playoff MVP before winning the Calder Trophy as rookie of the year. Dryden also won the Vezina Trophy as the NHL's top goaltender five times in those eight years. Such excellence was shared throughout the Habs' lineup, from Lafleur's three Art Ross Trophy–winning scoring championships, his two Hart Trophy–winning seasons as league MVP, and his Conn Smythe win, to Robinson and Gainey's Conn Smythe wins, plus Robinson's two Norris Trophy wins as best defender and Gainey's four Selke Trophy wins as best defensive forward.

The Game, Dryden's 1983 memoir about his life with the Canadiens, is regarded today as the best hockey book ever written. In it, he recalls what motivated the Habs during his final season as the team pursued its fourth straight Cup:

> When a team wins once, it is for one central reason. When it wins for three consecutive years, nine times in fourteen years, it's for a crush of reasons. Winning brings with it such an immense momentum. Everything fits, everything works. Every new thing is made to fit and work. Everything just is. Reasons blur and disappear. It becomes a state of mind, an obligation, an explanation; in the end, an attitude.[14]

Guy Lafleur took a while to develop that state of mind. Drafted in 1971 after a record-breaking Junior career with the Quebec Remparts that ended with a Memorial Cup, the superstar right winger arrived in Montreal the very next season instead of playing another year in Quebec or honing his professional skills with the Nova Scotia Voyageurs, the Canadiens' farm team. Expectations were high: the Habs' long-serving captain, the great Jean Béliveau, had just retired after winning his tenth Stanley Cup. Béliveau's career had overlapped with Rocket

Richard's, connecting generations of classic Canadiens teams. In hockey-mad Montreal, where success was a given, the fans needed a new saviour, and Lafleur was the anointed one. So from the moment he arrived, he was expected to be the next Béliveau. At first, the legend himself even encouraged the rookie to wear his old number, 4, which Lafleur had worn throughout his Junior career. But then he changed his mind, wisely telling the young phenom, "Don't try to be a second Jean Béliveau. Be the first Guy Lafleur. Take a number and make it your own."[15] As legend has it, Habs trainer Eddy Palchak tossed Lafleur a jersey: number 10.

By most standards, Lafleur put up some decent numbers in his rookie season, scoring 29 goals and 35 assists for 64 points, with another 5 points in six playoff games. But this was Montreal. The Habs had picked him over another Québécois Junior phenom, Marcel Dionne. And Dionne was embarrassing Lafleur in his first two seasons with the Detroit Red Wings: He scored his first and second NHL hat tricks against the Habs. In 1972–73, Lafleur's scoring dipped slightly, to 28 goals and 27 assists. (As if to taunt les Canadiens for drafting the "other" Québécois star, Dionne finished that year with 40 goals and the best two-season point totals for a sophomore.) In 1973–74, Lafleur's goal total dipped to 21.* This three-year performance was fine for a third-line winger, a minor supporting player, but not for the Chosen One. After three years, media and fans were growing impatient. Was "the Flower" wilting under the pressure? Had Pollock and his scouting team blown it by choosing him?

While the pundits and fans were fretting, Bowman was still playing Lafleur. The veteran stars supported him. As he recalled later, "Henri Richard and Yvan Cournoyer were telling me one day, 'Stop listening to everybody, just play your style—you'll get your confidence back.' And that's what I did."[16] At some point, he decided to switch to a curved stick. After his third season, he made another decision that would change his fortune, and that of the Habs, for the next decade.

---

* Dionne slipped that season as well and soon had his own problems. By the following season he had worn out his welcome in Detroit, getting traded to the Los Angeles Kings. From there he would go on to have a Hall of Fame career—and the dubious distinction of being the best NHL player never to have won a Stanley Cup.

At the same time the league was moving toward mandatory helmet use, Lafleur got rid of the circular Lange head protector he had always worn, allowing his long, sandy-blond mane to flow behind him in the wind created by his speed. From the moment he hit the ice for the 1974–75 season, nothing was the same.

The Flower truly blossomed that season. Suddenly more confident to play his own game, Lafleur was determined to elevate his performance with a dazzling style to match the new look. First there was the smooth, deliberate skating to survey the ice ahead of him, then a gradually accelerating pace that used explosive speed and stickhandling to stun the opposition. Finally there'd be a quick slapper, a wrist shot or a deke, to fool the goalie. And it worked, again and again. Lafleur finished the 1974–75 season with 53 goals and 119 points, the first in a six-year run of 50-goal and 100-point seasons, all but the first totalling at least 125 points.

Four of those last five seasons coincided with a quadruple Stanley Cup reign, confirming that Lafleur was indeed the final piece of the puzzle in the Canadiens' return to dynastic greatness. During this period, he entered the pantheon of all-time NHL legends beside Orr, Howe, and his fellow Habs alumni, Richard and Béliveau. As the biggest hockey star in the world, he was recognized by his peers with successive Lester B. Pearson Awards as league MVP (on top of his other NHL silverware) and by both federal and provincial governments. In Quebec, where he was adored, they dubbed him "le Demon Blond." And across Canada, whether francophone or anglophone, boys who loved hockey and the Habs wanted to be like him.

Lafleur's prime hockey years unfolded while I was between the ages of eleven and sixteen, a period that ended with a late puberty and nascent awareness of my homosexuality. Over the years there would be no shortage of NHL stars I would lust after, but my favourite player growing up was never among them. Although handsome in a classic Gallic sense—that long flowing hair really did do a lot for him—and despite a charismatic combination of self-confidence and team-first humility that is always attractive in a superstar, Guy Lafleur did nothing for me sexually. His quietly brooding hetero masculinity, his chain-smoking habit, and his slightly larger nose disqualified him as fantasy material.* His appeal for me was entirely aesthetic: He was a hockey artist of inspiring creativity.

But as Dryden revealed in *The Game*, the Flower was also a humble man, the unpretentious product of a working-class upbringing in Thurso, Quebec, a tiny pulp-and-paper mill town along the Ottawa River. For someone like Lafleur, hockey was the only escape from a life of industrial drudgery.† But Dryden was still perplexed by Lafleur's singular sense of his own future. Interviewers seeking insight into his personal life, probing for his other interests, kept getting the same response: "Hockey's my life." So Dryden probed a bit deeper.

> I asked him to explain the unquestioning direction to his life he so often expresses in interviews—playing a little longer, retiring, staying on with the team, travelling the country as its ambassador as Béliveau has. He looked at me, surprised. "What else would I do?" he asked. "When you play as a kid you have no time to learn or study anything. After fifteen or twenty years, what else do I know?"[17]

As an adolescent during the peak years of Lafleur's hockey career, I had no idea of the differences that separated someone like him from a suburban middle-class doctor's kid like me. Because of my own fortunate upbringing, I never imagined what steely determination might be required to improve one's fortunes in life by believing that strongly in one's own talent. I knew I could never be like Lafleur in

---

* If any member of the Habs turned me on as a fourteen-year-old, it was dark-eyed, black-haired Scorpio Pierre Larouche, a twenty-two-year-old bad-boy cutie-pie who came from Pittsburgh in a trade for Pete Mahovlich. During his brief career with the Penguins, the team that drafted him, Larouche in his sophomore year became the youngest player to score 50 goals in a season. According to his hockey card, the Penguins exploited his stardom and good looks by offering a date night with him as part of a raffle. I had swooned over him ever since.

† I've been to Thurso once, out of curiosity, in 1984. It did seem like a town to move away from if you had grown up there.

any way, nor live the life he did. Regardless of class upbringing, players like him had always started early, as young as three or four, and had demonstrated their natural gifts from the moment they put on skates. I would never be a true athlete because I lacked the self-confidence to excel at sports in general. But that didn't matter when I was watching Lafleur work his magic on the ice. Like any other Canadian kid who loved hockey and the Habs—regardless of gender, race, or economic status—I tried to channel his energy into something I could try doing myself.

Whenever I saw the Flower turn opponents inside out with his skating and stickhandling, whenever I saw him bear down on a goalie during a breakaway or otherwise change the course of a game with a single brilliant play, making it all seem so inevitable, the excitement I felt made me want to play hockey, regardless of my limitations. It made me want to feel what le Demon Blond must have felt when he went on instinct, when he broke through the other team's defence to make all those great plays without even thinking about it. I felt I was approaching a kind of ecstasy simply by attempting to do those same things. Even if only in my dreams, I could feel what it was like to make that move, to take that shot, to score that goal. To be Guy Lafleur.

I would have to start on the back driveway outside our family home, and I would have to learn from my four older brothers, none of whom had played hockey on ice. For most of them, their rec league sport growing up was soccer. But they did enjoy road hockey, and it wasn't long before I did too. The driveway of our suburban family home was paved with smooth asphalt, one corner of it bordered with a cement wall that divided the pavement from a garden four feet above it. In that corner, the wall was rounded in dimensions not unlike one team's end of the ice. It was the perfect shape for a half rink, which is what my brothers created when they saw its potential. Placing a net six feet in front of the back wall, the same distance as in an actual rink, left just enough room to make plays from behind it.

That wall became "the boards," which no one wanted to bump into because it was solid cement six inches thick. But otherwise, you could use it like real hockey boards, bouncing the orange plastic ball off it to fake a defender and move around him or to pass to a partner. There wasn't enough space for a standard game of five shooters and two goalies per side, so my brothers played what we called a checking game. The half-rink playing area allowed for one or two shooters per side, with both sides shooting on the one goalie. In either case, faceoffs took place where "centre ice" would be. It was a bit like half-court basketball, with the two sides switching between offence and defence depending on who had possession.

After some time watching my brothers and their friends play this version of road hockey, I got my own stick and began playing with my friends from school. I enjoyed the checking game, which required the defender taking possession to bring the ball back to centre to switch to offence. The more I played, the more I discovered new ways to outsmart my opponents with good stickhandling. Two-on-two was more fun than one-on-one; as a player, you had someone to pass to, and for goalies, the saves were more impressive because they had to be more alert to a goalmouth feed. Whenever I was successful at faking out another player, making a perfect pass, or beating the goalie with a nice wrist shot, I was always channelling Guy Lafleur. By this point, I had learned how to skate, so it was only a matter of time before I started playing on the ice.

The Civic Arena was downtown Nanaimo's hockey palace, a grand old barn with a rich history. The rink's gala opening in 1940 was attended by Lynn Patrick, a member of that year's Stanley Cup–winning New York Rangers and, as a son of Lester Patrick, hockey royalty. Over the years, the Civic had become the launching pad for many a talented player who would go on to enjoy an NHL career, including local heroes Red Carr and his son Gene,* Al Hill, Mel Bridgman, and Gary Lupul. It was the home rink of the Nanaimo Clippers, whose teams under coach Larry McNabb in the 1970s were among the best in Canada at that level, winning three

* Gene Carr made the most of his celebrity status as an NHL star after being traded from the New York Rangers to the LA Kings in the 1973–74 season. He befriended Eagles member Glenn Frey, a dedicated season ticket holder with the Kings, and later speculated that the Eagles' 1976 hit single "New Kid in Town" (co-written by Frey, Don Henley, and J.D. Souther) was inspired by his own arrival in Los Angeles.

British Columbia Junior Hockey League (BCJHL) championships from 1976 through 1978.*

When I first set foot there in 1973, the Civic was a creaky old barn, its hallways and bleachers well worn after more than three decades of hockey, lacrosse, boxing matches, rock concerts, and Barnum & Bailey circuses. There was a gritty mystique to the arena, an atmosphere of passion and struggle, its storied history showcased on the walls with photos of past champions and performers. Every small town in Canada had a rink just like it—another kind of church, where instead of the Father, Son, and Holy Spirit, the "faithful" called up ghosts from classic games or spectacles past; where instead of incense, the air was thick with cigarettes, french fries and vinegar, old wood, and stale sweat.

Stepping onto the ice for those first tentative strides on skates, a late bloomer at age ten, I struggled to put one foot in front of the other without falling down. My mother, bless her heart, skated backward while holding both my hands and pulling me along, encouraging me to stand up straight and try not to bump into the throngs of other skaters swirling around us. I don't recall what music was playing on the arena's ancient sound system that day, but I do recall what I raced and swirled around to over the next few seasons, as I became a more self-assured skater: ABBA's "Waterloo," Elton John's "Bennie and the Jets," the Sweet's "The Ballroom Blitz," and the Bay City Rollers' "Saturday Night." These and other pop tunes thrilled my prepubescent heart as I found my skating legs and pretended I was Guy Lafleur. Before I even knew what it meant, gliding around to all of that jubilant pop music made me feel just a little bit gay.

During this time, I was impressed by the grace and artistry of figure skating but never considered trying it. For one thing, I wasn't coordinated enough to dare attempt those spin manoeuvres and jumps, which required a high degree of skill and discipline, including endless hours of practice. I was a timid child, terrified of the spotlight. What if I fell? What if I humiliated myself? Finally, there was something I understood about figure skating, even at age eleven or twelve, that made me

* Today, the Clippers play under the revised league banner of the British Columbia Hockey League (which was known as the BCJHL from 1967 until 1995).

The author at thirteen, playing for the Bantam Elks in the Nanaimo house leagues in his sophomore season, 1976–77

wary of entering that world. Somehow I knew that committing to figure skating would mark me as different, as outside of my peer group. I didn't want to make myself *more* vulnerable than I already was; I just wanted to belong. And it seemed much easier to gain a sense of belonging in the collective enterprise of a team sport, like the one I'd been watching on TV and mimicking in the back driveway. Yes, it was time I played *real* hockey.

By age eleven, I had never played an organized sport outside of PE class, and I had no interest in soccer. Rather than copy my older brothers, I wanted to go my own way. And so, with a carefree middle-class perspective that blinded me to the financial barriers preventing less-fortunate kids from participating, I told my father I wanted to play recreational hockey in Nanaimo's house league system. My wish was his command: During the summer of 1975, Dad signed me up for hockey school at the local curling club. One of the instructors was Wayne Bianchin, a Nanaimo-born Pittsburgh Penguins prospect who later cracked the big team's roster. The drills he put us through were challenging—playing with full equipment made the skating more laboured—but I loved hockey school and looked forward to playing in actual games.

For my first season, 1975–76, I played with the Buffaloes, a mixed bag of unformed hockey talent in the Peewee B division. Among my fellow twelve-year-olds, I might have been the only player who hadn't started at age five or six. I shot left-handed, so they put me on left wing, the position I've played ever since. I didn't score many goals, but I do recall my first one, a one-timer tap-in from five feet in front of the net after a great pass from a teammate behind it. Despite my limitations, I got just as much ice time as our best players until the end of the season, when we won the championship. The coaches applied just the right mix of learning and fun to make every boy's experience a positive one, so I came to love the game. I loved the feeling of cool air rushing around me as I picked up speed—though I wished we were helmet-less so I'd feel more like Guy Lafleur. I loved the thrill of making a good pass to a teammate or beating an opponent to the puck. And yeah, I loved winning, especially that last game and the trophy that came with it. Outside of school and Sunday mass at St. Peter's, hockey for a brief moment was the only organized activity in my life. The early-morning playing time was crazy, but my father, a family doctor well accustomed to the hour, didn't mind driving me to and from the rink.

For my second season, having aged out of Peewee at thirteen, I moved on to Bantam B hockey with a new team, the Elks. I also moved (as did the Clippers) from the Civic Arena downtown to the brand-new Frank Crane Arena at Beban Park, north of town. Looking at the team photo today, I don't recall much about the 1976–77 season or even my teammates, apart from the fact that Randy Geddes, our captain with the Buffaloes, joined me on the Elks. I must have had fun as my skills improved, but I don't recall the season being as big a deal as my rookie year had been. At that age, I suppose, I took the game for granted. Or perhaps playing in the antiseptic environment of Nanaimo's brand-new hockey rink, which lacked the gravitas of character and tradition I had enjoyed at the Civic, made the experience less memorable.* But when that season was over, I had no idea that it would be my last organized hockey action for the next seventeen years. Nor how much I would miss the simple pleasure—the innocence—of just playing the game.

---

* The Civic remained in use for another thirty years but ultimately fell victim to the whims of real estate. In September 2006, the arena was closed and two months later demolished to make way for a proposed twin condominium tower complex. But the condo development never materialized, so Nanaimo's most cherished hockey rink—a rich source of local history and childhood memories for generations of locals—ended up being sacrificed for a parking lot.

CHAPTER 2

Elbows Up—and Gloves Off

"Hockey doesn't build character—it reveals it."
—KEN DRYDEN

"A crusher who becomes a rusher soon becomes an usher."
—DON CHERRY

For all the joy I experienced in those first two seasons of minor hockey, by the end of them I was no longer so naive about the darker aspects of the adult game. A few years after I began watching NHL hockey on television, I could clearly see a tension within the sport and the philosophy surrounding it, a conflict between two different ways of playing that hockey's gatekeepers seemed not to regard as a conflict at all. The first approach focused more on skills and finesse. For offence, that meant high-speed skating, puck handling, and passing plays to outsmart and outscore the opposition. On defence, it meant controlling the play through puck possession, closing up the middle, using one's body to force opponents into the boards, and using one's stick to take the puck away from another's. The second approach focused on proactive aggression, including deliberate acts of violence. This meant slamming opponents into the boards before they knew what was coming, using the stick as a weapon to spear or slash an opponent, or starting a fist fight to beat up an opponent and intimidate him into submission.

From the first bench-clearing brawl I ever saw on TV—I don't recall which teams or players were involved—I always regarded fighting in the game as a stupid waste of everyone's time. Why did hockey allow it when other sports didn't? Whenever a brawl broke out, I used the stoppage in play as a cue to bolt for the kitchen to get a snack or to go outside and take a few shots with the orange ball, returning only when play had resumed. Of course, I wasn't expecting ballet on ice, as defenders of fighting often assumed of its critics. I understood that hockey was a high-contact sport that required some degree of aggression, if only to maintain possession, force a turnover, or prevent a high-danger scoring chance while defending. But the very best players could always meet those challenges without resorting to the cheap shot or the dirty play, without letting their emotions get the better of them. I was always most impressed by the players who could demonstrate their strength, resilience, and even toughness without having to go full neanderthal. A healthy regard for one's opponent is axiomatic to the principle of fair play. But in the NHL, it seemed, some players who were perfect gentlemen off the ice could turn into monsters when they were on it.

All this would make sense many years later, when Toronto's Summerhill Press published a groundbreaking work of academic inquiry into the world of competitive sport. Written by University of Toronto physical education and health professor Brian Pronger, *The Arena of Masculinity: Sports, Homosexuality, and the Meaning of Sex* (1990) was remarkable for its time. Described as "a popular merger of Foucaultian theory, sport, and sexuality," the book was a rare and provocative source of scholarship on the history, politics, mythology, and psychology of homosexuality and masculinity in sports.[18] In *The Arena of Masculinity*, Pronger identified three categories of behaviour that typify orthodox masculinity in sports: violence, struggle, and aesthetics. Of the latter, he noted,

> The least masculine sports are those where success is determined by the marriage of skill and aesthetic expression. Such sports are figure skating, diving, gymnastics, and bodybuilding. These aesthetic sports are the least masculine because they involve the lowest degree of aggression.[19]

In the middle category are sports in which struggle with one's opponents or oneself is a dominant characteristic—but without requiring violence. Typical sports in this category are baseball, wrestling, tennis, and swimming. Individual sports that involve non-violent struggle with the self are track and field, golf, archery, and weightlifting. But the sports considered the most masculine are those that involve violence: boxing, football, and hockey.

In singling out Canada's national sport as representing the peak violence of high-masculinity athletics, Pronger quoted Mr. Hockey himself. Detroit Red Wings Hall of Famer Gordie Howe once described hockey as "a man's game."[20] He would know. For all his offensive prowess—he remained the NHL's all-time leading goal scorer for nearly thirty years, until Wayne Gretzky eclipsed him in the mid-1990s—Howe could be as brutal as any typical enforcer. During puck battles along the boards, or in open ice, his elbows were notorious weapons. He never hesitated to use them to knock an opponent out of a game if it gave his team the edge. This, according to Howe's own sense of masculinity, was what being "a man" was all about.*

"Violence and fighting constitute major attractions to the game," Pronger wrote of hockey, "for it is in violence that masculinity shines."[21] Acts of violence might not be as crucial to hockey as they are to football, where the equipment is designed for more violent physical contact and where "each play consists of battlefield formations." But, he noted,

> Athletic competence is actually a secondary feature of hockey, especially in the NHL—the real appeal lies in its significance as "a man's game." The masculine aesthetic of hockey becomes almost sacramental through its violence and bloodshed.[22]

---

* Howe's elbows are so legendary that, nearly a decade after his death, Canadian Member of Parliament Charlie Angus popularized "Elbows up!" as a rallying cry of resistance against Donald Trump's tariffs, "fifty-first state" threats, and other attacks on Canadian sovereignty.

To emphasize this point, Pronger laid it on thick with a passage from Frank Rose's *Real Men: Sex and Style in an Uncertain Age* (Dolphin, 1980):

> The cold adds a subtle colouration to the violence that is one of the sport's special treats. There is an undeniable frisson to the sight of blood on ice—the spilling of the very warm onto the very cold, perhaps—that not even football can match.[23]

Reading that passage, I am reminded of Brian Spencer, a tragic hockey figure whose life story was first told in a sensational biography that became a TV movie.* Spencer, whose career bookended the 1970s, is the perfect poster boy for that decade's kind of hockey—the violent, goonishly masculine sort. Nicknamed "Spinner" for his wild, uninhibited skating style, Spencer was a capable scorer when he arrived with the Leafs. But he was better known for causing mayhem with a well-timed hit or a fight. Hockey's version of a wrecking ball, he had a bit of the Tasmanian devil about him. "I never believed in going around somebody," he once said, "when I could go through them."[24] Popular with teammates wherever he played and loved by fans and women, Spinner was cursed with a violent temper inherited from his father, Roy, that would prove fatal within a decade of his NHL retirement.

The night Spencer played in his first televised NHL game with the Leafs, his parents were looking forward to watching from their home in the remote northern BC frontier town of Fort St. James. But after hearing the CBC's northern affiliate in Prince George was broadcasting a Vancouver Canucks game instead of the Leafs–Chicago match, Roy Spencer called up the station and demanded that they switch to the Toronto game. Told that the station couldn't do that because it was a network decision, Roy got into his Ford LTD with a rifle, a pistol, several rounds

---

* The book was Martin O'Malley's *Gross Misconduct: The Life of Spinner Spencer* (Penguin, 1988). The film version, *Gross Misconduct: The Life of Brian Spencer* (1993), was adapted by Paul Gross and directed by Atom Egoyan.

of ammunition, and three hunting knives. Then he drove to Prince George and held up the station at gunpoint. When RCMP officers arrived, he shot at them, and they returned fire, killing him instantly. At that moment, his son was being interviewed as an intermission guest on *Hockey Night in Canada*.

Brian Spencer drifted through life after that. Taking his hockey career for granted, he blew all his money on cars, women, and good times, making no real plans for retirement. When his playing days were over, he descended into a life of drugs, alcohol, and crime while living out of his truck in Florida. Though he had his tender moments (he loved his five kids from two marriages, his twin brother, Byron, and the Bellamy Brothers hit "Let Your Love Flow"), too often he flew into rages while getting mixed up with shady characters. After being busted for and charged with kidnapping and murder—which carried the death penalty in Florida—Spinner received character references from former NHL teammates and was acquitted. He vowed to change his life, but three months later, while buying crack cocaine, he was shot dead, meeting a similar fate as his father.

In *Gross Misconduct*, Martin O'Malley captured Spencer's addiction to fighting in an article he wrote early on in the player's career—an article Spencer had saved and still kept in his attaché case when he was arrested many years later:

> Some men have grown to old age without ever having been in a fist fight. Others can remember three or four. Brian Spencer is only twenty-two but he has been in so many fights he really can't remember all of them. They are a blur of hot blood and sudden rapid punches.[25]

In his explanation to O'Malley of the best fighting strategy for hockey players, Spencer's enthusiasm came through, as if he were advising the listener to follow his example:

> You're wearing maybe twenty-five pounds of equipment, so first you have to throw your gloves down. And you can only hit the guy in the

> face. You can't hit him anywhere else. I mean, what's the use? You might break your hand. You've got no footing so you try to anticipate what the other guy's going to do. Try to brace yourself and keep upright, because if he puts you on the ice he has an advantage. Try to block him, stay on your feet, maybe throw him on his back and get a few in. You use discretion, of course, but I can take all kinds of punches and I know I'm not going to get hurt. If he hits you with a stick, fine. You bleed a little, you get sewn up.[26]

Spinner was thirty-eight when he died, a couple of decades before we learned about chronic traumatic encephalopathy, when science confirmed the long-term impacts of repeated hits to the head through hockey fighting. One can't help wondering how well Spencer would have aged had he not met his end in a drug deal gone wrong. His story was difficult to read and even more so to watch—I saw the Egoyan film—because I found it impossible to identify with this man as a human being. While I felt compassion about the loss of his father—how crushing that must have been for him, and how destructive the path it led him on—everything about Brian Spencer's life seemed to be rooted in violence, which he took for granted as the go-to solution for all of life's problems.

I was only twelve or thirteen when I was confronted by one of the most shocking acts of hockey violence in NHL history. This wasn't something I saw on television or live at a hockey rink; it was an incident captured in photographs. What deeply shocked me as a child was the public record of a sickening event that took place three years before I began watching hockey, back in the days when few players wore helmets. A stick-swinging duel between two players, it was a brutal encounter that left one of them with a compound skull fracture and brain damage caused by a vicious blow to the head with a hockey stick. Fans of a certain age will recall this horrible moment as the Ted Green / Wayne Maki incident.*

On September 21, 1969, the Boston Bruins and the St. Louis Blues were playing a pre-season exhibition match in Ottawa. Halfway through the first period, Blues winger Wayne Maki dumped the puck into the Bruins zone and skated after it. When Boston defender Ted Green arrived in the corner to retrieve it, Maki caught up and slammed him into the boards. Angered by the hit, Green pounded Maki onto the ice. As the referee was calling a penalty on Green, Maki—still on his knees—speared the Bruin in the groin before standing up. Green then swung his stick at Maki, hitting him on the arm and knocking him to the ice again. As Green was turning toward the penalty box, Maki pursued him. Swinging his stick at Green's head, he smashed him in the right temple with its heel, sending him crumpling to the ice.

Long before I knew the sequence of events, I understood what had happened from a brief description and three photos I came across one day in a magazine. The first two showed Green and Maki swinging their sticks at each other; the last showed Green lying on the ice, his face contorted in a dazed grimace while his body convulsed. He couldn't get up because the blow had crushed part of his skull and left him partially paralyzed, a gruesome injury that would require two operations and the insertion of a plate in his head. Later I would learn that the game had continued after Green was wheeled off the ice. He and Maki both received game misconducts (academic, in the semi-conscious Green's case) and were later fined one hundred dollars each. Ottawa police charged both men with assault, the first

---

* Permission to publish these photos in this book was stymied when I was informed by the *Ottawa Citizen*, which published the images captured by a staff photographer, that permission for a reprint fee would only be granted subject to approval by the NHL. I wrote to the NHL but heard nothing back. Why the NHL would presume jurisdiction over a work of journalism is anyone's guess. But it's telling that the league's brand protection efforts extend to events that occurred fifty-seven years ago.

time NHL players had faced criminal charges resulting from on-ice violence. Both were acquitted. The NHL suspended Maki for thirty days.*

The first time I saw those photos, I couldn't believe my young eyes. How could two grown men playing a sport meant to entertain the masses have so completely abandoned their senses? How could they have descended into such primitive barbarism, endangering each other's lives for the sake of a little black piece of rubber (and in an exhibition game no less, with nothing at stake)? What kind of men were they to succumb to that kind of rage in service of their competitive edge and partisan loyalties? And what did it say about the NHL that the game was allowed to continue after Green lay catatonic on the ice? A year later, what did it say about the Vancouver Canucks—a new team on the verge of entering the NHL—that they were willing to overlook Maki's horrifying assault on Green and claim him in the expansion draft?† The Green/Maki incident was a rare case of NHL players engaging in lethal combat with their sticks. But there were other acts of violence beyond fighting that brought hockey into disrepute. And when they happened on an international stage, where the stakes were highest, hockey's Canadian gatekeepers preferred to look the other way.

---

* Green missed the entire 1969–70 season, which ended with Boston's first Stanley Cup win in twenty-nine years, but he resumed his playing career in 1970–71. He went on to play eight and a half more seasons with several teams before retiring at age thirty-eight and moving on to enjoy a long coaching career. He died in 2019 at age seventy-nine. Maki was not so fortunate. After the Blues demoted him to their American Hockey League affiliate, the Vancouver Canucks claimed him in the 1970 expansion draft. Turning into a valued goal scorer, he enjoyed two and a half seasons in Vancouver before being diagnosed with brain cancer. He died in 1974 at age twenty-nine, living half a century less than the man whose brain he had injured. The Canucks retired his number, 11, but twenty-three years later—over the protests of Maki's family—they allowed Mark Messier to un-retire it. It was re-retired following Messier's unsuccessful three-year stint with the Canucks.

† In this century, other players wearing the Canucks uniform have become victims or perpetrators of newsworthy hockey brutality: Donald Brashear the former, following a stick-to-the-head assault by Boston Bruins player Marty McSorley in 2000, and Todd Bertuzzi the latter, with his behind-the-back punch and pile-on against Colorado Avalanche player Steve Moore in 2004.

For most Canadians older than sixty, the Summit Series of 1972 is a defining moment in our collective history, right up there with the Normandy invasion or the driving of the last spike of the Canadian Pacific Railway. Pitched in our national media as a battle of two political systems, the great hockey showdown between Canada and the Soviet Union captured our attention for twenty-seven days that September. After Game 1, a humiliating 7–3 loss for Canada, the country seemed to hold its collective breath, wondering if our boys would redeem themselves. Billed before the series as overwhelming favourites, they had been badly outclassed by the Soviets.

A month shy of my ninth birthday, I watched those games like everyone else, but I don't recall much about them. Just the novelty of hearing the famous voice of legendary Hall of Fame broadcaster Foster Hewitt, who had come out of retirement at age seventy to call the play-by-play for this historic event. I also recall the thrill of Game 8, which I watched at school with my Grade 4 classmates: our excitement when Paul Henderson scored the winning goal late in the third period, and our relief when those final thirty-four seconds ticked away, the final buzzer ending the game with Canada winning the series. Other than that, I recall only the nervous tension in the family room at home while we watched the games played in Canada. It felt as if we'd all die if Team Canada lost. I remember that the Canadians, exposed as out of shape and overconfident, had trouble adjusting to the Soviets' superior fitness and disciplined play. To turn the series around, Team Canada had to play a more aggressive style, with hitting. I cheered for my country but secretly preferred the enemy's style of play.

It was only decades later, after reviewing the games on YouTube and seeing interviews with surviving players for the fortieth- and fiftieth-anniversary commemorations, that I learned just how desperate Team Canada had been—how far the players were willing to go—to win the series. Canada's play after the devastating Game 1 loss was much rougher, with lots of big open ice hits and scrappy play along the boards. The Soviets stood their ground as best they could, sometimes hitting back. But there was a limit to their physical play. The Russian game was all about systems and finesse, a disciplined style that emphasized passing accuracy and five-man units where coordination—not individual heroics—was the priority.

The Soviet players had been whipped into shape with practice drills in which they had to remain in constant motion. This "assembly method," as it was known, had been developed since the 1950s by coach Anatoly Tarasov, a brilliant hockey innovator whose methods established the Soviet Union as an international hockey powerhouse.* In this system, physical contact with the opponent was never a factor, because the Soviets were supposed to simply weave their way through the offensive zone unmolested. Team Canada, seeing this gap in their game, took advantage by hooking, slashing, boarding, and cross-checking the Soviets at every opportunity, getting in their faces.

But after five games, it wasn't working. Although Team Canada's players had come together as a group since Game 1, had worked on their fitness, and were playing better, they were down 3–1–1 in the series after the first game in Moscow. This meant they had to win all three of the final games—in enemy territory—to take the series and redeem Canada's reputation as the world's premier hockey power. They needed something new to give them an edge. Many of the Soviet forwards had been effective in dominating the Canadian zone, and none more so than Valeri Kharlamov. A deadly threat all series, Kharlamov had scored two goals in the opener, earning player-of-the-game honours. Since then, he had been causing no end of headaches for the Canadian defence. On a hunch, assistant coach John Ferguson gave an order that would change Team Canada's fortunes, a turning point in the series triggered by a deliberate act of violence.

Ferguson, who had retired as a player in 1971, was a veteran hockey pugilist. His main job as an enforcer with the Habs had been to protect captain Jean Béliveau from aggressive defenders. Now, in his new coaching role on behalf of his country, he was applying his own style as a former player to the Team Canada

---

* Known as "the father of Russian ice hockey," Tarasov was one of the first Russians to be inducted in the Hockey Hall of Fame when he was selected in the "builder" category in 1974. He had been fired after the 1972 Olympics, despite leading the Soviets to another gold medal victory, so he was not the bench boss for the Summit Series. That honour went to Vsevolod Bobrov.

strategy. Halfway through the second period, he called Bobby Clarke to the bench and pointed at Kharlamov. "I said, 'Bobby, try to tap that ankle of his and break it,'" Ferguson recalled years later, "'and we'll slow him down.'"[27] Clarke, a scrappy young centre from the Philadelphia Flyers, happily obliged. Chasing Kharlamov as he carried the puck into Team Canada's zone, Clarke wound up with both hands on his stick and whacked the Russian's left ankle, breaking a bone. Kharlamov laboured for the rest of Game 6, sat out Game 7, and was ineffective in Game 8. Canada barely won all three games, as required, to win the series. Notwithstanding media criticism of the unsporting behaviour such a dirty play revealed, Clarke had no regrets about what he had done to gain competitive advantage. "If I hadn't learned to lay on a two-hander once in a while," he famously told hockey journalist Dick Beddoes after the series, "I'd never have left Flin Flon."[28]

Another shameful stick incident during the series happened in the first period of Game 8. I don't recall seeing it while watching the game on our classroom TV. Perhaps the dramatics of the third period drowned out that part of my viewing experience as a nearly nine-year-old. (As well as Henderson's winning goal and Phil Esposito's heroic leadership in driving the Team Canada comeback, there was also the spectacle of Summit Series organizer Alan Eagleson getting roughed up by Soviet state police.*) Perhaps I had gone to the toilet and missed it. Or perhaps I was merely distracted, like my classmates and most other Canadians, by the larger purpose of the patriotic narrative uniting us at that moment. I wanted Canada to win.

Earlier that day, Team Canada learned that the Soviets had chosen Josef Kompalla, over their objections, as one of the two referees for the final game. In Game 6, a lopsided tally for penalty minutes—thirty-one for Canada and only four for the Soviets—was seen by Team Canada as being more about Kompalla's

* Eagleson, seated in the stands near thousands of Canadian fans, had stood up and walked down toward the ice, shouting in rage because the goal light hadn't gone on to signal Yvan Cournoyer's tying goal. The cops were trying to lead Eagleson away when Pete Mahovlich and other Team Canada players skated up to the boards near them and began lifting their sticks. They let Eagleson go. As the players escorted him across the ice, Eagleson could be seen on television flipping the bird in the Russian goal judge's direction.

pro-Soviet bias than about their own lack of discipline. Born and raised in Poland, Kompalla was a championship-winning blueliner who emigrated to West Germany at the end of the 1950s and eventually became a referee.* Apart from two exhibition games in Sweden (the first a win for Team Canada, the second a tie), he only co-officiated for two of the final four games in the Summit Series—both Canada wins. But series legend has never quite shaken the idea that Kompalla had it in for the Canadians.

This seemed especially the case in Game 8, when our boys were penalized twice in the first three minutes and fell behind early when the Soviets scored on the power play. Forty-six seconds later, the Canadians were still on the penalty kill when a Soviet player carrying the puck out of his own end got pulled down by forward J.P. Parisé. Kompalla blew his whistle and gave Parisé two minutes for interference. "You bloody German referee!" Parisé shouted, protesting his innocence. "He's carrying the puck!" Kompalla blew his whistle again. "You've got ten more!" he replied, giving Parisé an unsportsmanlike misconduct penalty.

Parisé went berserk. He skated around for several seconds, slamming his stick on the ice, before returning to the bench. Then he got back on the ice and approached the penalty box. Suddenly he spun around in a circle and took a running lunge at Kompalla, who was backed up against the boards. At the last moment, Parisé swung his stick at Kompalla, stopping just short of whacking him in the head. Kompalla could be seen raising a leg and cowering in fear. The game had to be stopped for several minutes as Parisé received a game misconduct on top of his other penalties while his teammates regrouped.

In the wake of the series, some Canadian media commentary excused Parisé's reckless act of rage in the same manner they exonerated Clarke for his mugging of Kharlamov. According to one view, such violence reflected the virtue of necessity; the Summit Series was a showdown between two political and socio-economic

---

* Some chroniclers of the Summit Series have gotten Kompalla's nationality wrong, erroneously recording him as an East German posing as a West German. This mistake might have been caused by credulous interviews with Team Canada players who assumed he was East German.

systems, so Clarke and Parisé had demonstrated civic heroism through their intense fighting spirit. The morning after Game 8, a jubilant Team Canada was boarding a flight to Prague when they learned that Kompalla was on the same plane, sitting up front.* Parisé, seizing an opportunity for mischief, left his own seat to sit directly behind the hated ref. He then grabbed Kompalla by the cheek, squeezing it hard. "I told him I just wanted him to know I was here!" Parisé recalled on the fortieth anniversary.[29] Twenty years earlier, in a commemorative documentary, he had shared what seemed an honest appraisal of his behaviour in Game 8. "Maybe sometimes you don't understand who you are," he said. "Never would I have realized that I would become such an enraged man for two weeks."[30]

By the mid-1970s, a battle was raging in the NHL for the soul of hockey itself. The forces of good were represented by the Montreal Canadiens, who exemplified pure skill at its finest. The forces of evil were led by the Philadelphia Flyers, whose reputation for dirty, violent goonery was well earned. By 1974, the year Philadelphia won the first of its two consecutive Stanley Cups, Bobby Clarke was captain of the team and led by the same example he showed in the Summit Series: Do anything to win, even if it means injuring an opponent. Take away the other team's will to win through intimidation. In this team philosophy, Clarke had a willing co-conspirator in head coach Fred Shero, a cynical pragmatist who knew he'd get better results by throwing opponents off their game than by trying to beat them with pure skill alone.

As Ken Dryden put it in *Game Change*, his 2017 book on the implications of fighting-related brain injuries for the future of hockey,

* After the Summit Series, Team Canada would stop in Prague for an exhibition match with the Czechoslovakian national team before returning home. The game ended in a 3–3 tie. Kompalla was not one of the referees.

> Intimidation had been a strategy used throughout hockey's history—by individual players, and by some teams against certain opponents. But for the Flyers, intimidation became the basic team approach. A superior player who is not focused completely on what makes him superior, but is instead distracted by concerns for his safety, is no longer superior.[31]

During this period, the Flyers were known as the Broad Street Bullies, a team Dave Bidini memorably described as a bunch of "greasy, snaggle-toothed pirates on a bad buzz who'd found a home in the lawlessness and unruly behaviour" that was hockey in the mid-1970s.[32] The "pirates" included Dave "the Hammer" Schultz, Bob Kelly, Don Saleski, and Jack McIlhargey. If those guys were in the sin bin, there were always more who could rough up the opposition or start a brawl: the Watson brothers, Jimmy and Joe, or defender Ed Van Impe, for starters.* These players did the heavy lifting of violence so that skilled players like Clarke (he was versatile), Bill Barber, Rick MacLeish, and Reggie Leach could do their damage on the scoreboard while Bernie Parent stopped the puck.

Walt McKechnie was a veteran of the first few NHL expansion years in the early 1970s. Recalling his playing days as a member of the Oakland Seals, he told Dave Bidini that the 1973–74 season was "nothing but brawls with Philadelphia." During one game at the Spectrum that season, he said, a young teammate named Barry Cummins, who had been called up from Oakland's minor league team, decided to go after the Flyers captain.

---

* Van Impe had the distinction of becoming the second member of the Flyers to assault Soviet superstar forward Valeri Kharlamov. Three years after the Summit Series, the Soviet Red Army team visited the Spectrum in Philadelphia as part of an exhibition series with select NHL teams. With 8:39 remaining in a scoreless first period, Van Impe had just served a minor for hooking when he stepped out of the penalty box and skated up to Kharlamov, cross-checking him in the back. The Russian fell to the ice, momentarily stunned. In protest, the entire Soviet team left the bench and went to their dressing room (prompting Bob Cole's famous play-by-play call "They're going home! They're going home!"). The Soviets returned only after being told that they wouldn't be paid if they quit the game. The Flyers won 4–1.

> As Clarke was skating away, he speared Barry on the forehead and opened him up. The kid went crazy. He chased him to Philly's bench, where he baseball-batted Clarke in the side of the head and knocked him out cold. The wolves on the Philly bench jumped the boards and went after the kid. Cummins cut two more of them with his stick before they jumped him. We jumped too, but our job was to try to pull the wolves off our player, who was getting savaged.[33]

During the early to mid-1970s, NHL players started getting bigger and tougher. Fighting in the game increased as the Philadelphia influence took hold. But after the Montreal Canadiens swept the Flyers in four straight games in the 1976 Stanley Cup final, beginning their four-year dynasty, the Broad Street Bullies' influence began to fade as teams placed a higher priority on speed and finesse. Still, the NHL would never abandon fighting. In one especially violent year, 1986, the Detroit Red Wings led the league with 154 fights, almost two per game. (Even the Flyers at their peak averaged only one per game.[34]) Many hockey fans who supported fighting insisted it was part of the game and should never be banned. More cynical supporters pointed to league revenues: Fighting made lots of money because a huge part of the fan base loved it. But there was yet another argument for fighting, a deterrence theory that defied all logic: If fighting were removed from the game, the thinking went, there would be an instant spike in dangerous stick infractions, because players would be deprived of an important outlet for their emotions.

For several decades, the loudest proponent of this argument was a guy named Don "Grapes" Cherry. Perhaps you've heard of him. For nearly forty years, Cherry had a national media platform with his Saturday night soapbox of "Coach's Corner" on *Hockey Night in Canada*. (Hosted mainly by the CBC but later a Sportsnet/CBC tandem broadcast, Cherry's reign ended badly in 2019, when he was fired for a racist comment about immigrants. But more on Cherry's non-hockey politics later.) Following a mostly successful coaching career in Boston—he was fired after the Bruins lost to the Habs for a third straight playoff year—Cherry spent only one more season behind the bench before deciding the Colorado Rockies were too lousy a team to coach.* His broadcasting career began in 1980, as soon as his coaching career ended.

Cherry's transition to television made sense. First, he was someone who, as Dryden put it, "had grown up in a working-class family, developed into a player of working-class skills, and become the coach of a team with a proud working-class identity," so he would have a significant fan base among *Hockey Night*'s sizable working-class viewership.[35] Second, "he was successful, cranky, and funny: a character; a blustering, ranting, syntax-challenged street kid who spoke basic truths. That was his schtick."[36] That "schtick" combined Cherry's two favourite subjects: love of country and love for a certain type of hockey player from that country. Over the years, his love for Canada was a constant distraction on "Coach's Corner," a segment supposedly dedicated to professional analysis of that night's hockey action from a coach's point of view.

Cherry typically opened his first intermission segment—or changed the subject partway through it—with a story or an issue that had nothing to do with hockey. He would talk about Canadian war veterans, the Royal Canadian Legion, community volunteers, or today's young Canadians serving in the armed forces. (Touchingly, he ended some segments with a roll call of Canadians recently killed in action, the screen showing their profile photos in military attire but with no soundtrack, only the sound of Cherry's voice in the background, often breaking with emotion, before fading to a commercial.) Born in 1934, Cherry was just a ten-year-old kid during the Normandy invasion. But you got the sense from watching "Coach's Corner" that he would have suited up and made the trip to Europe if he'd been just five years older, then lied about his age to join Canada's war effort. The guy simply bled red and white.

Decades before his reactionary populist opinions about immigrants got him cancelled, Cherry pretty much had free reign to talk about whatever he wished. The unthreatening Ron MacLean, his co-host for all but the first couple of seasons,

* The disdain was mutual, as the Rockies fired Cherry six weeks after the end of that one season.

became his foil and did his best to minimize Cherry's excess and get him back to the subject of hockey.* In the early days, Cherry's xenophobia was limited to non-Canadian hockey players in the NHL—particularly Swedes, Finns, and Russians. Europeans were too soft, he said, not tough enough to deliver the goods in the playoffs. (He would eat his words when Nicklas Lidström, Peter Forsberg, and forty-five others won Stanley Cups while Swedish, some of them multiple times; when Jari Kurri and Esa Tikkanen piled up ten Cups between them and sixteen others won Cups while Finnish; and when dozens of players, including a five-man unit on the Detroit Red Wings during the late 1990s, won hockey's holy grail, many of them more than once, while Russian.)

For Cherry, the ultimate test of a player's hockey mettle was his willingness to go into the rough areas (in front of the net, in the corners, and all along the boards—wherever puck battles took place) and his willingness to dish out a hit as well as take one, or, if necessary, drop his gloves and fight. Fighting was a noble sign of commitment to one's team, a matter of honour if it were to defend a teammate or to avenge a previous injustice. This was all part of "the Code," an unwritten set of guidelines agreed to by the players that set the rules for fighting, retaliation, and proper respect. The Code was a way for players to self-police their on-ice behaviour outside the NHL rulebook.† Cherry embraced and promoted the Code with his popular series of NHL highlight compilation videos, *Don Cherry's Rock'em, Sock'em Hockey*, which showed favourite high-velocity hits, fights, and scenes of hockey mayhem.

By the early 2000s, science was ruining the party for Cherry's rock'em, sock'em hockey ideology. Research on concussions in different sports began to

---

* One wonders how long "Coach's Corner" would have lasted with its original co-host, the more cerebral Dave Hodge, who was more pointed about his opinions than the man who replaced him. Hodge was fired from CBC in 1987 when he complained on-air about the network's decision to cut away from a national broadcast of a Habs–Flyers playoff game as it was going into overtime, famously throwing his pen in disgust.

† See Ross Bernstein's *The Code: The Unwritten Rules of Fighting and Retaliation in the NHL* (Triumph Books, 2006).

show a pattern for three in particular for which hits to the head were a common denominator. At first, researchers regarded the sports differently: In boxing, hits were a central aspect of the sport, whereas in hockey and football, hits were incidental. However, the results were the same and had to be taken seriously. In essence, the same three sports that U of T's Brian Pronger had identified in 1990 as having the highest perceived masculinity because of their violence—boxing, football, and hockey—were also the sports in which fighting-related brain damage occurred most often.* And there was more bad news for hockey fighting advocates. In 2023, a Columbia University study analyzed data on more than six thousand players from 1967 to spring 2023. It found that, on average, NHL enforcers died ten years younger than their fellow players who were not designated fighters.[37]

More than three decades ago, the NHL's two biggest generational superstars, Wayne Gretzky and Mario Lemieux, said that fighting should be banned from hockey. By 2026, all that remains for that to happen is a simple vote by the NHL board of governors and some leadership by commissioner Gary Bettman. But I'm getting ahead of myself here. More about Bettman, and his leadership style, toward the end of our story.

In late February of 1977, I was halfway through my Bantam hockey season with the Elks when Universal Pictures released a new Hollywood movie about my favourite sport that was destined to become a cult classic. *Slap Shot*, directed by George Roy Hill, starred Paul Newman as Reggie Dunlop, a minor league player-coach on the

* Hockey's 2011 "summer of death" played a big role in changing the narrative around fighting in the game. That off-season, Rick Rypien, Wade Belak, and Derek Boogaard—all players who had adopted an enforcer role with their respective teams—died after long struggles with cognitive difficulties, memory loss, depression, and concussion headaches. Steve Montador and others would follow, all of them posthumously confirmed to have chronic traumatic encephalopathy, a degenerative brain disease caused by repeated hits to the head. As well as Dryden's *Game Change*, another good source on the consequences of hockey violence is CBC journalist Jeremy Allingham's *Major Misconduct: The Human Cost of Fighting in Hockey* (Arsenal Pulp Press, 2019).

downhill slope of his playing career. He's the veteran leader of the Charlestown Chiefs, a bottom-feeding minor league team on the verge of bankruptcy in a town where the local steel mill is closing permanently, laying off thousands of workers. The Chiefs are plagued as much by their hostile fans as by their on-ice incompetence, so they adopt a more violent playing style to gain popularity and survive.

Slap Shot was billed as a satirical sports comedy, and it was, in some moments worthy of the slapstick label to rhyme with the title. But in its exploration of mid-1970s minor league hockey culture in small-town America, it was also pretty heavy viewing for an impressionable thirteen-year-old. Filled with graphic, even cartoon-like scenes of bloody violence during the play—and subplots revealing hockey culture's antiquated and bigoted views about sex and gender—*Slap Shot* was fully deserving of its restricted viewership rating. I watched it with my father, which was probably a good idea: At that stage of my intellectual and emotional development, I found it hard to tell whether the implied satire was true to its own spirit. Were Hill and screenwriter Nancy Dowd—who based the Chiefs on an actual minor league team called the Johnstown Jets—ridiculing minor pro hockey's descent into violent goonery? Were all those scenes of bare-knuckle fist fights, unprovoked muggings, knock-out punches, and bench-clearing brawls meant to disturb or entertain us? *Slap Shot* appeared to be attempting both at once.

There's no question that Dunlop is old school. He'll do whatever it takes to win, and when the Chiefs do start winning by channelling their inner Broadstreet Bullies, no one is happier than the popular old-timer. At many points during hockey action scenes, it becomes hard to tell the difference between the skill players and the goons, because everyone is taking part in the mayhem. Everyone, that is, except Ned Braden, the Chiefs' top-scoring forward.

The soft-spoken Braden is from a distinct minority in the world of minor league pro hockey: college educated, he doesn't need hockey to earn a living. Disgusted by Dunlop's decision for the Chiefs to goon it up, he refuses to take part in the violence. But he's also miserable because his wife, Lily, hates living in Charlestown, and their marriage is on the rocks. It was in these personal details that it dawned on me, watching the film again a few decades later, that *Slap Shot* isn't really about hockey; it's about straight men's insecurity about sex, sexuality, and gender. The film is riddled with homophobic and misogynistic references, but in every case, the joke is more on the character telling it than on his target. (There are no "out" or visibly gay characters in the film, because gay men wouldn't be caught dead in the same beer-soaked milieu as the uncouth ruffians who populate the Chiefs' universe.)

Here's just a sampling of those references:

- A local fashion show featuring members of the Chiefs shows young defender Billy Charlebois walking the runway, modelling the "Omar Sharif look." Billy is the team's blond pretty boy—every team has one—who doesn't have a word to say but is often seen enjoying the amorous attentions of various women. Meanwhile, two of his rougher, less attractive teammates are in the green room throwing a fit. Sickened by the fashion show and what they're supposed to wear for it, they refuse to go onstage. "I look like some cock-sucking faggot!" cries one.
- Dunlop and goaltender Denis Lemieux are in a bar with the rest of the team, talking about Braden's marital problems and his unwillingness to fight. "He could be a faggot, ever thought about that?" Dunlop suggests, to which Lemieux, incredulous, replies nonsensically, "Are you kidding? He has a big cock—like a horse!"
- Dunlop is in bed with Suzanne, wife of Tommy Hanrahan, goaltender for one of the Chiefs' main rivals. She asks Dunlop if he's ever thought of sleeping with another man. Dunlop says no, he's around naked men all the time and hasn't been tempted. She tells him she slept with the wife of another player, first drunk and then sober, and found it beautiful. Dunlop can relate because, of course, "Women's bodies are beautiful." But Suzanne says when Tommy found out about it, he slapped her around until she had to be hospitalized, because "If I was a dyke, that made him a queer."
- In the Chiefs' next game against Tommy Hanrahan's team, Dunlop uses what Suzanne told him to throw the goalie off his game. Skating around his crease, Dunlop chirps Hanrahan repeatedly: "Suzanne sucks pussy! Hey, Hanrahan, she's a dyke! I know, I know! She's a lesbian!" Hanrahan skates after Dunlop, and the Chiefs score on the play.

- In a meeting with team manager Joe McGrath to discuss the future of the Chiefs, Dunlop reminds his old friend that he once caught him dancing in drag, wearing frilly underwear: "I'm sexually liberated. I don't care who's a fag no more. I mean, who cares? It's natural, it's all around us." But his comment is intended as an implied threat; Dunlop will "out" McGrath with this embarrassing story if he allows the team to fold.
- During a radio interview, Dunlop tells listeners he's putting a bounty on the head of Syracuse player-coach Tim "Dr. Hook" McCracken, promising to pay a hundred dollars to the teammate who takes him out. When McCracken and Dunlop meet in the hallway before the game, the burly Syracuse player snarls, "Dunlop, you suck cock!" Dunlop, before entering the Chiefs' dressing room, flashes his best smile and retorts, "All I can get!"
- During a meeting at her home, the Chiefs' owner, Anita McCambridge, informs Dunlop that she's not selling the Chiefs but folding the team as a tax writeoff. She adds that she has never let her children watch a hockey game. ("Children imitate what they see on a TV screen. If they see violence, they'll become violent.") First Dunlop says she's "fucked" for throwing his players onto the street. Then he insults her son (who's not present). "Your son looks like a fag," he says, heading for the door. "You'd better get married again, or he'll have someone's cock in his mouth before you can say Jack Robinson!"

In *Slap Shot*'s penultimate scene, the themes of sex and violence come together in the Chiefs' final game of the season, the championship match against Syracuse. Dunlop has told his teammates before opening faceoff that the team is folding. Too dispirited to fight, they skate out for the first period and get clobbered on the scoreboard—and in the fights. During the intermission, McGrath comes in and has a screaming tantrum, telling the Chiefs that NHL scouts are in attendance and were expecting to see winners in action, not "pussies."

The players respond in the second period by scrapping their way back into the game. Everyone is brawling except, of course, Braden, who sits alone on the Chiefs bench. The team's return to form is gleefully noted by announcer Jim Carr, small-town America's quintessential self-important radio broadcaster, complete with plaid suit and bad hairpiece. "Well, this is more like it," he enthuses. "Just makes me feel really glad to see the Chiefs back on the warpath again, to coin a phrase." (The next time we see Carr, he is rabidly sharing the crowd's bloodlust for all the fighting: "Everybody's on their feet, screaming 'Kill! Kill! Kill!' This is hockey!") Braden, looking up into the crowd from the Chiefs bench, sees Lily with Francine Dunlop, Reggie's estranged wife. The two women are clearly enjoying themselves and cheering for the Chiefs. How can he impress Lily if he's not going to fight? Then he gets an idea.

Leaving the bench, Braden skates out to centre ice. He pulls off his jersey and starts removing his equipment, piece by piece. Some fans start whooping it up as he continues circling the ice. The high school marching band, enlisted to perform the national anthem that night, perks up from the bleachers and begins playing "The Stripper," an instrumental piece that famously evokes striptease acts. The other players, still fighting, are eventually distracted by Braden's act of protest. As he sashays his hips, an older woman in the crowd is seen enjoying a good look through her binoculars.

But play-by-play man Carr is disgusted. "I don't want any youngsters out there to get the idea that this is the way to play hockey," he says, morally affronted by Braden's nudity but not by the violent brawl. "This is a lascivious display." McCracken too is horrified. The Syracuse player stops fighting and complains to the ref: "Stop that, it's disgusting! Get that pervert off the ice!" When the ref refuses to stop the striptease, McCracken punches him hard, knocking him to the ice. The ref stands up, blows his whistle, and ends the game, declaring the Chiefs the winners. He's about to hand the championship trophy to Dunlop when Braden, now clad in nothing but his jockstrap, skates by and grabs it from him. Beginning a lap around the rink, naked Ned holds the trophy high above his head as the fans cheer. His bare buttocks are clearly visible as he leads his teammates off the ice.

I was still about a year and a half away from realizing my own sexuality when I first saw *Slap Shot*. But I was silently thrilled by the striptease scene. Actor Michael Ontkean was perfectly cast as the earnestly serious Ned Braden. Throughout the film, the viewer wants Braden to loosen up but appreciates his predicament as a talented, non-violent player. He only comes out of his shell—revealing his courage, humour, and individuality—in that over-the-top scene. I already knew where I stood on hockey violence, so the striptease seemed a perfect way to send it up. Of course, it's Hollywood, so Ned and Lily are reconciled at the end. But I still felt a kinship with Braden as someone who felt different and didn't fit in.

Also, I couldn't help noting that he just happened to wear number 10.

Guy Lafleur's number.

My number.

CHAPTER 3

Adult Survivors of *Hockey Night in Canada*

"They shout over the boards while I train. They whisper in my ears as I leave the ice and head to the locker room: 'queer, sissy, faggot.' The whispering is worse than the shouting. But it has become so normal to me that I just assume that this will be part of my life for, well, the rest of my life. I do not know any different and so I expect nothing different."

—WILLIAM BRIDEL, "'What Do You Mean You Don't Play Hockey ... You a Queer or Somethin'?"

The homophobic scenes in *Slap Shot* were my first clue that the sport I loved could be tainted by bigotry, which went hand in hand with the violence many fans insisted was part of the game. Only thirteen and still playing Bantam hockey when I first saw the film, I identified with Ned Braden's sense of otherness because I too felt a sense of difference. It was around this time that I began suffering from a nervous stomach, feeling nauseated whenever meeting new people, attending a formal event, or travelling to a new place. I was still too young to realize that the kind of bigotry I saw in *Slap Shot* might one day be directed at me, and for no other reason than the desires I had yet to realize or comprehend. So I kept on loving hockey, despite its most poisonous aspects, because my experience of the game up to then had been only positive.

Decades later, I learned that other gay men's childhood experiences of hockey bore no resemblance to mine. None of these men recalled their youthful impressions of hockey with wistful nostalgia. My friend Eric, who worked for a local arts organization, gave me a hard no when I first invited him to my apartment to watch a Canucks game on TV. "You must be joking," he said, offended by the notion. "I'm an adult survivor of *Hockey Night in Canada*." By this he meant that Saturday nights in his family home during hockey season had been deeply oppressive. His father had made *Hockey Night* mandatory viewing, regardless of whatever else was on TV or whatever other activities the family might have planned. Eric was not alone in hating hockey for this reason. I met other gay men with similar stories, a bushel of bad memories associated with *Hockey Night*. The tyranny of a drunken father or bullying brother pre-empting everyone else's idea of how Saturday night should unfold. Zealous possession of the remote to keep the channel fixed on the game. The family room monopolized for three hours as the "men" tuned out everyone else while expecting the women to fetch more beer and pretzels.

For those haunted by such memories, *Hockey Night*'s anthemic opening music—Dolores Claman's "The Hockey Theme"—was hardly the stuff of reassuring nostalgia. Instead of conjuring up memories of great hockey action, the CBC sportscasters' powder-blue jackets, or intermission features like "Showdown" or Peter Puck, that triumphant music became a trigger for traumatic recollection. To gay men in the making for whom hockey was an unwelcome intrusion, that repetitive opening horn riff had sinister cadences, every creepy note portending the aggressive and possibly menacing male bad behaviour to come.

Quite apart from its oppressiveness in childhood, TV hockey didn't have a lot to offer the adult gay male viewer, either. Unlike other team sports such as soccer, rugby, or Aussie rules football (whose uniforms expose plenty of skin on the male athlete, showing off beefy arms and legs thanks to high-cut, taut-fitting shorts that leave little to the imagination), there was nothing in the visual presentation of the hockey player to attract the disinterested gay male observer.* For one thing, the player's physical beauty was invisible: His entire body was armoured with equipment that concealed his physique, conveying nothing remotely erotic.

Even if there was a pretty face beneath the helmet, you'd likely be disappointed when that player was interviewed between periods on *Hockey Night*. This was partly due to the medium itself, which prevented reporters from asking anything too interesting lest the response be controversial. The hockey player interview became such an infamous cultural trope, with its cliché-ridden, irony-deficient banalities ("We gave it 110 percent," "If we work together as a team we know we can win," etc.) that every clip was potential fodder for bitchy gay ridicule. The refreshing exceptions—Ken Dryden for his sharp intelligence, Brett Hull or Jeremy Roenick for their candour and outspokenness—were few and far between. And even those guys weren't exactly homosocial. They weren't surprising us, for example, by sharing their favourite Maria Callas arias or name-dropping novelists like Christopher Isherwood, now, were they?

If I couldn't get my friend Eric to watch hockey on TV, there wasn't a snowball's chance in hell of getting him to attend a game at the Pacific Coliseum (or later, when the Canucks moved downtown, at General Motors Place before it became Rogers Arena). The hockey rink, when filled to capacity for its main purpose, could feel like a throbbing mass of heteronormative, conservative Canadian culture.† When gathered in crowds, hockey fans never looked or sounded like people you thought might be gay. If you eavesdropped on their conversations during intermission, you wouldn't hear a lot to suggest you might bump into these same folks at the opera, public library, or a boutique fashion store the next day.

---

* At least not in mainstream media, until *Heated Rivalry* came along. In gay porn, the hockey player stripped down to his jockstrap and shoulder pads has always been something of a kinky subgenre for hot athlete sex scenes. By 2025–26, some *Heated Rivalry* critics actually complained that Shane and Ilya don't fuck with their equipment on. But as our discussion of the series demonstrates (see Chapter 12), most viewers find their sex scenes smoking hot, regardless of what they're wearing (or not).

† And outside the rink, in the streets of Vancouver, when a Stanley Cup Game 7 was involved—at home (2011) or away (1994)—you could add "riotous" and "unhinged" to that heteronormative energy.

And what a strange anachronism that every NHL team made it mandatory to have the national anthem sung before every game, even though the hockey action was professional rather than a contest of nations. And that the anthems were sometimes accompanied by a military presence. These were just a few signs that the live hockey game was not a queer-friendly space.

Among gay men who have been alienated from hockey all their lives, no one has had it worse than the figure skater. If there were such a thing as a Purple Heart for adult survivors of my favourite sport—some form of official recognition of the courage it took to resist hockey's hegemonic hold over the experience of Canadian boyhood—its most deserving recipients would be the men who, as boys, had the courage to choose figure skating over hockey. Targeted for homophobic abuse regardless of their sexuality, these men made themselves vulnerable as boys just by being who they were and wanted to be and by expressing themselves artistically on the ice. Ridiculed by other boys, the male figure skater was subjected to abusive bigotry for no other reason than the stupid idea that figure skating is just for girls.

Hockey players in particular resented the male figure skater for choosing the silent inner world of a low-masculinity individual sport (more of a creative pursuit) over the compulsory camaraderie of a high-masculinity team sport. As if the queer male figure skater's effeminacy, his visible gayness, was not enough of a threat to their own sense of manhood, hockey players could not fathom how another guy could prefer a sport that emphasized aesthetics over aggressive physical contact. And they were jealous of these "homos" for being better skaters than they were.

One of the most revealing personal accounts of this experience is that of William Bridel, a sports sociologist and former competitive figure skater.* Bridel

* For Bridel's story, I have drawn from his essay "'What Do You Mean You Don't Play Hockey ... You a Queer or Somethin'?': Reflections on Life as a Non-Hockey Playing Canadian Boy," published in *Overcoming the Neutral Zone Trap: Hockey's Agents of Change*, edited by Cheryl A. MacDonald and Jonathon R.J. Edwards (University of Alberta Press, 2021), 229–245.

was that rarest of creatures in the small Ontario town where he was born and raised: a nondisabled white male who not only never played hockey in his youth but also never attended a single hockey game at any level. Nor, as an adult, had he watched an entire NHL game on television. Not even Olympic hockey games when Canada was playing the US. On the final day of the 2010 Winter Games, when most Canadians were glued to their screens watching their men's hockey team win gold, Bridel was teaching a yoga class in Kingston. *Sidney Crosby in overtime? Yawn. Whatever.*

Bridel came by his anti-hockey snobbery, his purposeful indifference to the sport, honestly. From early childhood until his peak years in competitive figure skating, he was taunted, bullied, harassed, and even sexually assaulted by Canadian boys and young men who played hockey. His story should be familiar to any male figure skater who fails to comprehend the appeal of a sport that has done nothing but oppress them all their skating lives. As Bridel recalled, his problems began at age five when he got his first pair of figure skates, a hand-me-down from his sister—they were white. Boys at the local rink, waiting to play hockey after his skating sessions, teased him about those skates. "The problem, it seems, is that white skates are for girls. *Everyone knows that*," he wrote.

By age eleven, Bridel had

> endured six years of being called "queer, sissy, faggot" on a more or less daily basis. I am frequently shoved around, punched, and on occasion kicked. This mostly happens during recess at school, but the boys who bully me are hockey players so it is pretty much guaranteed that if they miss me at school, they will find me at the rink.[38]

And on it went, throughout adolescence and into young adulthood. At one point, Bridel was invited to a sleepover under false pretenses by a hockey player he was attracted to—only to become the victim of a degrading group sexual assault by that player and his teammates.

Stories like Bridel's illustrate why so many gay boys of his generation and older had no interest in hockey whatsoever. And it partly explains why those of us who did play the game as boys rather than pursuing figure skating ended up running away from hockey as adolescents. In those days, such alienation from the sport was the inevitable result of societal homophobia, something we could no longer endure in the hockey community. Today, that seems more of a generational problem, an issue bound to disappear with increasing societal awareness of the diversity, equity, and inclusion (DEI) principles I'll address later. But from those of us who did experience that estrangement, there is much to learn about how bad hockey homophobia could get and why gay men like me felt we needed to cancel hockey before hockey cancelled us.

Of course, not all of us had the same reaction. Some gay boys who were far better hockey players than me actually picked up figure skating as a way to improve their game—only to find that, as competent figure skaters, they were soon under pressure to exploit their talent and fully immerse themselves in that world instead of hockey. One such hockey player was Robert Thompson from Thornhill, Ontario. Thompson, whom I interviewed in Toronto in the fall of 2025, was never a superstar but was a solid positional defender who received good coaching from his father. He was smaller at five foot eight but learned to use his strength and balance well. Today, still playing at sixty-three, he attributes his skating excellence to the two years he spent as a preteen pursuing a sport his fellow hockey players dismissed as only for girls and homos.

"I wanted to improve my skating overall, so I took some figure skating," he told me. "I got all of my badges in the first year ... In my second year, they started me into dance because I picked it up so quickly. But I was teased a lot. I was getting teased by the hockey players who found out—I was still playing hockey—and I was teased by people around me. I was one of two males, everyone else was female. And I wasn't effeminate in any way."

Wait, he was teased even though he was masculine presenting?

"I always had a soft edge to me, but I wouldn't call myself a masculine guy, or a masculine kid, but I was absolutely not feminine either. I was middle of the road. I was in tune with my emotions, things bothered me more than others. I was sensitive, but I guess I *was* masculine presenting because I wanted to fit in with everyone."

Many years later, his mother told him she had wanted him to pursue a figure skating career because his coaches thought he could go all the way to the Olympics. "They didn't talk to me, they talked to my mother," he said, contemplating what might have been. "But I was talking about getting out because I was getting teased. So I excelled at it but only lasted a couple of years in figure skating." He continued with hockey, playing in the Ontario Minor Hockey Association's competitive leagues before deciding to move down to house league selects at sixteen or seventeen. He never quit hockey, unlike so many other gay boys; instead, the figure skating he left behind would become a gift to his hockey play that kept on giving.

"What I got out of that was that I was an amazing backward skater, because you have to skate on your heels and not on your toes. And I could do things the other players couldn't, so even with my stature, I was put on defence because I was very good. To this day, even at my age, thirty- and forty-year-olds have a hard time getting around me. I've had people challenge me, and I've been able to beat them, even the young ones. I've slowed down over the years, but I still have that ability to skate, so thank God I did [figure skating]. I don't ever regret that experience. I regret my mother not telling me about the Olympics, because if she'd done that, maybe I would have changed my course."

For some of us, hockey in early childhood provided comforting reassurance through its ubiquity; it was part of classic Canadiana. The sight of players interacting, the sound of sticks and skates scraping ice, the commentators giving us the play-by-play, and artistic renderings of the game—from James Duncan's mid-nineteenth-century watercolour *Skating on the St. Lawrence* to Molly Lamb Bobak's World War II–era *La Partie de Hockey*—reinforced the sentimental notion that we were somehow united as a people because of that cold game on ice. But making the transition from aesthetic appreciation to direct participation is another matter. For some gay men, early childhood appreciation of hockey was a fascination they outgrew. This proved to be the case for Peter Thomas, an old acquaintance I decided to interview after he showed me a championship plaque he had won as a ten-year-old in 1961.

The plaque, a simple wooden piece, bears a circular image of a boy hockey player in action above a bronze plate that reads "K of C" (Knights of Columbus) above the words "HOUSE LEAGUE" and "1960–61 CHAMPS." So, what was the story with the plaque? Thomas won it during his final year playing hockey. He recalled having to sit out the third period of the championship game, benched in favour of a better player who helped his team win. I felt sad for Thomas, but he said he never felt bad about it. He was even okay with the fact that his name wasn't on his plaque, while his teammates each received one with their name on it. I would never have kept a childhood memento with such a sad story attached to it. But Thomas kept his plaque as a reminder of his individuality, which ultimately drew him away from hockey before it could become emotionally damaging.

Thomas, who worked in international development and now lives on Bowen Island in BC, is a transplanted Ontarian born and raised in Toronto. His earliest memory of hockey, like mine, was watching it on television with his family as a preschooler. "I always found, as a kid, that hockey was just there," he told me. "It was part of your life, and at that time, I couldn't distinguish a Canadian from a European lifestyle. I found it kind of meditative and soothing. It was just always in the background. When I watched it on TV, it was a kind of sedative. I don't know if I was mesmerized or not by the puck, but I never really followed it. And when everyone else went, 'He shoots, he scores!' then I'd wake up."

At age six or seven, all of Thomas's friends at his Roman Catholic school in Etobicoke played hockey with the Knights of Columbus team, so he wanted to play too. "But when I got there, I didn't care about the hockey, really. I was just there for the socialization," he said. "The hot chocolate machine was really important, but I hated getting up really early in the morning and having to go to practice." He enjoyed the skating but hated the cold. Then there was the hockey itself: not what he expected. He was put on defence without being asked, and he didn't enjoy the experience. "I found it really, really awkward with all the hockey gear on, and then putting it on and taking it off—I hated that part," he told me. "I didn't want to get bodychecked, and I didn't want to fall. I wanted to play, but I didn't want to play."

Survival badge: Peter Thomas's championship plaque, 1960–61

From his recollection, it's clear that Thomas lacked the basic priorities a hockey player needs to succeed in the sport at its most basic level. "You get on the ice, and I'm like, 'Oh, don't give me a breakaway or anything like that, because I probably couldn't handle it well,'" he said. "You know, I wouldn't know what to do with the puck. I was more interested in who was in the bleachers." On one occasion, both his parents attended one of his games, and he found himself on an actual breakaway. Halfway through it, he stopped to wave at his mother in the bleachers: "Look, ma, I've got a breakaway." Inevitably, an opponent easily stole the puck from him.

Before our interview, Thomas had spoken with his older sister, who remembered how the family listened to hockey games on the car radio while driving back from the cottage on winter weekends, as well as how frustrating Thomas's interest in hockey had been for the family. "You wanted to play hockey because your friends were there," she reminded him. "All you wanted to do was go there and hang out with your friends, but you weren't very good at it, and it ruined Sundays for us."

Thomas remembered the day he decided to quit, after his team won that championship. "There was this clinic, a special clinic for hockey players at the outdoor arena," he explained, meaning a hockey school. "My parents said, 'Go check it out and sign up if you want to be a good hockey player. See if you want to do this.' So I went, and oh, it was awful. It was really, really hard. I just watched—I didn't go on the ice with the class." The players, he said, were put through a series of "fancy" drills, including proper checking. It sounded just like the hockey school I attended in Nanaimo fifteen years later. I had loved it, but Thomas was horrified by the very idea of skills development. "I said, 'I can't do this, I don't want to do this,'" he said. "Then I met up with my mom and said, 'No, I'm not going to do it. I want to take up skiing.'"

From that point on, Thomas lost all interest in hockey, including as a spectator. Thanks to a client of his father's, he was lucky enough to receive comp tickets to Leafs games, which he shared with a friend. But once they arrived at Maple Leaf Gardens, they would sell the tickets and go see a movie instead. (This stopped after the client, watching a game on TV one night, saw someone other than Thomas and his friend sitting in their seats.)

Our interview revealed just how different Peter Thomas's experience of hockey had been from mine. Here was a gay man who had been fascinated with the sport as a child, just as I was, except that his early appreciation of it was more ethereal, almost abstract: He enjoyed its "soothing" or "sedative" effect—the last words I would ever associate with such an intensely physical sport. Here was a Toronto native who came into consciousness during the mid-1950s, both watching and listening to Leafs games, but he didn't know who Foster Hewitt was. (He did say the name sounded familiar.) He was also a bit vague on legendary Leafs owner Conn Smythe. ("Did he play as well?") At various points during our conversation, he struggled to recall the right words for basic hockey concepts. When he was in college, a hockey-playing friend got him a job at an arena "where I had to keep the scoreboard, or the light board, or something." (He was the timekeeper.) But all he really wanted to do was drive the "Jamboozie" (the Zamboni). When he played, he didn't want his teammates to "shoot toward me" (to pass). Thomas had never truly embraced the game enough to care about it. As difficult as it might be for some Canadians to imagine, he was hardly alone in this.

My own youthful alienation from hockey was a gradual process. At first, my exclusion from the sport was involuntary. After two seasons of minor hockey in Nanaimo, I was suddenly pulled away from the game at age thirteen by having no place to play it. After my Grade 8 year, my parents were concerned about my vulnerability as a sensitive, prepubescent child. Worrying that two more years at my rough public junior high school would have harmful effects, they sent me down island to a private all-boys boarding school for Grades 9 and 10. At this school, hockey was available only to elite players for its varsity program—boys cherry-picked mostly from Grades 11 and 12. Only one Grade 9 student made the team. It wasn't me.

By the time I came back home and returned to public school in the autumn of 1979, I had just been through a summer of rehab after corrective surgery to both my hips following a rapid pubescent growth spurt. More than two years had passed since my last hockey action. Once recovered from the surgery, I tried to imagine going back into Nanaimo's minor house league system and found I was no longer interested. Was I worried about my hips? Not at all. My body had the bounce-back typical of a healthy sixteen-year-old, and I would soon be back on the ski hills with relish. Had I lost my passion for hockey or assumed my skills had atrophied? No again. My avoidance of organized hockey in 1979 was all about survival.

During my final semester at boarding school, about six months before turning sixteen, I finally reached puberty after an excruciating delay. Along with the sudden physical changes came new awareness about my sense of difference. I now understood why I suffered from a nervous stomach, always vomiting before new adventures, and why I never talked about girls the way other boys did or thought of them as anything but friends: all my sexual fantasies involved boys. Boys from my dorm. Boys from my class. Boys I'd seen in the dining hall or showered with after PE. And Hollywood cuties like Leif Garrett, Robby Benson, or Scott Baio (before the politics). Because of delayed puberty, I was small for my age. During rugby, I was often pummelled into the ground by stronger, more developed classmates. Afterward, in the showers, I endured the humiliation of my unmanly privates being exposed for all to see. Back home and blooming months later, I had left that problem behind. But now there was a new one: What if I got near naked boys again—in public showers or after a swim at the lake—and a cute guy caught me checking him out? What I wanted most was what I feared most.

Then there was hockey itself. What was once a simple pleasure, the joy of sport, was now dangerous. As I discovered through school conversations, organized hockey was a serious business for sixteen- and seventeen-year-old boys. If you were still playing the game at that age (especially in Nanaimo, where the Clippers were a feeder team for the Western Hockey League's Victoria Cougars), it was probably because you were competing to get to some higher level. There was hitting in the game now, and goonery, which had never been a factor in the minor hockey house leagues where I had last played. The stakes were higher. Such a serious level of the sport was out of the question for a non-athlete ungifted with talent. I was no Nick Foglietta, that's for sure. Not even close.*

But even if I had played non-competitive rec hockey in the same age group, with career competition a non-issue, the dressing room presented a problem that hadn't been there in Bantam or Peewee. At age twelve or thirteen, the hockey dressing room was a safe and supportive space for most boys. We were all just kids having fun, with nothing to prove. But once you were sixteen or seventeen, the dressing room became a hornet's nest of jacked-up testosterone, full of exploding hormones and aggressive male energy needing release. Now, words like *faggot*, *homo*, *queer*, *pansy*, and *cocksucker* were part of the pre- and post-game banter, as well as the on-ice trash talk. In the interests of team bonding, such words were casually thrown around to dismiss the opponent, with the assumption that none of them—in their true meaning—applied to anyone in the room. For if they did, the object of the epithet would swiftly be taken outside.

To be sure, hockey was not the only factor in my decision to remain in the closet. There was also my enslavement to Catholic guilt and, after 1981, the fear of AIDS. But hockey's cultural influence meant that the homophobia surrounding it was not confined to the rink. Many hockey players in their mid- to late teens felt compelled to prove their manhood at every opportunity—including outside the rink. Of course, not all hockey players were like this. During Grade 8, my one year of public junior high school, I recall witnessing an incident involving Barry Pederson, a Grade 10 student and underage star with the Clippers who would go on to a successful NHL career. Intervening to stop a schoolyard fight, he pulled the larger kid off the one he was beating up and told him to pick on someone his own size.† Pederson was a decent fellow.

---

* Nick Foglietta grew up near the same Nanaimo neighbourhood I did and attended the same public schools as me, from kindergarten through Grade 12. A natural athlete, he worked hard at his hockey game and didn't seem to take success for granted. I always respected him as someone from our part of town who made it to the Clippers and had a few good seasons with them.

† It pains me that Pederson, whose best NHL years were on Rick Middleton's line with the Boston Bruins, was the player the Vancouver Canucks received in the Cam Neely trade, arguably the worst in Canucks

But some of them were idiots. On one occasion at our family home, another member of the Clippers showed up uninvited to a party my younger sister was hosting while our parents were away. When the party was over and everyone was leaving our house, this hockey player with the swaggering attitude refused to go. One of my brothers insisted he leave, so he puffed out his big chest and challenged him to a fight. My brother was surprised, less by the Clipper's bravado than by his sense of entitlement. When two friends joined my brother to find out what was going on, the hockey player took one look—they were both bigger than him—and changed his mind. He walked out the door, sulking. Before he showed up, I had privately thought of this guy as a bit of a hottie; now I thought of him only as a hothead. A fool. Not attractive at all.

According to the homophobic logic of late-1970s and early-'80s Canadian suburbia, boys who liked other boys could not possibly become "real" men, and those most visible in their sexual preference—the demonstrably effeminate—should be made to suffer for it. The first gay bashings I ever heard about were delivered by late Midget* or Juvenile hockey players preying upon some unfortunate queen who happened to be in the wrong place at the wrong time. At that age, I was fortunate enough to be straight presenting in my comportment, making me less of a target for violence. But I wasn't completely safe. The one time I was taunted with drive-by catcalls of "Faggot!" was while walking down a busy road with fellow thespians, still fully made up and ecstatically in character after a theatrical performance. Hockey taught me a sad lesson: If I wanted to survive in the real world, I would need to be straight *acting* as well as presenting.

---

history. The Bruins failed to inform the Canucks that Pederson had undergone two surgeries to remove a benign tumour in his shoulder, the second of which required the removal of muscle tissue. He put up some decent numbers during his first two seasons in Vancouver but was nowhere near as dominant as he had been with the Bruins. Meanwhile, Neely went on to become a Hall of Fame superstar in Boston. The Bruins also received the Canucks' number-one draft pick as part of the Pederson trade, which got them future star defender Glen Wesley

* *Midget* was once used to describe the age category for hockey players younger than eighteen. Considered derogatory to people with dwarfism, the term was abandoned in 2020–21 when Hockey Canada changed the division name to U18 (under 18).

I still hung out with the same peer group I'd enjoyed playing ball hockey with before my departure for boarding school. These guys were around during the summers and after my return home for Grade 11, so we picked up where we'd left off. But something was different about those checking games now. Because of the changes in me, I no longer found ball hockey as carefree an activity as I had before puberty. One of my acquaintances was suddenly more attractive than when I'd last seen him. A new player who joined us was disturbingly hot, as well. Hyperaware of this problem, I was determined to keep it a secret, and that took work. The stealth of avoiding detection required constant acts of subtle hetero mimicry, such as lying or being vague whenever asked about my non-existent sex life.

Unlike other closet cases who projected their insecurity in obvious ways, I was careful not to overcompensate with excessive displays of fraudulent macho posturing. Apart from requiring too much energy, such a strategy would have been unconvincing from such a little nerd as me. But I did succumb to the whims of peer pressure, such as drinking beer and smoking weed before, after, and once even during a checking game. The one time we got wasted during the play, refreshing ourselves with cold beer instead of water—as if that would hydrate rather than dehydrate us—and then smoking a joint, the results should have been predictable.

At first, we played harder under the influence: exerting ourselves to exhaustion, struggling for possession along the cement "boards," running quickly to the net, and taking big slapshots regardless of our ill-protected goalie's safety. But inevitably, the more pissed and stoned we got, the sloppier our play became. After six or seven beers and a bit of reefer, some of us ended the game covered in scrapes and bruises, battered from bumping into and falling over each other and tripping into the wall, the pavement, or the goalie. We also knocked out a lot of stucco that day, violating my father's directive not to use the side of our house like the "boards." I was only sixteen or seventeen then. But after that game, I never drank or toked up again while playing any kind of hockey. A good lesson learned once I did return to the ice.

For the first five years after I left home in 1983, I avoided the ice completely. I even stopped playing road hockey, with the rare exception of family reunions, when my brothers hit the pavement for some shinny. It was only when I landed my first job in journalism, as the reporter/photographer for a Fraser Valley newspaper, that the game drew me back in an unexpected way. Now twenty-five and still a virgin, I was tall, skinny, and earnest: just the sort of fellow a young woman could take home to the parents. At the *Hope Standard*, I was the only man on staff, joining four women. At the end of my first day, the ad sales rep, a spunky and quick-witted Australian, stopped me before I left the newsroom. "This is a small town, and everyone knows everyone else's business," she warned me. "You're the only reporter here, so people will want to know more about you. Who you are, where you're from, what you're into. So if you don't have a girlfriend within two weeks, we'll know you're gay." She was kidding, but her candour was so refreshing that I couldn't help deadpanning as I walked out the door: "Don't hold your breath." She opened her mouth wide in silent shock and then smiled.

My colleagues had my back. I knew they would protect my secret and was pretty sure they did. But that didn't make the small community any less of a fishbowl. Hope was a much smaller town than Nanaimo. Other than my one-bedroom rented apartment in a 1970s-era low-rise near the train tracks, a dreary retreat darkened by a thicket of fir trees, there was nowhere to hide from the locals I depended on for good quotes and primary source material. My spunky Aussie colleague was right: People *did* want to know about my personal business. Where was the little lady? Why didn't I have a wife and two kids? I soon tired of the intrusive questions and my own Rock Hudson mask, the fraudulent reassurances that I just hadn't found the right woman.

In the closet for nearly a decade, I was desperate to break free but couldn't come out just yet. Not in this town. But after about the tenth time I was asked about a girlfriend, I found a solution: signing up for drop-in hockey at the local rink. Once it got around that I was on the ice every week joining scrimmages with local men—including loggers, truckers, mechanics, and gas jockeys—all the questions stopped. Suddenly, I no longer got strange looks for confirming my single status. The message? *Relax, everyone: If this reporter guy plays hockey, he can't possibly be a homo.* Part of me was relieved. The strategy worked, and the pressure was off. But another part felt like a total hypocrite. In high school, I had walked away from hockey because of its culture of bigotry. Now I was walking right back into it, using that same toxic culture to my secret advantage. Hiding in plain sight.

The adult men's version of rec hockey in Hope was a club that wouldn't have had someone like me as a member had it not been for my Oscar-worthy performance in passing as straight. These were God-fearing, Conservative Party–voting, salt-of-the-earth, small-town family men, working-class guys without post-secondary educations who sprinkled every other sentence with "fuck." What would they have thought, had they known the truth about their local newspaper reporter/photographer: That I had abandoned organized religion and hoped one day to be delivered from the misery of small-town existence. That I preferred the Russian to the Western version of our favourite sport. And that I had no sexual interest in women and inside, was screaming for release by bedding as many hot young dudes as possible.

The hockey part was easy. It was great being back on the ice again, finding my skating legs, rediscovering the skills I'd picked up at hockey school and in Peewee and Bantam. This was drop-in, so most of the players knew each other, and the on-ice action was friendly. We all shared a healthy regard for our opponents—not a hint of goonery, and no cheap shots—knowing that we had to get up for work the next morning. But the dressing room was not so easy. There was constant small talk to avoid the silences that straight men find discomforting while naked in each other's presence, chit-chat about family activities for the coming weekend. I'd invent vague plans to visit out-of-town friends. Otherwise, I kept my head down and my mouth shut—all I needed to do, I was certain, to emerge from this experience unscathed.

But that was before a cocky nineteen-year-old Rob Lowe look-alike returned to drop-in after a short absence. A skinny white boy with black hair and smooth tanned skin, his big brown eyes were deep pools of mystery I couldn't resist staring into a few times. Once or twice, he caught me doing this and turned away, avoiding my gaze. I quickly pivoted, feigning indifference. Too late, I thought, convinced my cover was blown. Surely the rumours would begin circulating. Even if not, I knew it was going to be difficult to be in the same room as this little hottie without some kind of incident occurring between us—a fist fight, say, or, when no one else was around, a blow job. Or perhaps both. Such is the cost of being so deep in the closet.

I had recently seen *Youngblood*, a 1986 Hollywood hockey melodrama about a talented seventeen-year-old forward, played by Rob Lowe, who dreams of NHL stardom but is not considered tough enough for the Big League. Dean Youngblood, who happens to wear number 10, is tormented by his biggest rival, a ruffian named Carl Racki, who calls him "Pretty Boy." Changing in that dressing room at the Hope Arena with *this* Pretty Boy, then playing with him on the ice before returning to the dressing room to shower beside him, was dangerous. I kept picturing Rob Lowe in one of those slow-motion scenes from *Youngblood*, the sweat dripping from his flowing black hair and immaculate pecs. I had to get out of there. Fast.

Before long, I came up with a credible excuse to drop out of drop-in: nagging pain from a non-existent previous injury. Within a few days, the time I'd been spending on the ice was all taken up by the time it took to drive to Abbotsford for my first gay and lesbian club meetings in a private basement, clandestine gatherings safe from the prying eyes of the Valley's sizable Jesus crowd. Not long after that, barely six months into my first reporting job, I won the lottery: I was the last cub reporter chosen for a summer internship program at the *Vancouver Sun*. I wouldn't stay long with the *Sun* before going freelance, but I would always be grateful for that summer gig. It was my ticket out of Hope and out of the closet at last.

By then, I was certain that my hockey life was over as well.

PART 2
HOW I RECLAIMED THE GAME

CHAPTER 4

A Gay Games Sport

"Remember, no one wins on a march; no one tries to. We all march forward together."

—IAN MCKELLEN, closing address, Gay Games IV (1994)

One afternoon during the summer or fall of 1989, I was skimming through the local gay and lesbian monthly rag when I spotted a story about a big sporting event being planned for Vancouver the following year. Celebration '90: Gay Games III & Cultural Festival would be the third edition of an Olympics-style competition founded by Tom Waddell, an American physician and former decathlete who had competed at the 1968 Summer Olympics in Mexico City. Waddell, who later became an active member of San Francisco's gay bowling league, wanted to create a gay and lesbian version of the Olympics that emphasized fair play and goodwill, inclusiveness, and individual achievement—but without the toxic politics of the globally recognized original brand. Waddell and his new federation also had a public relations agenda: As more gay men had begun dying of a mysterious disease linked to their sexual activity—a connection established the year before the first event—the Games would present gay men and lesbians as healthy, wholesome, striving for excellence, and, in a few cases, capable of setting world records.

Not surprisingly, the International Olympic Committee (IOC) wanted nothing to do with this. The IOC sued to prevent Waddell's organization from using the word *Olympics* for its name and branding. This was obvious discrimination, given that the Special Olympics, Nude Olympics, Police Olympics, Dog Olympics, and other events using the big *O* name had not suffered the IOC's wrath. Predictably, mainstream media coverage of the lawsuit was mostly homophobic. And that only mobilized support from within the communities Waddell was trying to reach. Gay Games I (1982) and II (1986), both held in San Francisco, drew enthusiastic crowds and support from progressive media. Vancouver had won the bid to host Gay Games III, marking the movement's debut outside the US, so the event was becoming a big deal in my newly adopted home city as the one-year countdown to opening ceremonies began.

I had first learned of the Gay Games during the fall of 1988 while living in the Fraser Valley. Every now and then when I was bored, I'd pick up a fundamentalist Christian newspaper and scan the alarmist headlines for amusement. One front-page banner had really stood out: "Sodomite Invasion Planned for 1990." The story warned all good Christians about the moral depravity and bacchanalia sure to consume Vancouver in the flames of hell, should the Gay Games be allowed to proceed. But there was also a partisan purpose to those Christian alarm bells: mobilizing Burnaby voters to unseat New Democratic Party Member of Parliament Svend Robinson in the upcoming federal election. Since his dramatic coming out earlier that year on CBC's *The National*, Robinson had been targeted by homophobic media and hate mail from across Canada. Blaming him for the Gay Games—as if the country's first out gay politician must have been the lead conspiracist—the Bible thumpers were hoping the "end of Svend" would also herald the end of the Games. Instead, Robinson was easily re-elected—and would be many more times—and the Games were held as planned from August 4–11, 1990.*

* As a bonus, a writers group I would join that summer was inspired to appropriate that newspaper headline, reclaiming it for a new gay men's literary journal, *The Sodomite Invasion Review* (1990–94).

Since moving to Vancouver, I had anticipated Celebration '90 as a final public way to celebrate my own coming out. Little did I know what a triumph it would turn out to be. At first I assumed my involvement with the Games would be limited to "athletic supporter" (pun intended): I would take in a few events as a spectator, and perhaps volunteer for one of them, but not participate directly. At twenty-six, I was a non-athlete—or at least, an untalented athlete—who did not excel at summer sports. Despite being a more-than-capable swimmer, I was in no state of fitness or training to compete in a race. But one day, I dropped by the gay and lesbian centre to visit the Gay Games office and find out how else I might get involved. When I first walked in there, I was hoping to be conscripted as a towel boy for men's swimming, diving, water polo, Greco-Roman wrestling, or some other aesthetically pleasing event. But when I picked up a brochure and scanned the list of scheduled sports, my eyes popped at two words.

Ice hockey. I couldn't believe it. Hockey at the Gay Games? In August? And not just for lesbians? Yes, Canada's national game—one of the most homophobic sports—was being introduced as a Gay Games event, including for the men it had alienated as boys, allowing us to reclaim it. This seemed too good to be true, an inspired example of self-empowerment through cultural resistance. The very essence of gay liberation. Like the lonely soul who thinks he's the only homo in the world until amazed to find out otherwise, I almost shouted out in that office, "You mean I'm not the only one?!" Unlike the other listed sports, for which talent and skill level would be deterrents, I had no hesitation about embracing the participatory spirit of a Gay Games event for hockey, a sport I first played at age twelve. This despite the fact that any self-assessment of my skills as a forward, based on those few turns around the Hope Arena ice during drop-in, at best labelled me a lifelong intermediate.

Hockey's inclusion as a Gay Games sport meant, for one thing, that organizers were confident there would be enough teams for a tournament. Thanks to hockey's homophobic reputation, it was also fair to assume that such an event would have no Gretzky- or Lemieux-calibre, elite-level talent on display. Few, if any, highly skilled gay male hockey players had received the institutional or community support necessary for their talent to flourish in the game's top tier. And even those fortunate few, if they did exist, would be too closeted to risk exposure by participating in such a high-profile gay pride event. For this reason, I was confident that even the best hockey players at the Gay Games would be several rungs below elite level, meaning that even a plodding beer leaguer like me faced pretty good odds of cracking the Team Vancouver lineup. Among the men who registered, we'd have in common our love for the game and, since puberty, our estrangement from it. Count me in!

Seeking more information, I turned to my first contact at the Gay Games, office manager Mary Brookes: a butch lesbian with a thick British accent and a brush-cut mop of spiky brown hair dressed in a white tank top bearing the Gay Games logo, always with a lit cigarette dangling from her fingers and a good one-liner at the ready. I asked Brookes where to sign up for hockey, and she said I would need to contact the LA Blades, Southern California's gay men's hockey club, as they were the tournament organizers. After getting over my amazement that Los Angeles had established a gay hockey team before Vancouver had, I asked why an American hockey club was organizing a tournament taking place in Canada. Her answer was that the Games organizers couldn't find anyone from the host city interested in doing it.

"I'll do it!" I exclaimed, without considering the implications of such a commitment.

Brookes smiled. "I'll get you their contact info, love."

From then on, hockey was back in my life, fully reconciled with my adult sense of self.

How novel, the prospect of playing my favourite sport, with sexuality being beside the point! Once I reached the LA Blades by phone, they were happy to return organizing responsibilities to the host city and instead concentrate on winning gold. I shared their response with Brookes, who then began searching for a local lesbian hockey player to co-organize the event with me. Once they found Holly Pruden, she and I split the duties for tournament logistics and contacting registered teams. (In the cosmopolitan spirit of the Games, teams represented cities instead of countries.) But when it came to player recruitment for the host city, there was an uneven playing field: While Pruden had a team of local lesbians already registered for the Games and more individuals who hoped to play, my search for gay men to form a second Vancouver team was a Sisyphean task.

For all my excitement at stepping back into hockey as a newly liberated gay man, I had forgotten how counterintuitive this new enterprise would seem for so many other men in my community. While some of my gay brethren were impressed to learn that hockey would be in the Games and wished me good luck, others regarded me as a sad and pathetic figure, like some deluded street-corner preacher trying to sell bibles on Davie and Thurlow. *Hockey?! You mean that bloodsport where men beat the living shit out of each other? The sport with all the fighting and dirty stick work—all that whacking and hacking? And the homophobic taunts? Why on earth would any self-respecting gay man want to participate in such an activity? Self-loathing, much?* These were some of the first adult survivors of *Hockey Night in Canada* I would meet, gay men whose childhood grievances with the sport had been well founded.

With hockey proving such a tough sell in the gay village, there was little I could do but write about it. Riffing on a then-popular book that satirizes masculine stereotypes, *Real Men Don't Eat Quiche*, I published an essay titled "Real Fags Don't Play Hockey" in the April 1990 edition of *Angles*. My point—to undermine the stereotype implied by the headline—was confronting community resistance to the idea that hockey could be reclaimed as a gay men's sport. "Canada's most popular team sport inspires stereotypical, macho attitudes among straight and gay men alike," I began. "Perhaps it's heterophobia, or a need to separate gays and straights by what they do in their spare time, but there seems to be an unwritten assumption that, to be a truly self-actualizing fag, one must choose between two polar opposites: the barbaric or the aesthetic."

My argument was simple: A recreational, non-contact version of hockey could be a safe place for gay men to be ourselves while embracing our athletic side and enjoying hockey's best qualities. And what were those qualities? High-speed breakouts with tape-to-tape passes. Artful set plays that lead to beautiful goals. Skilful defence that relies on stick checking, shot blocks, and safe, well-timed body checks instead of slashing or dangerous elbows to the head or body slams into the boards. Great goaltending that cuts down the angles and challenges the shooter, making full use of the body to keep the puck out of the net. "The way its critics describe it, you'd think hockey was just sixty minutes of fighting and spearing," I wrote, forgetting to mention the role of *Slap Shot*—the 1976 Hollywood film mentioned earlier—in reinforcing that stereotype.

"What about the playmakers? What about the skaters?" I pleaded. "When Gretzky circles the entire offensive zone unchecked before setting up a perfect play from behind the net, is that not poetry? When Stéphane Richer moves past a defender by faking a shot and then slipping the puck through his legs, is that not art?" To gild the lily, I appealed to the reader's appreciation of certain NHL stars' hotness—always the talented "finesse" players, the "gentlemanly" Lady Byng Trophy candidates, never the goons—as extra motivation to watch hockey. (At the time, I had a thing for "Lucky" Luc Robitaille and other lean, smooth-skinned players like him.) I anchored the piece, naturally, with a pitch to join me on the ice at the Gay Games.

Apart from a few readers offended by the ironic "fag" references, the essay was well received. I began hearing from men who'd played hockey as young boys but abandoned the game at puberty. They said they'd love to give it another try but didn't know where to find affordable equipment or gay-friendly ice time. The equipment solution was easy enough: There were plenty of sporting goods stores, including a few used-equipment outlets, in the Lower Mainland. But ice time was more complicated. In the *Angles* piece, I mentioned drop-in hockey at the West End Community Centre. But that option, despite its location, was a mainstream hockey milieu where straight men played before going out for beers. So how safe was it, really?

My lesbian co-organizer, Pruden, didn't even have to leave Commercial Drive to find players. Lucky for her, there was no shortage of East Side dykes willing to show up at Britannia Rink to join the already registered women's team for scrimmages. But I was on my own in the West End, a hockey desert for gay men, and growing desperate to fill my roster. With only a few weeks to go before the

Games opened, on the last possible registration date, I finally found enough players through the *Angles* article and word of mouth to arrange an ice rental or two. I was grateful to Pruden for sending me the few women I still needed to complete my roster.

I recall nothing of the pre-tournament scrimmages. But I do recall my alarm at the closetedness of some of my male teammates—their discomfort, the closer we got to opening ceremonies, about the prospect of media covering an event for which they had signed up of their own free will. It was here I learned one of my first sobering political lessons about gay liberation: Despite our shared desire to be free, we all have different levels of anxiety and ways of coping as gay men, especially when it comes to the pressures and expectations of orthodox masculinity in mainstream culture. For me, the matter was simple: After a long hibernation, I had come out at last—not screaming my sexuality from the rooftops but no longer hiding it, either. My politics were typical of an earnest human rights activist, with all the militance one might expect of a lapsed Roman Catholic recently unshackled from his Vatican chains. I was getting on with life by living without compromise, more than happy to be witnessed in a gay milieu.

Zealously prescriptive, I wanted everyone to achieve and celebrate the same hard-won liberation I had. My assumption was that all participants regarded the Gay Games the same way: as a public expression of celebration, a shared rejoicing in the simple fact of being ourselves. I thought we all felt, or sought to feel, the same way: fearlessly confident and happy to be seen by our friends and families, who were allies in embracing the moment of our own becoming. But such a perspective was far too idealistic. As a couple of my teammates would demonstrate, true liberation is never as simple as one declarative statement or a single event. One player was forced by his own experience of hockey bigotry to adopt a personal survival strategy of quiet discretion; another, from a powerful family, feared media exposure.

The first was the best player on our team, a gifted skater with offensive talent who had once been a referee in the Western Hockey League (WHL). For years, Russ Neely had moved up in the game as a ref, advancing in every level of on-ice officialdom until reaching the pinnacle of major Junior hockey. Neely had every reason to believe that those green lights would keep going for him all the way to the NHL, where he could become part of the world's top refereeing fraternity. His WHL colleagues told him as much. However, the walls were closing in; his career ambition was colliding with his desire to be true to himself. He had grown up in the heart of the Fraser Valley Bible belt, in a town where evangelical homophobes typically spewed their bigotry at any sign of unorthodox male behaviour. And so, from elementary school onward, he had put on a survival mask of pseudo-straightness. This mask would serve him well in hockey, especially in the black-and-white world of the zebra-striped ref, where poker-faced inscrutability was a necessary component for projecting impartiality.

The pressures of being a ref in the WHL, a significant feeding source for the NHL draft, are heavy for anyone, regardless of sexuality. The fan abuse to which all refs are still subjected today—abuse that includes homophobic taunts and epithets—has long been seen as part of the game. Straight presenting and masculine, Neely had a good cover; he doubted that anyone in the hockey world suspected his secret. During his first season of reffing in the "W," both teams in a division final asked him to officiate. But by the time his second season began in 1984–85, Neely—already hiding his homosexuality from fellow on-ice officials, players, team staff, and rink personnel—was finding the pressure unbearable. Every night, he could hear the mobs of drunken fans screaming at him from the stands. "Whenever I heard shouts of 'You faggot ref!' I wondered if my mask might be slipping," he told me recently, breaking a public silence of four decades. "I may have had the courage to referee for league finals, where games drew as many as fifteen thousand fans, but not to do it as an openly gay man. Even if I did possess such courage, I knew that opportunity would not exist if I were true to myself. So I decided it's either hockey or it's me, and—to borrow the title of Derek Sanderson's book—I decided, 'I've got to be me.'"*

* See *I've Got to Be Me* by Derek Sanderson with Stan Fischler (Dell Publishing Co., 1972). Best known for his play with the Boston Bruins during their early-1970s Stanley Cup glory years, Sanderson stood out from most of his NHL colleagues with his larger-than-life personality and independent ways. These qualities later got him into trouble off the ice, a period captured in his second memoir, *Crossing the Line:*

In January 1985, Neely called up the WHL's executive director and supervisor of officials and told them he was quitting. He was met with shock: "After all the training and sacrifice, you now decide to quit when you're this close?" The only explanation he gave was that he wanted to pursue a different path. Five years later here he was, signed up for the Gay Games where he could enjoy hockey as a player without putting himself in the crosshairs of unwanted attention. At the time I hoped he would share his story with any media covering the Games, failing to appreciate how raw this traumatic experience still was for him. Now he was coming out at his own pace by participating in a more positive sort of blending in: the solidarity of shared experience through gay sports. After the hell he'd been through as a ref, there would be good karma for Russ Neely. A few years later, he became one of the few guys in my little hockey world who met their future husbands by playing on the same team.

The other player was the son of a prominent personality in Canada's media aristocracy, a highly intelligent young man of my age who worked in high tech and had moved to the West Coast from Toronto. He was friendly and seemed to embrace the unique camaraderie we shared as gay teammates. But one day, just before registering for the Games, he approached me to talk about confidentiality. Who would see his name in the Gay Games office or on the roster sheets? Terrified at the thought that his identity would be revealed and his participation exposed, he was afraid of bringing shame upon his family, who did not know he was gay. This surprised me, as I understood his father to be on the more progressive side of the federal Liberal Party. Respecting his request, I did my best to ensure his anonymity. I made sure he didn't appear in any photos. I kept him away from media, keeping an eye open whenever news reporters were at the rinks. But I could not prevent his name from appearing on the roster sheet; every Games participant had to be on the record with their own personal ID. In the end, he was not exposed, and I'm certain he enjoyed himself during the Games. But once the event was over and I

The Outrageous Story of a Hockey Original (Triumph Books, 2014), co-authored with Kevin Shea and with a foreword by Bobby Orr.

was looking to build a team for the future, I think he moved away. He was a good guy. I hope he found happiness.

One of the problems gay hockey players faced in the struggle for self-acceptance was a lack of cultural representation. Apart from the rarest exposure in the queer press (a US gay sports magazine had profiled the LA Blades), in 1990 there were no images of us in popular media playing the game we loved. So if the public didn't see gay hockey players, then we couldn't possibly exist, right? But the Gay Games were coming up. There would soon be more opportunities to crowd the public sphere and change the narrative. Or at least try to.

Early in 1990, I was invited by local photographer Daniel Collins to model for his *Gay Athletes* exhibition, to be held at a Yaletown art gallery during the Games. Each of us who posed for Collins was a registered Gay Games athlete representing our respective sport. There were no rules as to how we presented ourselves; the purpose was to challenge conventional thinking about those sports and who played them. Honoured to be ice hockey's model, I showed up with most of my gear and a Montreal Canadiens jersey. Given the high degree of media interest in the Gay Games, I knew that whichever image Collins chose for my *Gay Athletes* photo would get exposure beyond the gallery display. And so, from the moment I arrived at his studio, I thought about what message to send through my portrait.

This would be my final, no-turning-back gesture of coming out, so I had to get it right. At first I tried all the predictably masculine poses: Standing in the faceoff position, looking directly at the camera, leaning over and holding my stick with both hands. Standing up straight with my stick to the side, holding its knob with one hand. Raising my stick to the sky with both arms up, as if celebrating a goal. And more of that kind of thing. As I tried different poses, I knew the audience was not just the general public or the gay community but also the mainstream hockey establishment. I was in a position to send a message about the culture hockey valorized while also demonstrating that I belonged in the game, and on my own terms. So I camped it up.

The author camping it up for the *Gay Athletes* exhibit, 1990

Of course, hockey's biggest homophobes would be disgusted by whichever "faggoty" pose I came up with. But I didn't care. I was happy to rub my sexuality in their faces after enduring so many years of their shitty expressions of hetero culture being rubbed in mine. As Collins aimed his camera, encouraging me to step out of the orthodox, the first person I thought about was Tiger Williams. Yes, David "Tiger" Williams of Vancouver Canucks / Toronto Maple Leafs fame. The most penalized player in NHL history. Tiger's pugilistic skills were legendary in the hockey world, where violent play was culturally acceptable masculinity. Like most NHL ruffians who brought some offensive skill to their game (he was a leading scorer in his Junior days), Tiger loved scoring goals. So much so that he'd come up with a ritual to celebrate his best tallies: After scoring, he would take a few hard strides away from the net and, turning his stick around and keeping its blade flat on the ice, sit on its leaning shaft and take a nice long glide down the rink, taunting his opponents and their fans by waving and pointing at them with one hand while holding the knob of his stick with the other. High theatre.

Queering up the Tiger Williams goal celebration was a lot of fun, as Collins snapped away at me in his studio.* Not that anyone would have recognized whom I was lampooning; I was wearing a Habs jersey, and Tiger had never played for Montreal, so the reference would be lost on most viewers. But the Tiger Williams pose was the one Collins chose for my *Gay Athletes* portrait. Months later, during the week of the Gay Games, when the exhibition was open and drawing attention, I happened to meet Brian Pronger, the University of Toronto academic whose new book, *The Arena of Masculinity*, would be on its way to the printer in a few weeks. Pronger, who was in Vancouver to attend the Games, was invited for brunch—along with a small group of local culture vultures that included me—to the Kitsilano home of UBC French lit professor Floyd St. Clair and the novelist David Watmough. A booze-soaked midday affair highlighted by Floyd's excellent

* Collins, later expanding on this motif, would photograph another model riding my stick—naked, except for my helmet, skates, and gloves, his notable tumescence dominating the frame—and call it *High Sticking*, one of a subgenre of photo projects he would categorize as "humo-erotic."

cooking and David's fine gossip, the brunch featured much talk about the Games and what they meant for our liberation. At one point, I told our esteemed guest that I was co-organizing the hockey event. Intrigued, Pronger said he was still compiling images for his book and asked if I knew of any good photos of gay hockey players. I told him about the *Gay Athletes* photo by Daniel Collins: a black-and-white portrait of me in full hockey gear, camping it up while riding a hockey stick. I said nothing about Tiger Williams.

"Oh, do have him send it to me," said Pronger.

The photo was published, along with other images from *Gay Athletes* and more photos taken by Collins around the city during the Games, in *The Arena of Masculinity*. To Collins's and my amusement, after the exhibition was over, the photo of me also appeared in *Angles*, *Xtra! West*, the *Vancouver Sun* (twice, including with my review of Pronger's book), and on the cover of *Parallelogram*, an arts magazine. In its naughty reclaiming of classic Canadian iconography—the hockey player's bending ass and sarcastic limp wrist, the masturbatory innuendo of his other hand on the stick, and that cheeky, come-hither gaze at the camera—the photo struck a nerve.

This was Pronger's take in *The Arena of Masculinity*:

> Dan Gawthrop was one of the organizers of the hockey tournament at Gay Games III. Hockey is traditionally seen as a powerful expression of orthodox masculinity. As a gay hockey player who eschews that orthodoxy, Dan has here taken the traditional symbols of athletic masculinity and undermined them with camp sensibilities that give full expression to the paradox.[39]

So far, so good, I thought. *He's nailed it*. And then this:

> The question remains open as to whether the stick he is riding should be read in its phallic significance or in reference to the broomstick of the Wicked Witch of the West in *The Wizard of Oz*.[40]

Ha! I hadn't thought of the *Wizard of Oz* connection. But then, I wouldn't have; while the importance of *Oz* to gay culture was well known, no one of my generation used *Oz* references (i.e., friends of Dorothy) as cultural code for gayness. So Pronger was aging himself a bit with that cheeky broomstick reference, and it could be argued that taking the piss out of Tiger Williams undermined orthodox masculinity even more than Pronger imagined. When his book was published, I was thrilled to be identified as a gay athlete through that photo and was generally impressed by his commentary on sport. But when I first read his passages about the game of hockey, my immediate reaction was defensive.

According to *The Arena of Masculinity*, my favourite sport was inherently violent. But didn't hockey's appearance in the Gay Games prove the opposite? Were there not many advocates, and not just gay men, calling for an end to fighting in hockey? If Pronger's contention that hockey was innately violent were true, then how could someone like me have embraced the game so completely? I had never fought and rarely got even a two-minute penalty for minor infractions like holding, hooking, or tripping. I wanted the game to be a safer place for gay men and all people who felt unwelcome in the sport. I hadn't quite formalized the idea in my mind at the time, but any success toward that goal would also serve to improve the game itself.

The hockey action at the Games was as predicted: With a mix of skill levels, the atmosphere throughout the tournament was upbeat, and everyone had fun. Why wouldn't we? There was something liberating about making plays, gaining the offensive zone, and going to the front of an opponent's net knowing you weren't going to get throttled into the boards, flattened with a dirty mid-ice hit or cross-checked in the head for being too effective. From the "D side," it was confidence inspiring to know you could lift an opponent's stick with your own to prevent a shot or beat them to the puck with more effort, and they weren't going to cheap shot you or call you nasty names. There was lots of laughter on the ice, collective recognition that we were enjoying hockey the way we'd always wanted to, even laughing at ourselves when we fucked up because we knew we wouldn't get benched for it. This was a welcome change from the kind of hockey where, even in the beer leagues, some players took themselves far too seriously.*

Like the Olympics, the Gay Games were held every four years. Once again, I would struggle to find enough players to build a Team Vancouver for Unity '94: Gay Games IV in New York City. But thanks to the recruiting and organizing skills of a good friend who came to the rescue—more on him in the next chapter—we did send a team to New York. Then we did it again for Gay Games V in Amsterdam (1998), Gay Games VI in Sydney, Australia (2002), and the first World Outgames in Montreal (2006).† While I did join the team for the New York, Amsterdam, and Sydney Gay Games, I did not make the trip to Montreal for the Outgames.

By 2006, I was freshly married and in my early forties. No longer craving the adrenalin rush of the throbbing party circuit that the Gay Games experience offers single men, I had also grown bored with it. By this time, I had been out of the closet for seventeen years; the Games had long since fulfilled their purpose, for me, of affirming my sexuality. Though my gay identity remained important, I had lost

* Considered the tournament favourites before the Games, the LA Blades had to settle for silver after losing gold to Team Seattle. My team, the Vancouver Real Puckers, won bronze.

† The Outgames event was organized by a splinter group that had left the Federation of Gay Games over several issues, mostly surrounding disagreement over the budget for the Montreal event. When the Federation responded by stripping Montreal of Gay Games VII and awarding the event to Chicago (on the dates originally planned for Montreal in 2006), the queer sports movement split in two. The anti–Gay Games group, led by Canadian Olympic gold medal–winning swimmer Mark Tewksbury, formed its own federation, the Gay and Lesbian International Sport Association (GLISA), and scheduled the first Outgames in Montreal for the week after Gay Games VII. The Cutting Edges sent a team to Montreal, while a Vancouver women's team played in Chicago. (Their story is told in Chapter 8.) The World Outgames held two more events (in Copenhagen in 2009 and Antwerp in 2013) before GLISA collapsed. On the eve of the fourth Outgames in Miami in 2017, most events were cancelled, triggering fraud investigations. As of 2026, the Federation of Gay Games stood alone as the international queer sports organization of record. As this book went to press, Gay Games XII was scheduled for València, Spain, from June 27 to July 4, 2026.

interest in seeking solidarity around it through international community sporting events, a milieu I had come to find too politically conservative. And, since my big coming-out party at Celebration '90, I had soured on the particular assimilationist politics the Gay Games embraced.

It's fair to say that Tom Waddell's original concept of the Games represented progress for the gay and lesbian liberation movement. Insofar as they pushed the "coming out" envelope at the beginning of the AIDS pandemic, the Games were an affront to mainstream sensibility. In almost every other respect, however, the Games would eventually pander to mainstream sensibility. Beneath the surface of an admirable liberation agenda was a problematic ethos: Rather than defiantly embracing and promoting diversity within gay, lesbian, and bisexual expression (this was before trans people were widely recognized), the Gay Games sought the approval of mainstream culture by presenting an acceptable face of homosexuality, a more palatable image for corporate America, whose funding it sought. Needless to say, this required a degree of compromise that undermined the goals of gay liberation in multiple ways.

During the lead up to the Vancouver Games in 1990, big advertising dollars were available—for the first time in the city's history—to promote this large, unprecedented event. But some suppliers were antsy about having the words *gay* or *lesbian* appear on their ad displays. Instead of challenging this homophobia directly or exposing it in local media, the Vancouver Gay Games' board of directors caved to the advertisers. The official Celebration '90 ad images showed wholesome athletes with the message "Come celebrate with us!," which offered no clue as to what was being celebrated. Daniel Collins, the photographer for these ads, was not impressed by this cautious approach to the event's mainstream ad campaign. "It's closeted," he told Stan Persky for his "Mixed Media" column in the *Vancouver Sun*. "The more closeted we are, the more we're going to be treated like sissies. It's time to be brave and proud."[41]

The Unity '94 Gay Games in New York City coincided with the twenty-fifth anniversary of the Stonewall riots. There were complaints that racialized and disabled people were underrepresented in Games advertising and that the Federation's mainstreaming of the Games also marginalized the transgender community. Given that these very same minorities had led the protests that gave Stonewall its significance, the Federation's marketing strategy was shocking in its obtuseness, oblivious to the historic political struggle being commemorated that year. Games officials also cautioned pride parade attendees not to be too butchy as lesbians or too queeny as gay men. Visible agitators like Dykes on Bikes and ACT UP were relegated to the back of the parade. Not surprisingly, such prioritizing of straight-looking, straight-acting homos did not go over well in New York City.*

But the Federation saved its worst betrayal for Amsterdam. On the eve of the '98 Games, the first held outside North America, the Federation cancelled the same-sex pairs event in figure skating because the International Skating Union (ISU), which regulated figure skating, had ruled that same-gender teams violated its definition of a "team" as one man and one woman. In response to the ISU's threat to punish skaters and judges who participated, including with a permanent ban, the Federation had one job: to stage a media conference to condemn this homophobia and commit to holding the event for teams willing to participate. They should also have lawyered up to challenge the ISU in court for any punishment of skaters or judges. Instead, they caved. The event was held as an exhibition, devastating athletes who had come from around the world to join a legitimate competition and celebrate their pride. These athletes were reduced to a novelty act by a Gay Games board too timid to stand up for the rights we had all fought for.

All the hockey teams at the Amsterdam Games were happy to have found a safer place to play our game and celebrate our liberation. But we were there to celebrate *all* queer athletes. How sadly ironic that another group of queer athletes (including the gay male figure skaters, who were arguably more courageous than us gay hockey players, given that their sport exposed their sexuality rather than hiding it) were denied having the safest space possible by their own community,

* For my part, I was happy to join ACT UP's "die-in" outside St. Patrick's Cathedral. Apart from its political purpose of raising awareness about a homophobic religion's response to AIDS, the die-in achieved the added virtue of pissing off cardinal John O'Connor by stopping traffic for several blocks surrounding the cathedral.

punished from within for pursuing free expression in a sport long presumed to be the domain of women and gay men.

Gay pride is great. Gay shame? Not so much.

CHAPTER 5

The Cutting Edges

"When the Cutting Edges hug, they really mean it."
—A STRAIGHT HOCKEY PLAYER

During the week of Celebration '90: Gay Games III & Cultural Festival, while playing in the hockey tournament I helped organize, I had a chance encounter with an acquaintance that would lead to events that finally produced the safe gay male hockey environment I'd been seeking. I had just finished a game at Britannia Rink with the Real Puckers, one of the host city's two teams at the Games, when I heard someone call out my name from the bleachers as I left the ice. Smiling and waving at me from the stands was *Vancouver Sun* reporter Kevin Griffin.

I had met Griffin during my brief stint at the *Sun* the previous year. We had worked on one story together but never gotten to know each other personally. I had heard it through the city's lavender grapevine that he was one of a handful of gay men at the paper. (In those days, one had to be discreet about sexuality in a big-city newsroom. The *Sun* was managed by rugged Brits and other aging white men, their faces flushed with the whiskey of their liquid lunches as they ogled the young female staffers.) I hadn't seen Griffin since early January, when I was last in the newsroom. Now here he was, notepad and pen in hand, covering the Games in his capacity as the *Sun*'s multiculturalism reporter, a fact we both found highly amusing.

"Dan, this is great!" he enthused. "I had no idea they had hockey. I wish I could have played!"

"Well, maybe you can next time," I replied. (A throwaway line, really, since I had no confidence there would be a "next time.")

Over the three years that followed, Griffin and I became good friends. But other than joining a few drop-in sessions here and there, we didn't do much on the hockey front. In the wake of Celebration '90, there was no urgency to build a new hockey team. The struggle to build a roster that first time was still fresh in my mind. But during the fall of 1993, when Gay Games IV organizers in New York City ramped up their call-out for registrations, Griffin and I got serious and put our heads together. The Real Puckers no longer existed, but a few of the players were still around. One of them, a lesbian realtor, offered to host a meeting at her apartment west of Denman. Griffin and I, along with one other player, attended this meeting with her.

She wanted to play in New York at the Games and was willing to help put together a roster. I shared my frustration that there'd been no momentum from Celebration '90, no realistic way to keep the Real Puckers together to continue playing on a regular basis. I didn't want to start over from scratch every four years, assembling a team for the Gay Games only to disband it when the event was over. Griffin agreed that we should try to build a team that would last. At the same time, we discussed the importance of the team name to its identity. Real Puckers was a bad pun—cute for the moment, but as random and temporary as the roster I had assembled in 1990. A few straight friends and relatives had suggested "Gay Blades," a tired sixties slang reference I knew was bad because, well, straight people had thought of it. In any case, the team from Southern California had already taken Blades for their name, so we weren't going to be copycats.

Meanwhile, there was the question of where to play after the New York Games were over. Given the challenge just to assemble a team for the same event every four years, the notion of an all-gay league in a city like Vancouver did not seem realistic. Even if we did stay together after Unity '94, it was pretty clear we would have to compete in a regular beer league against mainstream (i.e., straight) teams. What were the options, apart from the rec leagues run out of municipal rinks? Griffin told us there was a duffer league at the Thunderbird rink on the Point Grey campus of the University of British Columbia (UBC). This was recreational, non-contact, safe adult hockey for all skill levels. Perhaps playing on the grounds of an educational institution would be a safer route for a gay team than a regular beer league run by the municipalities, offered Griffin. But if we wanted to sign up for this league in time for the next season, we would have to investigate the idea as soon as possible. If UBC turned out to be a good fit, we could be signed up and ready to go for our first season right on the heels of Gay Games IV.

"Wow, guys!" exclaimed the lesbian realtor. "That would be amazing, getting into the UBC league as a gay team. I mean, that would be really cutting edge."

Those last two words jumped out at me. "That's it!" I said. "We have our name right there."

The name Cutting Edges would telegraph our hipness, our relevance as groundbreaking gay hockey players competing outside our safety zone of the gay ghetto. It was a good hockey name too, incorporating the idea of the damage that skate blade edges can do. In a team name, such a double entendre implied a menacing opponent. Griffin endorsed it, and so did the realtor and the other player present. Soon my boyfriend at the time—a graphic designer for a local architectural firm—got to work on a logo and team colours. We ended up going with a teal, black, and white scheme similar to the early branding for the San Jose Sharks. The logo design featured a gender-neutral silhouette of a hockey player winding up for a slapshot, their body on the left side of a teal-and-black triangle that looked like a West Coast mountain or a reclaimed pink triangle symbol. "CUTTING EDGES" slid in from the right in giant block letters, one word above the other.

The logo and jersey design were impressive—much slicker than the barebones stick figure design and one-colour amateurishness of the Real Puckers logo (which, if memory serves, was designed at the last minute by the company selling the jerseys). But the Cutting Edges had branding before we even had a team; once again, as in 1990, player recruitment was a challenge. This time Griffin took charge, picking up where I'd left off. "I remember being desperate, especially to get people to go to New York," he told me in an interview three decades later. "Putting up little pieces of paper, with 'Players Needed' and a phone number to tear off and call, at Little Sister's and all those places.* I don't know why I didn't think of doing that at hockey rinks. It was only later, when we needed players for the league, that I did it out at UBC."†

Ideally, any hockey team competing in a tournament should have at least thirteen skaters and a goalie.‡ But as the countdown to Unity '94 approached the registration deadline, we were well short of that number. Many people we contacted wanted to join us but couldn't afford the trip to New York or the time off from work to attend the entire week of Gay Games IV. In the end, we sent eight skaters and a goalie to the Big Apple. We didn't have a hope of reaching the podium like the Real Puckers had, but we did manage a 3–3 tie with the eventual bronze medal winners from Detroit. In our four other games, all losses, we managed to keep the scores close.

Back in Vancouver after Unity '94, Griffin got to work recruiting players for the Cutting Edges' inaugural season at UBC. This time, he expanded the outreach effort by papering public hockey rinks with the "Players Needed" bulletins he had used for the Gay Games recruitment drive. "I thought, 'Oh, I'm putting up a gay thing here,' so there was a little trepidation," he recalled. "When you hear the pucks hitting the boards, and it's cold, and it's this kind masculine-assertive

* Little Sister's Book and Art Emporium, Vancouver's LGBTQ+ bookstore, was then located on Thurlow Street. "Those places" included the West End Community Centre on Denman and the Gay and Lesbian Centre on Davie.

† To his credit—and my undying gratitude—Griffin included his own phone number, becoming the Cutting Edges' main contact person.

‡ A thirteen-skater roster has three forward lines and two pairs of defenders.

environment, and you're doing something new in that situation, that's a little stressful." But he pressed on with the clandestine advertising campaign, putting up the bulletins at UBC's Thunderbird rink, Britannia Rink in East Van, and the West End Community Centre's rink.

"Did people seeing them tear them down? I have no idea," he said, still amazed he didn't receive a single crank call, homophobic message, or sexual come-on after leaving his own phone number for a gay hockey team in so many visible places around the city. But at the time, he was less concerned about invasion of his privacy than about player recruitment, still an all-consuming struggle. The Edges were breaking out of the gay ghetto by playing in a straight league, and that made it harder to find people. "I had some idea there were a lot of players who were gay and had played hockey but stopped for whatever reason," he told me, "so the question was how to get in contact with them." By the time season one began, the Cutting Edges had found enough players for a full roster of thirteen skaters, with a few spares on call. The team registered for a Monday night division playing at the UBC Thunderbird Sports Centre's Father Bauer Arena.*

In the beginning at least, our mere existence was indeed cutting edge. At the first league meeting Griffin attended, he informed UBC and all the other team reps that the Edges were gay. "For a moment, everything stopped, and no one said a word. Then the chair just nodded at me and moved on to the next agenda item," he recalled. "I made a point of speaking up because I wanted there to be no doubt in the mind of league organizers what the Cutting Edges were all about. I didn't want them or anyone else saying afterward that we weren't up front about who we were from the start. We were. It was like coming out once and being done with it." Once the inaugural season began, the team had something to prove. The Cutting Edges' opponents knew all about the team's identity and connection to the Gay Games, but the chirping, or trash talk, was confined to the harmless kind with few,

* Named after Father David Bauer (1924–1988), a player, coach, educator, and Roman Catholic priest whose program to develop players for the national men's ice hockey team led to his induction as a member of the Order of Canada, as well as the Hockey Hall of Fame, Canada's Sports Hall of Fame, and the halls of fame of Ontario and the International Ice Hockey Federation.

if any, homophobic epithets thrown around the UBC rinks. (Those we did hear we reported to the league. Eventually, the rules incorporated homophobic taunts as grounds for a game misconduct, joining racist or misogynistic taunts.)

Trevor MacNeil, who joined the Edges in season two and has served in multiple board positions, including president, remembered how the team gained respect around the league. "In the early years, most people thought we'd be a pushover," he told a UBC student documentary filmmaker for a course project. "But then it was like, 'Oh, some of these guys can really play hockey,' and we competed with the other teams. Some of them were a little better—there's always someone better than you—but most of the time, we competed, and that earned us the respect, I guess."[42] The Cutting Edges proved we could play, so we belonged. Soon we were sharing after-game beers with our opponents, and before long, the Edges were just another part of the larger hockey community. Joining a straight league turned out to be a learning experience for everyone, ourselves included. And, of course, there was humour.

Griffin recalled a moment at the Thunderbird lounge, while enjoying a few beers after a game one night, when he heard our opponents talking about us. They knew we were listening when one of them said, "Yeah, when the Cutting Edges hug each other, they really mean it." It seemed a witty acknowledgment of cultural difference, not a judgment. "It was just in reference to 'Oh, they like each other,' whereas when straight guys hug, it's just a recognition of camaraderie or something," he told me. "'There's a little extra because they're gay, the Cutting Edges, and we don't have that little extra—we're still men,' or something like that. I didn't think it was homophobic. It was clever—a nice line—and I thought, 'Okay, I like that.'"

The Cutting Edges became a registered society on March 10, 1998. After electing our first board of directors, the club began sponsorship relations with several organizations and donated to good causes—including Vancouver's Dr. Peter Centre in support of its work at the time providing comfort care and day programs for people living with HIV/AIDS. After team contributions reached $20,000, the Centre dedicated a dressing room in its gym to the Cutting Edges. Throughout all this, the club kept growing. Over the years, the Edges would expand to add more

Members of the Cutting Edges entertain crowds at the Vancouver Pride Parade during the late 1990s teams. At one point in the late 1990s and early 2000s, there were four teams in different divisions at UBC. Meanwhile, as part of the network of LGBTQ+ teams in North America, we competed at tournaments in Calgary, Toronto, and Montreal, as well as in Seattle, New York, Boston, Chicago, and Denver.

We eventually hosted our own tournaments in the Lower Mainland, as well as sending teams to the Gay Games. And we became a popular presence at Vancouver's pride parades. Early appearances featured a rollerblading routine that players would interrupt to mimic a hockey fight, first dropping our gloves and then ... embracing each other to kiss. In more recent years, the Edges connected with the Vancouver Canucks as the NHL team joined the city's pride parade while the Edges took part in in Pride Nights at Canucks games. More on this later.

While Griffin and I, along with MacNeil and a small core of dedicated players, were helping to get the Cutting Edges off the ground on Canada's West Coast in the mid-1990s, similar efforts to build queer hockey teams were happening in other cities throughout North America. By 2026, there would also be LGBTQ+ hockey associations in Calgary, Edmonton, Toronto, Hamilton, Ottawa, Montreal, and Halifax.* In the US, the pioneering LA Blades would be joined by active queer hockey associations in Boston, Buffalo, Chicago, Columbus (Ohio), Denver, Madison (Wisconsin), Twin Cities (Minnesota), New York City (and Albany), Palm Springs, Phoenix, Pittsburgh, San Francisco, Seattle, and Washington (DC). There were also ice hockey associations in Sydney and Melbourne, Australia.

---

* In fall 2025, William Bridel—whom we met in Chapter 3 as a former competitive figure skater who had been terrorized by hockey players in his youth—shared the joy of belatedly discovering that there had long been queer hockey in Calgary, his adopted city. A sports sociologist at the University of Calgary, Bridel published online his thoughts about Calgary's growing queer hockey scene and what he'd learned about the history of the Calgary Gay Hockey Association (rebranded the Calgary Inclusive Hockey Association in 2019) and the International Gay & Lesbian Hockey Association. See William Bridel, "Out on the Rink: A Brief History of Queer Hockey in Calgary," Calgary Gay History Project, October 2, 2025, https://calgarygayhistory.ca/tag/history/.

When I finally connected with Robert Thompson, co-founder of the Toronto Gay Hockey Association (TGHA), I learned that he and his colleagues were putting together an entire league at the same time the Cutting Edges were born. When we met for dinner in downtown Toronto in fall 2025, what I expected to be an hour-long interview turned into nearly three hours. Thompson had a lot to share, including one particularly weighty story. One of his motivations for starting the TGHA was to provide a safe hockey space that protected people rather than victimizing them—a dream he had kept close to his chest since being raped at age eleven by an arena attendant at the community centre hockey rink where he had his first job. Such an experience might have turned most kids off hockey arenas for good, but Thompson was fortunate. First, he managed to prevent a second assault by alerting his mother about the man and exposing the crime as soon as it happened, leading to the man's arrest, charge, and conviction. Thompson was then sent to a child therapist, ensuring that he could deal with his feelings about the incident right away instead of burying the trauma into adulthood.*

"That conversation I had to have with the police and my father was the hardest conversation at eleven years old I could ever have—what had happened and how it happened," he told me. "But it made me a better person in the long run, because then for the arena, I was hired to do all the hockey shinnies, the public skates, and all the power skating—and I was protecting kids." Thompson learned to be protective of younger children who came to the rink. But after his own experience of sexual assault and the teasing he later received from fellow hockey players for taking up figure skating (as told in Chapter 3), he also learned to build a self-protective armour. He did not come out as gay until his early twenties, after

---

* Other less fortunate victims of arena pedophiles, such as Martin Kruze, a whistleblower in the Maple Leaf Gardens sex abuse scandal, would ultimately be ruined by their experiences. After being invited to Maple Leaf Gardens at age thirteen to watch hockey games, practices, and concerts unchaperoned, Kruze endured seven years of sexual abuse by Gordon Stuckless, a part-time maintenance worker at the Gardens. After descending into a haze of drugs, depression, and therapy, Kruze eventually blew the whistle on Stuckless and became a public crusader on behalf of sex abuse victims. When Stuckless received a sentence of only two years less a day, Kruze, thirty-five, took his own life on October 30, 1997.

graduating from the University of Guelph with a history degree, when he took his first trip to California.

One night, he was casually chatting with the third man he'd ever met in a gay bar. The man, who had spent time in Toronto, took note of his interest in sports. "He said, 'You know, there's a lot of gay sports clubs in Toronto.' And I'm like, 'Really?' And he says, 'Yeah, there's basketball, there's swimming, lots of volleyball, badminton—lots of things.' And I'm like, 'Well, is there hockey?' So he goes, 'Probably.' I thought it was possible. I mean, if there's basketball and wrestling and all these others, then there has to be hockey. So the first thing I did after coming back from California was search up [gay] hockey, but they didn't have any hockey leagues." (Recalling my own uphill battle trying to find players in Vancouver during the early nineties, I couldn't believe he thought there would have been organized gay hockey in Toronto.)

After a couple of years, Thompson met two other gay men who wanted to play hockey, so they put an ad in *Xtra!*, the flagship paper of Toronto's Pink Triangle Press. The ad summoned anyone interested to show up and play shinny at an outdoor rink behind Upper Canada College on Sundays between two and four o'clock. "We started with two players and four players, and at first we didn't know who was gay and who wasn't gay because we weren't going to check," he recalled. "At that time, it would be very rare to find an effeminate hockey player ... Back then, if you showed up and you were playing hockey, generally you were straight acting." Thompson told me that 90 percent of the players who signed up for the TGHA in the early years would not appear in photographs and wanted no internet presence.

By 1993, word got out to Montreal's gay hockey team that Toronto was getting its game together. So a Montreal coordinator called them up and challenged them to a match. "We said, 'Great,'" said Thompson. "We called it the Friendship Games, and Montreal came to play. As soon as we had enough for three teams, we started the league in 1994. And New York was our first Gay Games. I had twenty people who wanted to go. We had to figure out who was going to go and who wasn't because it was too many people." I told him that was a good problem to have; the Cutting Edges had sent only eight skaters.

But even with all those players, the best Toronto could do was a bronze medal for the Huskies in the "open" division. "But I said, 'Don't worry, we're going to grow, we're going to get better,'" Thompson recalled. "So the next Gay Games, in Amsterdam, we ended up beating Montreal. That's when I think we had six or seven teams, maybe even eight, so we picked the best of those teams and won it all. I coached that group, and that was fantastic. And that solidified the league, the importance of the league and also the talent. From there I managed the league and grew [it]. We hit a wall fifteen years in when our mean age just kept rising. It was thirty-eight, thirty-nine, forty. I said, 'How do we get that mean age down?' So we started advertising in universities—all universities had gay organizations—and then we started to bring the mean age down."

Like me with the Cutting Edges, Thompson—who's a year older—still plays, and he's the longest active member of the TGHA. The league now has twenty teams and three hundred players, with a long wait-list to join. One change that should help accommodate the greater numbers is moving the league downtown. For years, the TGHA has been centred north of the city at York University. When the Maple Leaf Gardens complex was sold, the new owners decided to turn it into a playing centre. "So I was on them constantly," Thompson said. "We want[ed] to get their ice. The way our constitution works, the members have to decide—it's not just one person—to move downtown. Afterward I found out they were willing to give us the ice. So when we moved the league from up north at Jane and Finch, that's when we started to populate, playing in the heart of the city and the community."

When I brought up the contrast between an all-gay league, like Toronto's, versus a single queer association with a few rosters that play in different divisions within a mainstream (straight) league, like the Cutting Edges, Thompson said he was trying to split up the TGHA into divisions based on skill level. "I always said when we had twelve teams, I would split the league," he said. "The members fought it, but I'm pretty close this year." Why do they fight it? "Well, you have to look at it from the point of view of a person with not as much ability. There's a lot of really good players who have left. A whole team, half of them left because it wasn't competitive enough or they felt they were always expected to score goals." Thompson was hoping to produce an end-of-year survey in which people can identify their own skill level. "If you think you're advanced and you're not, you quickly figure that out."

And it's here that Thompson's protective instinct comes through: Inclusivity in hockey is ideal—until safety becomes an issue. One season, a player showed up who wouldn't rate his own skill level but said he understood hockey. When he went on the ice, it was clear he couldn't skate. His teammates had to hold on to him and bring him across the ice to put him in position. "And I think, 'Fantastic that you want to come out and everything else,'" he recalled, "[but] when I was skating backward, I almost ran over the guy." The player posed a hazard to himself and everyone else on the ice. "Thank God I saw him the last second, because I could have hurt him, or he could have really hurt me, if I didn't see him," said Thompson. "So if there's a real safety issue—and 'inclusive' means you can play—what we're saying is that maybe you need a little more experience. We want you to come out, we want you to be part of it, so let's help you get there. That's inclusive." But Thompson said the player's team dismissed that reasoning, citing the Association's non-discrimination clause in the constitution.

There's a lot less ambiguity when it comes to players who violate the very spirit of the safe space the TGHA was created to provide, and that's where Thompson's protective instinct comes down hard. "In the early days, when a friend would bring out a straight player, the straight players were ultra aggressive, trying to show their masculinity, and I had to kick a few of them out," he remembered, still amazed that people could be so obtuse about their responsibility as allies. "They became a liability—they were always in the penalty box, and they were very ultra aggressive. One of them turned out to be a good friend of mine. He was a great hockey player, but I said, 'I'm going to have to kick you out because it's too much—you're yelling at people, and that's not what our league is about. Our league is about friendly play. It's okay to get a little riled up—that's hockey—but not consistently, and not every game.'"

More recently, some of the higher-level TGHA teams have played games in a straight league, and ... well, let's just say that Toronto men's hockey hasn't had the benefit of the three decades of education the Cutting Edges have provided at UBC and now at Scotia Barn (8 Rinks) in Burnaby.* "This one guy started going off on one of our guys, calling him 'faggot' and everything else ... [Because] we don't say, 'Hey, we're a gay team!' and this was in a straight league, he probably thought we were straight and that it was safe to say." More of a head-scratcher is the conduct of queer community members who use the F-word to attack each other. "When I was running the league," Thompson remembered, "women asked if they could play, and I said, 'We'd love to have you. You have to understand though, that it is men's hockey. Men play the way they play, right?' For some women, they did not like it. For others, it attracted them because they were very aggressive. And there was one woman [who] was overly aggressive and saying slurs. She was, like, the biggest lesbian in the world, and she called me 'faggot,' so I gave her several warnings and ended up kicking her out."

For Thompson, who has stepped aside from running the league while continuing to play and coach, most of his experience with the TGHA has been positive. The worst moment was when a former treasurer stole all of the league's money. "I had come back on to the board because I didn't like the direction of the league—it didn't feel right to me," he said. "So a few months into that, I got a call from the bank. They said, 'You're overdraft.' I'd just written a cheque for the ice because I like to pay up front [for] a discount. I said, 'How could I be overdraft? We're supposed to have this much money in the bank.' So I started calling the treasurer, and he's not answering his phone." After calling the membership together and informing them of what had happened, said Thompson, he decided to fund the league himself until it was out of deficit.† "When I left again, they had $50,000 in the bank account and were totally set," he recalled. "It took me a couple of years to get it there." The whole experience was a black eye for the league but a learning

* Burnaby's largest hockey facility, 8 Rinks, was renamed Scotia Barn in 2019 after the property was purchased by Scotiabank and reopened the following year under the new branding. Because I try to avoid using corporate rebranding names where possible, and because most users prefer the original name, I call it 8 Rinks from here onward.

† Thompson, the owner of a large events production company with major contracts all over North America, could afford it.

experience for Thompson. "For me as a developing person—I was in my forties—it hit me hard," he recalled. "They said, 'Fold the league.' And I said, 'Why would I fold the league? I love the league. We'll carry the league until it can get back on its feet.' And thank God I was in a position that I could."

The Cutting Edges can relate. Like our Toronto counterparts, we too have been let down by teammates who took advantage of the club's goodwill by skimming funds for personal use. In the first case, just before the 1998 Gay Games in Amsterdam, a player volunteering at a fundraiser failed to turn over all the expected bar proceeds. Despite strong evidence that he had kept some of the money, he denied the theft and was cut from the Amsterdam roster. He never played with us again. In the second case, the thief returned money he had stolen—but only after another club member intervened on his behalf. Both players left the Edges after that.

Like any other community organization, we've had our share of heartbreak. In our first decade, at least three club members died within a few years of each other—two from illness and the third from personal crisis. The Cutting Edges sent a group of players to attend their funerals. One of those members who died was among the few women who played with us in our first decade, a defender who also played in a women's league. Older than most of us, she was a maternal figure in the dressing room, always encouraging teammates, never hesitating to help someone in need, and always the first to volunteer to drive an injured player to the hospital. Another player who died was the team comedian for a while, a funny guy who always had a good one-liner ready just when you needed it and was generous to a fault. Those two deaths were heavy events in the club's history. But the third was especially devastating and came as a shock.

Brad, I'll call him, was a popular young man, an A-list party boy who was well connected in the community. I had first met him during my short stint as founding editor of *Xtra! West* when he took out ads for his new business. Brad was with the Edges from the start, joining us in New York for Gay Games IV. He was on our first team at UBC and came with us to the Gay Games in Amsterdam and Sydney. Thoughtful and compassionate, he was a creative force whose sense of adventure rubbed off on everyone. To me, he seemed destined for a long life of success and contentment. But something went seriously wrong for Brad during the fall of 2003. Believed to have been plagued by business debts, he retreated further into himself over the holiday season while taking powerful antidepressants. On December 30, having decided he didn't want to see the New Year, he jumped off the balcony of his high-rise apartment.

The Cutting Edges have done a lot of good for a lot of people since 1994. Aside from the public-facing charitable donations that are part of any non-profit society's operations, the organization's basic purpose of providing a safe place for queer and gender-diverse hockey players (explored in more depth in Chapter 10) has made a difference in people's lives. Romantic relationships have been born in the dressing room, as have friendships and business or academic connections too numerous to count. Some players have regained their self-confidence by playing with the Edges; others say their team membership has led to healthier living. Some players have developed new skills not only in the game but also through various roles on the board.

For former board president Reid Hearsum, joining the Cutting Edges in 2016 was a liberating experience. Growing up in Winnipeg, he had always played hockey and had never stopped, because the atmosphere was friendly. But there was no queer hockey movement in Manitoba, so he kept the gay part of his life hidden from his hockey community. "Hockey was my social life, essentially, along with other sports. So when I moved to a new city, I wanted to make sure I found a place to play hockey," he told me in an interview. "And I thought if I could find a queer place to play, that would be great, but if not, I was sure I could find other places to play. I literally googled 'gay hockey Vancouver,' and the Cutting Edges popped right up." Hearsum joined the hockey organization before he even found an apartment in Vancouver.

"The biggest thing for me when joining the Edges—I didn't know what to expect, because I'd never encountered it before—was that it was such an intersection of two big parts of my life, the gay and the hockey," he said. "I didn't know what it would be like, what the quality of players would be like, and was very pleasantly surprised. It allowed me to become more comfortable as a gay man, not having to put on such a masculine face ... I just [felt] more relaxed, because you're not so stressed about presenting such a front."

In some cases, playing with the Cutting Edges has literally been a lifesaver. This is true of more than a few players who were (and still are) long-time survivors living with HIV. Late in the Edges' first decade, one of our teams even had a forward line some of us privately called "the HIV Line," in reference to the positive status of all three players. Non-contact recreational hockey with the Edges, it was clear, improved their overall health by increasing their fitness levels while reducing their viral loads. Of course, we didn't advertise this fun fact. While there was no risk to anyone else on the ice (and the HIV Line was assembled after the advent of protease inhibitors in 1996), there was still a great deal of AIDS paranoia and ignorance in mainstream society. So discretion was necessary in a league just getting used to the idea of having a gay team in the first place. But gosh, I would have loved to write a story about that trio—they had lots of swagger and could put together some pretty nifty passing plays.

CHAPTER 6

Pavel Bure and Me

"Bure is such a great talent. If only he could play with himself out there, it [would] really give the fans a show."
—TOM LARSCHEID*

As great as it was having queer hockey in Vancouver for the Celebration '90 Gay Games and then helping give birth to the Cutting Edges four years later, I never shook the feeling that gay men would always be ghettoized within our sport—and not only as players. As hockey fans and as commentators on the best professional hockey league in the world, we were invisible. As far as the NHL was concerned, there was no such thing as gay hockey opinion, and why would there be? In the eyes of most of the punditry in hockey's old boys' club, the sport's dominant culture of high masculinity was incompatible with a gay world they knew nothing about. This, of course, was narrow-minded. By the early 1990s—before the Cutting Edges

* Radio CKNW broadcaster Tom Larscheid, a colour commentator for Vancouver Canucks games during the 1990s, was well known for his many inadvertently homoerotic sayings about Canucks superstar Pavel Bure.

were born—it struck me as short-sighted that a major league as profit-driven as the NHL had no interest in targeting the potentially huge new market that fans like me represented, that they were satisfied with a boring status quo. *There are men, and there are homos. Never the twain shall meet.*

During the fall of 1991, something happened in Vancouver to change all that. As a writer, it would be my good fortune—a case of opportunistic media activism, you might say—to play a role in bringing the mainstream hockey world and gay sensibility together, however briefly, into the same conversation. As part of hockey lore and the sport's cultural narrative, it was a minor episode. Forgettable, even. But the way it took shape and the response of everyone involved said a lot about hockey's uneasy relationship with masculinity and homosexuality.

To say that the Russian Rocket was the biggest star the Vancouver Canucks have ever had, apart from Quinn Hughes, would be an understatement. Pavel Bure didn't just score more goals per season than any other player in team history; he also scored more goals per *game* than any other NHL player in the modern era not named Mike Bossy or Mario Lemieux. His talent was so off the charts that the Canucks would rename their Most Exciting Player Award after him. (This was after his induction into the Hockey Hall of Fame, when he became the only player to have spent most of his career with the Canucks to claim that distinction.) Bure thrilled fans every night with the explosive power of his skating, his electrifying speed, and his deadly shot. He scored on most of his breakaways—of which there were many—and he always found the right moment to bring fans out of their seats. He could skate around Norris Trophy–winning defenders like pylons, make Vezina Trophy–winning goalies look silly with highlight reel dekes, and reduce general managers to tears at the thought he could have been *theirs*.*

* The Canucks pulled a fast one to get Bure, selecting him 113th overall at the 1989 draft when other teams thought he was ineligible. That story has been told many times, most reliably by Brian Burke, who

On top of all this? The twenty-year-old Pavel Bure who arrived in Vancouver in the autumn of 1991 just happened to satisfy every other prerequisite for superstardom in the pop culture stratosphere: He was exotic, mysterious, charismatic, and drop-dead gorgeous. It was my privilege, toward the end of his Calder Trophy–winning rookie season, to join what I called the Pavel commentariat. These were local Vancouver writers, not confined to the sports media, who shared their thoughts on the phenomenon that was Pavel Bure and what it all meant.

My own fascination with Bure began with the Christmas morning–like atmosphere—the excitement of gift unwrapping—of his first media conference with the Canucks. In those days, the internet was still in its infancy, so there were few images of Bure in circulation. A subject of the Soviet Union just before its collapse, he was a highly gifted player whose progress international scouts had been tracking for years. But his media presence in the West was limited to a few grainy bits of footage from the World Junior Championships of 1990 and 1991, his features obscured by the cage of his helmet. So when he arrived in Vancouver after a cloak-and-dagger departure from Russia via the US, the mystery surrounding him only added to the anticipation of that media scrum, which was held two days before his first NHL game. Like most Canuck fans, I watched the whole thing on TV during that day's evening news sports report.

When Bure stepped into the room to reveal himself, the strobing effect of all the camera flashes going off had a Hollywood feel to it. Like Tom Cruise arriving on the red carpet for Oscar night. *What a stunner*, I thought. *A perfect 10 ... and oh, look, that's the jersey number they're giving him. Guy Lafleur's number. My number ...* Bure was dazzlingly pretty, his symmetrical Eastern European features worthy of a runway model. This was a presence seldom seen in the rough-and-tumble NHL, a league overpopulated with mullet-maned, meat-and-potatoes regular dudes. The blond-haired Bure was an Adonis with lips like rose petals and sparkling green-blue bedroom eyes. His astonishing beauty combined the cherubic

---

had a front-row seat to all the drama. See *Burke's Law: A Life in Hockey*, by Brian Burke with Stephen Brunt (Penguin, 2020).

androgyny of River Phoenix with the mystique of Rudolf Nureyev or Rudolph Valentino and the insouciance of James Dean. Smoking hot. Apart from being blown away by his looks, Canuck fans like me were left wondering how such features could survive the wear and tear of a lengthy NHL career. As we would soon discover, Bure's being faster than everyone else would help.

It would take the Canucks a long time to realize what they had. Too long, in my view. I did not begin writing about Bure until I saw what was lacking in their promotion of him. Once I did, I found there was plenty to say. In joining the Pavel commentariat, I soon learned that I was the only openly gay writer among its ranks. My interest began innocently enough: A hot young prospect arriving in town to save the Canucks from chronic mediocrity turns out to be much more than anticipated. Were the Canucks taking full advantage? Later I would be accused of stalking Bure with my interest, my "obsession," even. Apparently there was something tawdry—a breach of good taste—in an "older" man objectifying a defenceless young male athlete. But I was still in my twenties, like Bure, so the age objection was groundless. And this defenceless young male athlete also happened to be a millionaire, soon to be loaded with money, lawyers, agents, and media handlers. He had power and influence, while I had words. He was fair game.

I was not alone in thinking the Canucks' conservative marketing plan was limiting Bure's potential fan base. His NHL team played in Canada's third-largest city, which in the five years since the Expo 86 world's fair had seen a growing number of immigrants, especially from Pacific Rim countries. But the team's promotion of the Russian Rocket seemed targeted at the same white suburban Christian demographic that had been their bread and butter since 1970, when Vancouver entered the NHL as a much different city. With the exception of *Western Living*, which did a sexy fashion shoot, the early publicity around Bure was limited to the usual boilerplate PR stunts for every new signing. Pavel the celebrity chef, serving up pasta for a charity benefit, where his apron sold for more than $500. Pavel in a cornball radio ad for Marine Plymouth Chrysler, a rite of passage for every Canuck since Don Lever. And more of the same.

Where were the underwear ads? Where was shirtless Pavel in blue jeans, strategically placed in bus shelter posters on Robson, Denman, and Davie streets? Where was Pavel as heart-stopping runway model? If this were New York and Bure were a Ranger, there'd be a four-page spread in Andy Warhol's *Interview* magazine—or *GQ*, *Vanity Fair*, or *Cosmopolitan*. There would be Calvin Klein ads with black-and-white images of a sultry Pavel, shot by Herb Ritts or Bruce Weber. But none of this had occurred to the Canucks. Their image of the ideal hockey player was confined to the wholesomely earnest corn-fed exemplar of a prairie farm upbringing, such as the team's Alberta-born captain, Trevor Linden. Applying the same approach with Bure only exposed the sadly pedestrian sensibilities of the Canucks' public relations team.

So I decided to investigate by speaking directly with the Canucks—including, if possible, Bure himself. The interview would take place at the Pacific Coliseum, then the Canucks' home rink. My contact was retired Canuck and former Stanley Cup–winning New York Islander Steve Tambellini, then the Canucks' director of communications. He was gracious and helpful, freely sharing his thoughts about Bure when I asked how the team approached his marketing. "Pavel's Flash and Trevor's the Rock," Tambellini told me, stating the obvious contrast between the images of Bure and Linden. "There's a flair about Pavel that's special. It's that flash, the way he does things, that's exciting to watch ... There's so much talk about him because of what he does on the ice, plus the fact that he's a young guy, he's a good-looking guy. He's not a cocky person, so it's kind of refreshing." Tambellini also arranged an impromptu encounter with the player himself, right after practice, before Bure joined his teammates for lunch.

When he came out of the tunnel, Pavel Bure was freshly showered, his hair combed back in wet curls. He was wearing faded blue jeans and a tight-fitting white T-shirt that accented his bodybuilder-like frame. Because of his larger-than-life presence on the ice, I had forgotten that he was a few inches shorter than me. *Compatible, perfectly so, in fact. Uh-oh.* When another Canucks staffer introduced us, I collected myself to maintain professional decorum and make sure not to reveal any hint of the butterflies in my stomach as he gave me a firm handshake, his Botticelli face less than two feet from mine. Bure was still learning English, so it took him a while to understand me. I began by asking what it was like to receive so much fan adulation, not just for his talent but also for his looks and personality. Didn't he get tired of all the photos?

Bure shrugged, looking me briefly in the eye before turning away. "It's not hard for me," he said in his thick Russian accent, smiling bashfully. "Some people need my photograph, so it's not hard for me." I was about to ask him to expand on this when a teammate—I can't recall who it was—walked up and scolded him: "Come on, Pavel, time to go. The taxi's leaving." With apologies, Bure cut short our interview and left, ending the conversation when it was only just beginning.

The resulting story, published in the *Vancouver Sun*'s "Mixed Media" section of its Saturday Review on March 28, 1992, was headlined "Sex Sells, Like a Rocket." My take on Pavel Bure was that he was not just a charismatic hockey player but an object of desire who, unlike most NHL players, would not have looked out of place in one of those athlete/actor/model ads. I also noted a few responses from mainstream media men struck by the Russian Rocket's smouldering sex appeal. These included radio CKNW colour commentator Tom Larscheid, whose gushing appraisal of Bure's physical attributes was later lampooned for its unintended homoeroticism, and *Vancouver Province* reporter Tom Hawthorn, whose comparison of Pavel to a teen heartthrob could have been reprinted in *Tiger Beat*. (Two years later, *Sun* editors would amplify the titillation by running Ralph Bower's front-page photo of a naked Bure at training camp getting a physical. The visible part of his ripped physique ended at his waistline, just above the fold, requiring readers to open the paper to confirm there was nothing more to see.)

Three days after the *Sun* ran my story, Pavel Bure turned twenty-one. In a couple of weeks, I would be leaving for England to spend six months testing the freelance market in London. Encouraged by positive reader response to my essay, I decided on a lark to send Bure a copy of it on his birthday, cheekily including a postcard bearing that Daniel Collins photo of me taken two years earlier as part of the *Gay Athletes* exhibition for Gay Games III. Even cheekier, I scribbled on the back of the card an invitation to my going-away party. There wasn't a hope in hell that Bure would be interested, but I was feeling naughty. Why *not* invite him into my world—a world surely more interesting than his own hermetically sealed

NHL existence? Without the glamour, to be sure, but at least with art, agency, contingency, and irony?

Many months later, when I returned to Canada and the Canucks began another season, I came up with a story idea I planned on pitching to a glossy magazine. I conceived of a personality profile called "A Day in the Life of Pavel Bure," a kind of George Plimpton–meets–Roland Barthes essay describing what happens when a highly talented twenty-one-year-old elite athlete meets an out-of-shape twenty-nine-year-old intellectual for some rigorous workouts. The idea was for Bure and me to engage in a few endurance tests to reveal our contrasting abilities to comic effect: a skating race, a swimming race (his father had been an Olympian swimmer), and a climb up the Grouse Grind, a demanding mountain trail on the North Shore. These activities would bookend a visit to a West End juice bar, a bike ride around the Stanley Park Seawall, and a formal sit-down interview where I would ask Bure about his life in Russia, his feelings about the Soviet Union's collapse, and how he was adjusting to the West.

Pitching to Steve Tambellini once again, I sent the Canucks PR chief a two-page proposal. To accommodate the Canucks' and Bure's busy schedule, I allowed for two months' lead time in setting dates for our meeting. I also suggested supplemental interviews with Canucks general manager and coach Pat Quinn, Pavel's teammate and best buddy Gino Odjick, and play-by-play broadcaster Jim Robson. I requested a translator to ensure the best answers possible from Bure and a team photographer, if the Canucks preferred one of their own. Along with the proposal I included a tear sheet of "Sex Sells, Like a Rocket," to remind Tambellini of our previous contact and further burnished my journalistic cred by listing other publications I'd written for, including in the UK.

This time, he would not be so helpful.

Reviewing these events more than three decades later, poring through the clippings and correspondence, I am struck by the audacity of my younger self—even as an openly gay freelancer convinced he had nothing to lose. I had forgotten about that postcard invitation to my going-away party. (Spoiler alert: Bure did not attend or reply.) Regardless of what he may have thought of the *Sun* article, if in fact he had read or understood it, it was highly likely that the Russian Rocket wanted nothing more to do with me. Even if most of the story proposal had sounded reasonable and Tambellini had pitched it to Bure, that part about swimming—which would have required us to be in the water together, clad in nothing but Speedos, perhaps with only a single change room at the rec centre—just might have been the deal breaker.

As for Tambellini himself? The Canucks PR chief must have felt ambushed by the *Sun* article. His earnest comments about Pavel's "flash" were juxtaposed with references to male beauty of the like seldom written by men in mainstream Canadian newspapers in 1992. For a regular guy from Trail, BC, all of that must have seemed weird enough. But on top of this, some of the details of my "Day in the Life" proposal strayed into TMI territory. There wasn't a word about my sexuality, of course. But there didn't need to be; it was all there in the *Sun* piece. For a wary publicist, my proposal for "A Day in the Life" contained more than enough hints that its author might regard his follow-up encounter with Bure as more of a date than an interview. So Tambellini, having read the *Sun* essay, must have cottoned on to the fact that he was dealing with a homosexual who wanted more face time with the Canucks' most prized asset.

When I didn't hear back from him after a few days, I faxed him twice and called his office four or five times. Finally, about two months after my pitch, Tambellini left a stammering message on my answering machine, awkwardly informing me that it would "not be possible" for Pavel Bure to participate in this project. No explanation. *Click.* I was disappointed, fairly certain I knew the reason for the brush-off. But since there was nothing I could do about it—and, as an openly gay freelancer who had experienced more than a few unexplained rejections from mainstream journals whose reasons I could never prove—I let it go.

For a while, at least. Over the next year, I watched as one journalist after another—all straight, both men and women—were granted full access to Pavel Bure. These included Mark Leiren-Young and Lisa Fitterman, both competent journalists. Leiren-Young was a prolific playwright and freelance writer who used his face time with Bure to generate two lifestyle profiles in *TV Week* magazine. Fitterman, a *Sun* reporter, used her interview with the Russian Rocket to produce a front-page profile that left no doubt she'd relished every moment of their encounter, even describing Bure's lips as "strawberry." One night, at a party of *Sun* staffers and freelancers in Kitsilano, I engaged her in a good-natured back-and-forth about Bure's physical attributes, chiding her transparent lust for the player and correcting her on his lips ("Rose petal, not strawberry!"). The banter was friendly until Fitterman, tiring of it, ended our chat with this: "I think that Pavel is into *women*." She said it with such emphasis that the intent of her message was clear: *Stay in your lane, buster.* This only confirmed that sexuality was indeed an important consideration for deciding which journalists should have access to an attractive male athlete and which ones should not. As I had suspected all along.

It was this encounter that convinced me to jump right back into the Pavel commentariat.

"Desperately Seeking Pavel" ran in *Xtra! West*, Vancouver's biweekly gay and lesbian newspaper, on November 5, 1993. My essay, a form of media satire masquerading as a love letter, poked fun at everyone involved: the author, his subject, the Vancouver Canucks as an organization, and other journalists covering the Russian Rocket. Written in the second person as if directed to Bure himself, the article was accompanied by another Daniel Collins photo of yours truly. In this one, taken on a rainy autumn afternoon, I was clutching a heart-shaped box of chocolates while leaning adoringly into a bus shelter poster of Bure in action. The ad altered the Russian Rocket's image, photoshopping a small jet booster to his back in a cheesy take on his nickname. The accompanying text read "We have lift-off."

My "letter" was filled with the kind of bitchy irony expected of a gay columnist, typical of much pop culture commentary of that period. (Today, irony remains an article of faith for queer intellectuals of a certain age.) The main irony of "Desperately Seeking Pavel" was that I was engaging in an act of culture jamming, casting aside the apparent incongruence of hockey and gay cultures by ignoring the mutual stereotyping that had long separated those two worlds. By recounting the failed attempt of a gay journalist to get a second interview with Bure (having noted his beauty after the first one) while straight scribes were getting easy access, I was deliberately playing the homophobia card—possibly implicating but never explicitly accusing Bure himself. And I was testing that homophobia by going directly to the subject. In op-ed journalism, such an open appeal to a celebrity is considered low-hanging fruit.

"Dear Pavel," the piece began, "you don't know me, but we've met before ..." With the chatty and breathless tone of a fan still delighted with his idol, I went on to describe our brief encounter at the Pacific Coliseum during his rookie season, including my recollection of his appearance. I then reminded him of the Saturday Review essay in the *Vancouver Sun*, of that bold invitation to my going-away party, and of the proposal I had sent to Steve Tambellini for the "Day in the Life" feature. It would have been, I said, "a wonderfully postmodern ... kind of essay ... [that] would have made you seem really hip and ironic. Me? I'd come off pretty sexy as a result." After listing all the activities I had described in the proposal, I "told" Bure that he and I would have then debriefed

> at a West End health food bar where I'd introduce you to all my friends, who of course would instantly adore you (thus guaranteeing the Canucks a brand-new market). You would especially like my friend Alan, who has all kinds of neat books on the Russian monarchy—a subject that apparently turns you on.

The rest of the "love letter" summarized my ill-fated second interview request, the Canucks' willingness to grant full access to Leiren-Young and Fitterman, and the not-so-subtle suggestion that I knew the reason why. "What makes me such a threat," I asked, "when the whole world knows you can bench press two hundred pounds fourteen times? I only weigh 160." (Ah, to be thirty again.) And then this: "So please, Pavel, tell Canucks management that an injustice is being done—that you don't believe anyone should be denied an interview because they're a fag." Knowing the decision might have been his, I signed off this way: "So c'mon, Pavel—whaddya say we do an art gallery tour ... and then go for cappuccinos? Forever yours, DG."

The response to "Desperately Seeking Pavel" was outrage. Not from Bure or the Canucks, who probably weren't in the habit of reading the queer press, but from my main target audience, the gay community. *Xtra! West* ran a few letters to the editor in response to the piece. "So much for fostering understanding and compassion toward gays," sniffed one correspondent. "You just scared away an entire major league hockey team. Articles such as this do nothing to endear us to straight communities." In the next issue, another reader declared his satisfaction that he "wasn't the only person disgusted by the article on Pavel Bure ... I would have expected to find this article in the other newspaper" (a swipe at *Angles*, Vancouver's monthly left-wing queer journal). Some months later, I received a five-hundred-word letter from a woman in Redondo Beach, California, along with a business card identifying herself as a "correspondent–journalist."* The letter arrived courtesy of *Xtra! West*, who ran most of it. "The purpose of this letter," it began, "is to make you aware of some of life's little facts that I don't believe you have a clear understanding of." I could not expect to be granted every interview I sought, she informed me, adding that straight men didn't like being admired by gay men. Pavel had freedom of choice and had chosen "girls," so I had "crossed the lines of ethical journalism" by embarrassing him.

In the spring of 1994, the Vancouver Canucks made it to the Stanley Cup final for only the second time in their twenty-five-year existence. Not surprisingly, it was the electrifying performance of you know who that launched the team on a deep playoff run after its improbable recovery from a 3–1 series deficit in Round 1. Pavel Bure's dramatic overtime goal in Game 7 lifted the Canucks past Calgary,

* Decades later, a Google search of her name turned up nothing.

exhilarating his team and the city. As well as his own deadly threat, the Canucks were empowered by the courageous resolve of captain Trevor Linden and the stellar netminding of Kirk McLean, a solid defence core led by Jeff Brown and Jyrki Lumme, and a talented supporting cast that included Geoff Courtnall and Cliff Ronning. This was a much better team than the muckers and grinders who were swept by the New York Islanders in 1982. But in the New York Rangers, they faced an opponent whose Stanley Cup drought was more than twice the length of their own. Stacked with former Edmonton Oilers led by captain Mark Messier, and with a brick wall defence featuring Brian Leetch and the goaltending heroics of Mike Richter, the Rangers had cruised to first place and—motivated by that fifty-four-year curse—were considered heavy Cup favourites.

After the Canucks beat the Toronto Maple Leafs in the Western Conference final, punching their ticket to the Big Apple, I was on top of the world. Apart from enjoying my favourite team's first trip to the Cup final in a dozen years, I was a few days away from publishing my first book and winning a magazine award. I was enjoying a relationship I thought would last, and—with my friend Kevin Griffin doing most of the heavy lifting—had put together a Vancouver hockey team, the Cutting Edges, to compete at Gay Games IV, which just happened to be in New York City. The Gay Games were set to begin a couple of days after the scheduled Game 7 of the Stanley Cup final, also set for New York. By great coincidence, two of my worlds were coming together in a most dramatic way.

While the Canucks were still in New York for Games 1 and 2, I wrote an op-ed for the *Vancouver Sun*. The piece celebrated the joyful coincidence of my own Vancouver hockey team heading to New York within a day or two of the Canucks completing their series with the Rangers, hopefully with a first Stanley Cup win in their back pocket and a big parade to follow.* Headlined "Hockey Not Just Domain of Macho," the piece described how Griffin and I were part of a team that

* By 2026, the Canucks' Cup-less run was at fifty-six years and counting—the length of the team's entire existence.

would soon be competing at Unity '94: Gay Games IV & Cultural Festival, our hockey action taking place on Coney Island. Tongue firmly in cheek, I began the piece by suggesting that Canucks coach Pat Quinn and I were travelling down a similar road, "both determined to establish Vancouver's hockey supremacy over the big boys back East." I described our respective objectives as equally honourable.

> Mr. Quinn's is to show the world that a young team with good chemistry and great goaltending can beat the best team money can buy; mine is to show the world that hockey doesn't always have to be the domain of macho straight men and that the greatest qualities of our national sport—skating, passing, playmaking finesse—can be demonstrated without having to intimidate one's opponent.

There wasn't a word about Pavel Bure in this piece, but I did mention someone else.

> It's true that I probably have very little in common with the guys who were revving their engines on Robson Street in celebration of the Canucks' triumph over the Leafs. And my own lifestyle and social milieu don't exactly fit the Canucks marketing profile of the average fan. But gosh darn it, I'm just as Canadian as anyone on *Hockey Night in Canada*, and nothing I've ever worn in drag could possibly equal the sheer campiness of Don Cherry's wardrobe.

The op-ed ran on Friday, June 3—the day before Game 3 in Vancouver, with the series tied. One of my first phone calls that day came from the *Globe and Mail*'s Miro Cernetig. He was calling to talk about the op-ed but had also seen my previous commentary on the Russian Rocket. The next day, hours before puck drop for Game 3, the *Globe* hit newsstands with his article, "All Vancouver Coming Out to Support Bure," describing me as "a local author and gay activist." Such labelling was a common mainstream media practice in those days, when a queer person's willingness to be out in public or quoted on the record was enough to qualify them as an "activist." But I was okay with that. Unlike some folks in the gay community, at least Cernetig knew what I was up to in my writings about Bure.

The piece began by describing my "one-man mission" to steer the Canucks away from their meat-and-potatoes marketing of their biggest star in favour of a more cosmopolitan approach. Recognizing the NHL's resistance toward any expression of male behaviour that deviated from the most orthodox masculinity, Cernetig noted the league's response the previous season, when Ottawa Senators star Alexandre Daigle, posing for a hockey card photo, dressed up in drag as a female nurse. (The Senators promised that such gender-bending playfulness would never happen again.) Cernetig's article contained quotes from "Sex Sells, Like a Rocket," "Desperately Seeking Pavel," and "Hockey Not Just Domain of Macho," making it a kind of greatest hits of my queer hockey commentary. Zingers included the line calling on Bure to tell Canucks management that no one should be denied an interview "because they're a fag," my thoughts on how he'd be marketed if he were a New York Ranger ("you'd be expected to pose for *Details* and *Vanity Fair*—not stammer your way through Plymouth Chrysler ads on AM radio"), and that saucy line about Don Cherry's wardrobe.

Hours later, the Canucks hit the ice for Game 3, their first Stanley Cup action in Vancouver since 1982. Watching the game on TV with friends, I could feel the almost combustible atmosphere inside the Coliseum—the energy of the crowd, thunderous in greeting their Canucks, and of the players themselves, who came out storming. On his first shift, Bure took a nice feed from Linden at the Rangers' blue line and raced in on a breakaway, shooting the puck between Richter's legs to give the Canucks the early lead at one minute and three seconds. But that would be it for the Russian Rocket and his team that night. The Rangers scored twice before the first period was over and 3 more goals after that to beat the Canucks 5–1. All this thanks to a five-minute major and game misconduct, late in the first, by Bure for colliding with Rangers enforcer Jay Wells; Bure had whacked Wells in the head with his stick, cutting his face.

As the first period ended and the intermission began, my friends and I were fretting about the Canucks' chances after losing Bure for the rest of the game.

Then *Hockey Night* turned to its usual instalment of "Coach's Corner" with Don Cherry and host Ron MacLean. Three minutes into the segment, Cherry put on some reading glasses, picked up a newspaper, and began reading passages from Cernetig's *Globe* article. He began by making fun of my comment about Bure's Rudolph Valentino mystique: stealing a line from an anonymous Canuck staffer Cernetig had interviewed, Cherry said the baby-faced Russian Rocket looked more like *Home Alone* child star Macaulay Culkin. But the real reason Cherry was reading my story on air (he mispronounced my name as "Gar-thop") was what I'd said about *him*. Feigning ignorance, Canada's most celebrated redneck asked the more erudite MacLean what I meant by "campiness" (MacLean: "sort of tacky ... cool") and "worn in drag" ("going out in ladies' clothes"). Cherry said he didn't understand what I was talking about (Yeah, sure!) but that his "construction buddies wanted to know."

This segment of "Coach's Corner" was remarkable for a couple of reasons, apart from Cherry's decision to engage with a gay writer. The first was that, while quoting from Cernetig's article, he made a point of mentioning my team's participation at the upcoming Gay Games, effectively providing free publicity on national television for a gay hockey team. The Cutting Edges were so impressed that Kevin Griffin drafted a press release thanking Cherry for the plug. In response, Cherry not only read the release during Game 4's "Coach's Corner" but also privately sent us a card bearing a photo of himself and his beloved English bull terrier, with a message scribbled in black felt: "To my pals on the Cutting Edges: Good luck! Don & Blue."* One of my teammates, watching from his parents' home, accidentally

* Cherry's seemingly earnest goodwill toward the Cutting Edges was notable given that, after thanking him for mentioning us, we criticized his comments on another issue he'd raised in the Game 3 segment: his contention—apparently serious—that Sikhs should respect the Royal Canadian Legion's hats-off policy by removing their turbans before entering the premises. Cherry, taking our critique seriously, argued with it in his Game 4 segment until MacLean cut him off. By November 2019, it would be Cherry's perceived expectations of non-white immigrants—not sexual minorities, women, or Europeans—that would prove his undoing on *Hockey Night*.

Pavel Bure in 1997, less happy times in Vancouver

came out to them by exclaiming, "Hey, that's my team!" when Cherry mentioned our name.

The other significant part of Cherry's Game 3 commentary happened early in the segment, but the moment passed before it could register with viewers. He had begun by reading the kicker from Cernetig's article: "A Vancouver gay activist is urging the Canucks to market star forward Pavel Bure in all communities." Turning to MacLean, he said, "Funny, eh?" MacLean shrugged. "I don't think that's funny." Cherry replied, "No, but he just got kicked out of the game, that's what I mean." MacLean might have asked him to elaborate but didn't, so Cherry continued quoting from the story. So what *did* he mean? What did Don Cherry think was funny about gay fans making a big deal about Bure, and what did this have to do with his game misconduct? Was Cherry seeing paradox in all this gay affection for a player who had just broken open another player's face with his stick? Or was he speculating on the reason for the violence, implying that Bure might have been rattled by all this attention from homos and felt the need to prove his heteronormative masculinity by giving Jay Wells a two-hander in the head?

Either answer would have been more interesting than what followed. But Cherry and MacLean were playing the story for laughs (like a Martian landing—how else could they have treated a homosexual intervention in the Stanley Cup final?), so perhaps the real story got buried. Or was I overthinking all this? For a second opinion, I later called up Cernetig to ask if he'd heard anything about Bure's response to his article. He said that he'd been at the Coliseum for the game day practice and heard other Canucks teasing Bure about it. "Are you going to ask him out on a date?" one apparently said, as other Canucks giggled. Bure, not in the best humour, reportedly walked away from his teammates after telling them to fuck off.

To this day, I can't help wondering if my words were a factor in the Canucks' falling behind in the series. Could I have doomed their Stanley Cup quest by throwing their biggest star off his game? I mean, poor Bure—he already had more than enough on his plate. First, there was the performance anxiety of delivering on hockey's biggest stage in the most important moment of his NHL career, the pressures of expectation while living in the fishbowl that was Vancouver. Then there were the nasty rumours that he was yet another Russian hockey star susceptible to

Mafia grooming and that he had threatened to sit out the Cup final if a new deal could not be reached for that big contract extension he was close to signing. At that moment, the last thing he needed was the pestering of some smartass homo who couldn't take no for an answer.

By this point, I was already done with Pavel Bure as subject matter and had long since moved on. The problem was that the story wasn't done with *me* yet. In the wake of the *Globe* and *Hockey Night* coverage, I received phone calls from *LA Weekly* and *Village Voice*. I had nothing new to add, other than to concede the obvious (I couldn't prove why the Canucks had turned me down) and to note that homophobia made the pro sports world reluctant to permit contact between its athletes and out gays and lesbians. I told *LA Weekly*'s Paul Feinberg,

> The possibility exists—and it's a very strong one—that ... the Canucks are so reluctant to allow gay men in the dressing room [because] they perceive that gay interest in an athlete suggests sexual orientation on the athlete's part. This [would] create the impression that Pavel is gay, and that's part of the panicked response.[43]

Decades later, the most telling part of Joe Clark's "Jockbeat" column for *Village Voice* ("Pavel Gazing," August 16, 1994) is a quote from the *New York Daily News* in which former Canucks executive and then NHL vice-president Brian Burke was asked what he thought about the gay attention around Bure. Shrugging off the question, Burke replied, "I'm just a hockey guy." The message was clear: hockey and homosexuality were two different worlds, the latter of which Burke knew nothing about. Take note of that response: Thirteen years later, as we'll see in Chapter 11, Burke would have much more to say on the subject.

But back to Pavel Bure. Early in 1999, the Russian Rocket was traded to the Florida Panthers. A few days later, I received a phone call from Toronto sportswriter Mike Ulmer. He wanted to know what I thought gay fans in Florida could expect from Bure. I couldn't believe it—this was still news? At the time, I was in the middle of writing a book about the boreal forest for the David Suzuki Foundation, so I don't recall exactly what I told him. Ulmer's article described how the stories

I'd written long ago had "exposed Bure as a hunk of burning hockey love among gay as well as straight fans." To his credit, Ulmer became the first reporter to get a response from Bure on the subject. When he reminded the new Panther of Vancouver gay men's "love" for him, Bure replied with false modesty: "I don't think they thought I was the most incredible guy in the world." Did he have a problem with their interest in him? "Why would I have a problem? If people like you and treat you with respect, that's great. That's how I treat them."[44]

By this time, however, the bloom was off the rose. Since the '94 Cup run, there had been so many reports of Bure's contract complaints, shadowy business associations, and alleged reasons for wanting to leave Vancouver that my later writings about him shifted from the playful to the critical. Assigned by the *Vancouver Sun* and the *National Post* to review an investigative biography by Kerry Banks, a somewhat surreal experience given my own mention in it, I found myself focusing less on Bure's hockey brilliance and aesthetic appeal than on the character issues that had tainted his final years in Vancouver—a period typified by the sight of Bure in his luxury sports car speeding out of the Canucks' parking lot to avoid autograph-seeking fans.*

In fairness, I never did speak to Pavel Bure about any of this. Nor did Banks or, to the best of my knowledge, anyone else apart from Ulmer. The Rocket remained silent throughout all the rumours and innuendo, making it that much harder for his fans to get a true measure of the man. So what did any of us really know about Bure and his desires? By 2013, after his induction into the Hockey Hall of Fame, he buried the hatchet with the Canucks by attending a ceremony at Rogers Arena in which the Canucks retired his number 10 jersey. The next day, they named their Most Exciting Player Award after him. All was forgiven—with the Canucks, at least.

---

* See Kerry Banks's *Pavel Bure: The Riddle of the Russian Rocket* (Greystone Books, 2003).

To this day, I do not regret a single thing I wrote about Pavel Bure. But I do regret what I was quoted as saying to Mike Ulmer after the trade to Florida in 1999: "Now when I see his face I think, 'That spoiled brat.'" For me to have said such a thing to a reporter, it must have been sour grapes. Like everyone else in Vancouver, I had wanted Bure to remain a Canuck forever. As for that long-ago pitch of an art gallery tour and cappuccinos? I can't imagine how such a "date" would go today. I am pushing senior citizenship, well north of sixty and greyer by the minute. Pavel is in his mid-fifties, his once immaculate face now etched with wrinkles, his once bright eyes dimmed by experience ... and the burden of being politically betrothed to Vladimir Putin.

But I will say this: Were such a rendezvous to happen now—and notwithstanding his marriage to the mother of his three children or my own twenty-plus years of marriage to a man from Myanmar—he and I would have much more to discuss, and of more mutual interest, than would have been the case had he accepted my "Day in the Life" proposal back in his sophomore season. It would be an enlightening discussion, I am sure. But it would be of far less importance than the conversations hockey's powerful establishment figures need to keep having about making the mainstream hockey world a more welcoming place for everyone while addressing the game's darker legacies.

PART 3

CHALLENGING THE GATEKEEPERS

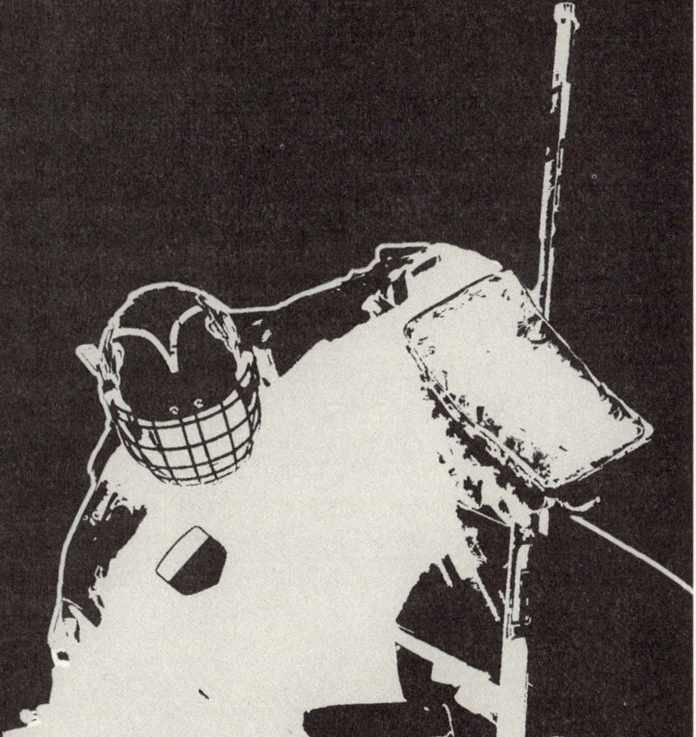

CHAPTER 7

Toxic Masculinity: Straight to the Dressing Room

"We are naked together in locker rooms four times a day and alone together on the bus for God knows how many hours, and it is ingrained in us that our teammates are our brothers ... When we look around the room, we see twenty clones of ourselves and we all know we are better than everyone else. This is our culture. We breed lions, and how do you tell a lion to stop being a lion?"

—A FORMER ONTARIO HOCKEY LEAGUE PLAYER[45]

When the 1991–92 hockey season began, I had been a casual fan of the Vancouver Canucks for just under a decade, charmed by their improbable run to the 1982 Stanley Cup final. In November 1991, Pavel Bure's arrival heightened my interest in the Canucks. But really, my heart had always bled for the Montreal Canadiens. In Grade 11, I wore a Habs patch on my sweater for the school's annual yearbook photo. (For Grade 12, I wore their white home jersey.) My favourite player had always been Guy Lafleur, and I had adopted his number 10 as my own whenever I played. As a hockey fan, I had twice attended games at the Pacific Coliseum to cheer for the Habs *against* the Canucks. Then, in 1990, there was that *Gay Athletes* photo exhibition for which I posed wearing the same Habs jersey I'd kept for so many years. But a couple of months into the 1991–92 season, I suddenly revoked my membership to Habs Nation.

My fandom became a casualty of some shockingly ignorant public statements in December 1991 that put my team to shame while shaking my emotions to the core. The first involved an inadvertent health scare resulting from the AIDS crisis. At a seminar in Montreal, one of the city's renowned AIDS specialists told those in attendance that one of his patients, a woman who had died of AIDS two years earlier, had disclosed that she'd had sex with about fifty NHL players—a figure "equivalent to about 10 percent of the combined rosters of the twenty-two NHL teams."[46] Although the woman had remembered each of the NHL players she'd had sex with and had notified "some but probably not all" of them to share her HIV status, the specialist's report freaked out the NHL community. Some called for mandatory AIDS testing of all players. Others denounced the doctor for not releasing the information earlier. Some players, especially the enforcers, were alarmed by the possibility that they could be at risk; these men shed each other's blood all the time while gooning it up.

One non-enforcer, a prominent member of the Montreal Canadiens whom I would name if I could only find the news story quoting him (it seems to have been scrubbed from the internet), said something to the effect that the woman must have had criminal intent or else she would have protected herself and not put at risk any of the men she'd fucked. In other words, the onus for accountability was entirely on the woman—whom he was blaming for spreading the virus—and not on the men. Nothing this player said allowed for the possibility that a player could have infected the woman; his comment exposed the misogyny of macho entitlement. I was disgusted by its Patient Zero–like logic and ignorance, the uninformed opinion of a hockey player who, until that moment, had likely assumed that only gay men could get AIDS.*

---

* "Patient Zero" was the clinical tag unfairly imposed on Canadian flight attendant Gaëtan Dugas, a person with AIDS whose sex partners epidemiologists linked to some of the earliest cases of what was to become a global pandemic. Thanks to media sensationalism and a damning—in parts fictional—portrait of Dugas in Randy Shilts's *And the Band Played On: Politics, People, and the AIDS Epidemic*

The second statement, part of the media's follow-up in response to the AIDS story, involved a doubling down on hockey homophobia by Habs coach Pat Burns. Asked for his opinion about homosexuality and sport, the Canadiens bench boss told Montreal reporters that an out-of-the-closet gay player in the National Hockey League would be unthinkable—and should be. "An avowed homosexual—that would never be accepted in hockey, never," said Burns.[47] At the time I was certain he was referring to popular Canadiens sniper Stéphane Richer, whose trade to the New Jersey Devils just before that season began had been implied by Quebec's yellow press to be more than a little suspicious. *Jeez*, I recall thinking: *the guy's had two fifty-goal seasons in the last four years and is one of Montreal's best players. Why would they have traded him? Were the rumours true, and they got rid of him because he's gay?*

In a biography of Pat Burns published three years after his death from cancer in 2010, Toronto columnist Rosie DiManno explained how the Richer rumours had started. For more than a year, she explained, Richer had allegedly been sharing a house with a male friend, the living arrangement vague enough to fan the flames of rumour and scandal. Tired of the media frenzy, a frustrated Richer had consulted with Burns, who encouraged him to dismiss the rumours by contacting reporters himself. And so Richer began by calling up *Le Journal de Montréal*.

> He was, in fact, quite the ladies' man, as teammates could well attest. "I was sick and tired of hearing that crap," Richer told reporters. "It wasn't fair for me and my family. I wanted it to stop. Me, I'm going out with a lot of different girls, but who says I have to be married?"[48]

Typical of those days, Richer's statement included no clarification that—regardless of his own sexuality, if he was telling the truth—there was nothing wrong

(St. Martin's Press, 1987), after his death, Dugas became known as the Typhoid Mary of AIDS. The term *Patient Zero* became code for seeking blame at a single source and demonizing that source based on morally righteous presumptions. Later scientific research exonerated Dugas of being the source of the outbreak.

with being gay. Meanwhile, he must have been relieved to get out of Montreal, where, as DiManno put it, "even the whispers could be shrill" and "the game exists in a heightened atmosphere ... a hothouse ecosystem of rumour and melodrama."[49] That must have been why he was traded. As for the rumoured "friend" he was apparently living with? The man not only didn't live with Richer but was not a "friend," either—they hadn't even met. A decade after the media circus, that man, Québécois singer Roch Voisine, used an interview with the *National Post* to declare his heterosexuality and put the Richer rumour to rest. He also apologized for not speaking up earlier: his late manager had counselled him to keep his mouth shut, convinced that Voisine would gain more fans if people believed that he and Richer were an item. Voisine said that he did not even meet the NHL star until a decade after the rumours first surfaced, when they recognized each other in public one day. They did not discuss the rumours, said Voisine, but if he himself were gay he would have said so and been proud of it.[50]

The Pat Burns quote about homosexuality—an affirmation of chest-thumping machismo by a former cop widely regarded around the league as "the dean of NHL coaches"—was a deal breaker for my Habs fandom, coming as it did right after a Montreal player's stupid comment about AIDS and sex workers. While such opinions were likely shared by many, if not all, among the NHL fraternity at the time, the fact these words came from the Habs—*my* Habs, Les Glorieux!—was a gut punch. At the very moment I had reached self-acceptance and reclaimed my love for hockey after the Gay Games, this felt like betrayal from what was supposed to be hockey's classiest organization. It would take a few decades, several coaches, and many roster transformations before I could open my heart to the Habs once again—and this time only as my *second* favourite team. I would not forgive so easily.*

* I came back to the Habs shortly after the Carey Price era began (2007). Interestingly, after the wildly successful launch of the *Heated Rivalry* TV series (see Chapter 12), a more enlightened Habs coach, Martin St. Louis, and two Habs players, Kaiden Guhle and Jake Evans, said the Canadiens would embrace a gay teammate and support him. See Jim Buzinski, "Montreal Canadiens Would Embrace a

My disillusionment with Les Canadiens was another oppressive reminder that hockey's mainstream establishment regarded homosexuality—the very idea of being gay—as the worst thing that could happen to a man. That same establishment defined a "man" as someone who eschews emotional sensitivity or vulnerability while embracing stoicism, competitive hatred, and homophobic belittlement of one's opponents. According to such logic, a man must, at all cost, avoid any trace of femininity within himself. Given this credo, which hasn't changed since 1991, compulsory heterosexuality goes without saying. "Even at the professional ranks," said Brock McGillis, a former minor professional player, "teammates and opponents alike feminize and homosexualize one another as a way to tease or blatantly insult one another." Noting the societal sexism that has always placed men above women, McGillis gained this insight during his career.

> If you wanted to put a man down, you called him a woman. The only thing as bad or worse than being a woman was being a homosexual. There was a bit of racism in there too but hockey was really mostly about feminizing and homosexualizing. So, they called each other that and it all meant that you were "less than."[51]

For McGillis, a goaltender from Sudbury, Ontario, hockey became problematic in his life at the very moment he should have been celebrating his rise to Junior prominence. When the Windsor Spitfires selected him in the Ontario Hockey League draft, he had recently broken his hand after getting into a fight during a ball hockey game at school. Another boy had called him a "faggot," spat on him, and kicked him. He couldn't play for Windsor the next season while still recovering, so he played in Junior B. Thus began a vicious cycle of hockey-related injuries and

Gay Teammate. 'Everyone Would Be Supportive,'" Outsports, January 23, 2026, https://www.outsports.com/2026/1/23/24126519/montreal-canadiens-jake-evans-kaiden-guhle-heated-rivalry-gay/.

illnesses that ultimately killed his NHL dream, from a torn meniscus and ankle ligaments and a nearly severed finger to mononucleosis and finally a concussion from his head hitting the goalpost. McGillis turned to painkillers and alcohol for relief.

But it wasn't just physical pain he was experiencing. McGillis was a closeted gay man conforming to a culture that conferred celebrity status on Junior hockey players in Canada. And he went along with the privilege that came with it: girls and women offering themselves for sex (he estimates having had more than seventy female partners), skipping lineups at bars and receiving free alcohol while underage, and being hounded for autographs by high school classmates. This homophobic culture also required him to share anti-gay jokes, which he did. Years later, he would conclude that his injuries and illnesses were psychosomatic because "they persisted as he continued to bury his feelings about himself" while pretending to be someone else.[52] This resonated with me, reminding me of the nervous stomach I suffered until I came out.

In Junior hockey, where NHL careers are made, there was a darker legacy to this pathologizing of gay men. In an all-male environment where orthodox masculinity rules—since women are mostly absent and openly gay men nowhere to be found—mentorship of the young gives great power to those responsible for their care. In such a milieu, predators thrive. In 1993, Harbour Publishing released a book honouring players, coaches, and builders from the Western Hockey League (WHL).[53] An entry for Graham James described him as a major contributor to Junior hockey in Canada, "one of the most colourful coaches to patrol the [WHL] bench."* (To illustrate this point, the authors recalled an incident when James responded to his team's blown lead in one game by starting to strip and throwing his clothes

* My apologies to the authors and to Harbour Publishing's Howard White for this reference. Like everyone else outside the hockey world's insular boys' club who were shocked by James's disgrace, Harbour couldn't possibly have seen it coming. James was named the *Hockey News*'s Man of the Year in 1989.

on the ice.) James's entry covers his rise in the scouting and coaching ranks from Midget to Junior A with the Moose Jaw Warriors and the Swift Current Broncos, the latter of which he led to a 1989 Memorial Cup victory. It noted that he was only forty after the 1992–93 season, with "a lot of coaching years still ahead of him."[54] But his hockey career crashed and burned during the 1996–97 season, ending in disgrace and infamy, all his accolades rescinded. His penalty box would be a jail cell.

Like a Roman Catholic priest who gets away with his crimes for years—a comparison I'll expand upon later—James was an expert at hiding in plain sight. He would ingratiate himself in every community where he coached, endearing himself to players, team and league officials, and the parents who placed their sons in his care. He was, after all, a great coach with connections throughout the hockey world. If James believed in a player's potential, he would do everything in his power to make sure he got drafted by an NHL team. Special favourites like Sheldon Kennedy would have to pay a price for it. Kennedy was fourteen when James first molested him in 1984 during the boy's first visit to James's home to discuss his hockey future. When Kennedy went public in 1997, he said the abuse had continued for years, with more than three hundred incidents of sexual abuse.

At the time, that last detail threw me off. Because hockey-playing teenage boys seemed to me to have more agency than younger abuse victims under the Roman Catholic Church's care (and perhaps in over-eagerness to see one NHL player, at last, identified as gay), I found myself speculating on the possibility of precocious sexual awareness in Kennedy when he first met James. Having never myself been a victim of sexual abuse, I knew nothing of the sense of powerlessness, of the coping mechanisms victims rely on to endure abusive and manipulative relationships.*

---

* These coping mechanisms can continue even after the sexual abuse has ended. Kennedy and another victim of James's abuse who went on to an NHL career (and whose story I'll tell shortly) both became investors in the Calgary Hitmen Junior team at James's urging. This was in 1994, long after both players had escaped from his direct control as their coach. Players under the influence of such predators often feel there's no way out of their situation. One of the more bizarre cases of such predator/victim dynamics in hockey is that of Mike Danton (formerly Jefferson) and his Svengali-like agent / former

Neglecting the many ways that James had threatened Kennedy as a teenager (and the significant pressure on the player as an adult after he went public), some of my own commentary on this case was offside. An essay I wrote after Kennedy's 1998 drunk driving accident cited the number of sexual incidents with James as possible evidence of his latent gayness.[55] Also used by James's lawyers as a reason to exonerate him, this observation was irrelevant and wrong-headed: Even if Kennedy *were* gay, he was in no position to consent to the adult who held power over him. However belated, let this serve as my apology to Kennedy.

It would take nearly a decade of reflection before the former NHLer was able to unpack the whole experience in a book of his own.[56] His 2006 memoir, *Why I Didn't Say Anything: The Sheldon Kennedy Story*, is a damning indictment not only of Graham James but of the hockey culture that enabled his predatory behaviour for so many years before he was finally caught. In the book, Kennedy spoke of hockey's unwritten codes of conduct, particularly those celebrating the stoic male. "Many of those codes, as anyone who has ever watched a hockey game knows, are based on demonstrating your physical and emotional toughness," he wrote. "You learn not to show anyone that you're in pain. If you get injured, you are expected to suck it up and brush off the pain with jokes and bravado. You never show weakness around the other players or your coaches. Doing so will get you labelled a baby."[57]

Looking back at the events a decade later, Kennedy was convinced that if he had exposed James while still playing for him, he would have been silenced, sent home, and shunned. The other players would have dismissed him as gay, and his hockey career would have ended before it had even begun. "Many people tried to shut me up when I wanted to go public about the abuse when I was thirty years old," he said. "I can't imagine what they would've done when I was seventeen."[58] Harder to accept was the tone of shock and surprise that greeted his

---

coach David Frost. Danton was playing with the St. Louis Blues in 2004 when he was arrested and charged with conspiracy to commit murder. It was revealed that he had tried to hire a hitman (who was actually a police dispatcher) to kill Frost, who had groomed Danton from age fourteen.

public disclosure of James's abuse. Everyone in the league, said Kennedy, acted as if they'd had no idea what was going on. But this was not his experience while he was enduring the nightmare, when "everyone seemed to know that I was shacked up with Graham." As he recalled, the verbal abuse of opposing players piled on to the sexual abuse he was suffering.

> It seemed like everyone in the entire league had heard about me and Graham. Players and coaches on other teams constantly accused me of being gay during games. On the ice, I just wanted to forget about Graham but even there I was marked as his property. I was taunted and catcalled. The other coaches would shout, "Hey, it's Graham's girlfriend!" The opposing players called me "faggot" and "Graham's little wife" every chance they got.[59]

Later in the book, Kennedy revealed more understanding of the distinction between homosexuality and predatory pedophilia than he was willing or able to express during the 1997 media circus that engulfed him. James's psychologist had argued that the coach was not a pedophile but a gay man who didn't realize he was abusing his authority as a coach by having sex with his players, who just happened to be minors. Kennedy called bullshit on this. "The fact that it is illegal to have sex with a fourteen-year-old and that homosexuality, like heterosexuality, has nothing to do with wanting to have sex with teenagers," he wrote, "did not seem to occur to Graham, his lawyer, or his psychologist."[60] He had similar insight into James's condition when he attended the disgraced former coach's October 1998 parole hearing.

> He was still using the same excuse he'd used when he was sexually abusing me: that he was a homosexual who could not come out publicly because he worked in the macho world of hockey. But this was not a case of being gay. Gay men do not have sex with boys any more than straight men have sex with little girls. To equate pedophilia

> and homosexuality is insulting to gay people everywhere but that's what Graham continued to do ... He never really admitted that what he had done was a crime that destroyed the lives of his victims. He didn't talk about his sick need to control every aspect of his victims' lives. He didn't admit he was a stalker, a manipulator, and that he used threats to get what he wanted. Worst of all, he didn't come clean about all of the other boys he molested.[61]

Theoren (Theo) Fleury was a fourteen-year-old Midget forward when James promised he would be drafted by the Moose Jaw Warriors, a promise James kept—after he began molesting the boy. In some ways, Fleury was even more vulnerable than Kennedy. First, his home life was a mess because of substance-abusing absentee parents.* Second, he was a small player (he stood five foot six) most scouts believed would never make it to the NHL. In the end, he proved them all wrong by enjoying an NHL career much longer and more successful than Kennedy's. After winning his only Stanley Cup in his rookie season, Fleury went on to become the all-time leading scorer of the Calgary Flames,† win an Olympic gold medal on top of Canada Cup and World Junior championships, and enjoy wide popularity as a skilled offensive force who could be tougher than players twice his size. But even as his career flourished, his personal life became a growing disaster that ultimately ended his hockey journey.

In 2003, Fleury was forced out of the NHL after repeated failure to comply with the league's substance abuse program, including frequent attempts to cheat on his urine tests.‡ Now on his third team in four years after being traded from the Flames, Fleury's life was a train wreck. By his own admission, he was addicted

---

* In one of the few happy endings in Fleury's hockey story, he later reconciled with his parents.

† Jarome Iginla eclipsed him as the Flames' leading scorer, ultimately totalling 1,095 points to Fleury's 830 points.

‡ Now called the NHL/NHLPA player assistance program, it deals with mental health and other issues not confined to substance use.

to alcohol, cocaine, and gambling, a stripper-loving party animal who, toward the end of his career, spent more time in casinos and nightclubs than on the ice, draining his bank account of the millions he had earned. Six years after his final NHL game, a recovered Fleury—aged forty-one—attempted a comeback with the Calgary Flames. He got into game shape and scored four points in as many exhibition games, but he was cut before the regular season began. A few days later, he published an autobiography in which he came out as another victim of Graham James, confirming what many had long suspected.[62]

Fleury has since become a leading figure for Canada's conservative Far Right. He's an anti-vaccine conspiracy theorist, was a supporter of the 2022 anti-mask and anti-vaxxer "Freedom Convoy" protest in Ottawa (and more recently of separatist Alberta premier Danielle Smith), and has been a promoter of various reactionary causes, the less said about, the better. However, a couple of observations from *Playing with Fire* are worth noting. When Sheldon Kennedy went public with his charges against James, the media learned that another player Kennedy refused to name had also pressed charges. Reporters asked Fleury if he was the one.* For months, his only reply was "no comment," and he refused all interviews on the subject.

"I knew if I said anything, it would become the focus of every interview, every media story, everything written about me again," he wrote.[63] Mindful of the media storm that had dogged Kennedy from the moment he went public, prompting his exit from the Boston Bruins and ultimately his NHL career, Fleury imagined the possible headlines about himself.

> "Theo Fleury scores his thousandth point despite growing up abused by his hockey coach." "Sexually molested hockey player Theo Fleury sets an NHL record for short-handed goals." This went on for nine months. I didn't want to deal with it in a public forum. I knew

* Fleury was not the other player who pressed charges in 1997. In fact, he did not go to the police until after his book was released in 2009, at the urging of Kennedy and others.

> I could get tons of sympathy, but I didn't need that. I needed to forgive myself, because I felt responsible. I'd allowed it to happen.[64]

Once he did decide to go public, Fleury chose the wife of a media contact he knew—not a hockey scribe—as his ghostwriter. Why not an established sports journo like Stephen Brunt, Bruce Dowbiggin, James Duthie, or some other erudite member of the NHL media fraternity? "I didn't want any of the usual sportswriters writing a book about me," he concluded. "I had trust issues with guys, and it would be tough to tell another guy about all the private facts."[65] There's that macho thing again: no vulnerability in the presence of other men.

The male hockey world's long-standing struggle with emotional transparency has finally been addressed over the last ten or fifteen years, thanks to programs aimed at helping players deal with mental health challenges. Hockey Talks, for example, was an awareness-building initiative the Vancouver Canucks launched after former Canuck Rick Rypien's death by suicide in 2011. Its purpose was to remove the stigma from mental health struggles and to encourage open conversation about difficult issues that most men are not accustomed to having. Hockey Talks began during the 2012–13 NHL season and soon expanded to include other NHL teams. TV sports networks for various teams adopted the program, with annual games to promote awareness, using the hashtag #HockeyTalks on social media.

One of the program's strongest advocates was Corey Hirsch, a former Canucks and New York Rangers goalie who became an analyst for Sportsnet and co-host of *Blindsided*, a podcast about mental health and other life issues that athletes face. In February of 2017, Hirsch, who had been diagnosed with purely obsessional obsessive-compulsive disorder (Pure O), shared his experience of the condition with the Players' Tribune, a media platform dedicated to stories seldom told from the athlete's perspective, of which *Blindsided* was an offshoot. Hirsch's essay became one of the site's most-read pieces. Until then, no NHL player had ever unburdened himself so publicly about his own mental health struggles. But, like much of the discussion around mental health that takes place in the conservative medium of sports TV, there weren't a lot of specifics about the dark thoughts Hirsch struggled with that caused such agony for him (including depression and suicidal ideation, chronic exhaustion, and weight loss) and confusion or frustration for legions of friends, family members, romantic partners, teammates, and coaches.

Five years later, Hirsch came out with a book-length version of his story that finally revealed what those thoughts were.[66] The memoir, which I reviewed for *The British Columbia Review*,[67] opens with a harrowing scene in which a suicidal Hirsch is in his car late at night near Kamloops, BC, determined to drive it off a cliff. He gets up to 140 kilometres an hour before his dark thoughts are interrupted, allowing him to slam on the brakes just in time to stop at the edge of the cliff. As I was reading, it occurred to me how difficult it was to be critical of someone sharing such deeply personal, private information for educational purposes while exorcising their own demons, especially when a mental health challenge like Pure O was involved. But for any adult gay male reader in the 2020s, it was also hard to fathom why it took the author five more years after his essay was published to share the big reveal that comes early in the book—even knowing that the dark thoughts he's describing occurred in the mid-1990s.

"I grew up in the culture of hockey," he wrote, leading up to it, "and everything I learned about being a man was taught to me on a ratty old bus rolling around the plains of Canada with twenty other guys between the ages of sixteen and twenty. We were taught to never, under any circumstances, talk about our feelings. You never, ever, *ever* cry."[68] Hirsch described the kind of "repetitive, distressing *what if?* thoughts" that once crowded his brain every day, thoughts he could only avoid while asleep or on the ice, prompting paranoid reactions that everyone would find out he was a monster and then he would lose everything and everyone he'd ever loved.

"Imagine those words being whispered over and over every three seconds into your ear for ten minutes straight without stopping. Really think about what that would feel like," Hirsch said. Then he shared the passing thought he'd had in a bar one night at the sight of another man:

> *Hey, there's a handsome guy.*
>
> But then my brain would just spiral out of control. It would go, *Hey, why did you think that? Are you attracted to him? Are you gay? Are you secretly gay, and you've been lying to yourself all this time? You must be gay to have thought that. You're gay and everybody on the team is going to find out. They're going to find out, they're going to find out, they're going to find out.*[69]

Hirsch acknowledged that the subject is difficult to discuss. "Historically, there has been so much homophobia in the sports community and in society at large, and that absolutely breaks my heart," he said. "The last thing I want to do is feed into that in any way. But if you want to understand what was happening in my brain, I have to take you all the way there."[70] In his recollections, he was talking about 1994, when "being outed as a professional athlete would have been a death sentence. So my brain seized on that irrational fear and spun it out of control."[71] He added that he subsequently went through therapy, which confirmed that he was not gay and that what was happening in his mind was more complicated than just sexuality.

Hirsch's long-awaited disclosure in his memoir only confirmed the hockey world's sick relationship with masculinity—a crippling homophobia that did not cause his mental health issues but exacerbated them. For this reason, I was disappointed that *The Save of My Life* did not include more reflection about homophobia in the NHL, a topic its author clearly understood. The book would have benefited from a deeper unpacking of the toxic masculinity that proved such a factor in Hirsch's mental health challenges. Seeing this as a missed opportunity, I said so in my review. As part of his growing awareness of the harm caused by homophobia, I noted, Hirsch might have expressed solidarity with players who happened to be gay. By doing so, he would find "parallels between closeted, self-loathing homophobia and stigmas surrounding mental illness as factors that prevent so many elite male athletes from being true to their authentic selves." Then I added, "Come to think of it, this would make a great topic for *Blindsided*, with

Nashville Predators prospect Luke Prokop, still the only openly gay NHL draftee, as Hirsch's guest."[72] I never heard directly from Hirsch about my review, but later I would learn that a few weeks after I posted it, Luke Prokop did indeed appear as a guest on the *Blindsided* podcast.*

A larger societal problem not confined to any one sport, sexual abuse is everywhere. But the nature of the problem in Canada's national sport—including the code of silence around it that hockey's gatekeepers maintained for decades, and the hush money long used to make the problem go away without addressing it—invites comparison to the Roman Catholic Church. In Canada, the Church's moment of reckoning—the scandal that blew the lid off all the secrecy—occurred with the Mount Cashel Boys' Home, an orphanage in St. John's, Newfoundland, run by the Christian Brothers of Ireland.† Hockey's Mount Cashel moment occurred in 2022, when Hockey Canada was revealed to have spent nearly $9 million to pay out settlements to twenty-one sexual assault complainants since 1989. During the same period, it was learned, Canadian Junior hockey players were the subject of fifteen police investigations for group sexual assault. This scandal—particularly the revelation that payout money came from player registration fees, including "from players as young as five or six years old in Timbits programs"[73]—exposed the culture of entitlement in Canada's male-dominated hockey establishment, shedding new light on toxic masculinity at the highest levels of our national sport.‡

* By the time I searched for it, Hirsch's interview with Prokop was no longer available on the *Blindsided* website. Four years later, Hirsch would express solidarity with gay players—including the Cutting Edges—in a very public way, as we'll learn in Chapter 11.

† It was at Mount Cashel during the late 1980s and early '90s that some three hundred cases of physical and sexual abuse were revealed to have occurred, an early case that led to investigations into similar crimes in other Roman Catholic organizations and dioceses around the world.

‡ Sponsored by Tim Hortons, which produces the bite-sized doughnut holes for which the program is named, Hockey Canada's Timbits Sports is a set of on-ice programs aimed at introducing children

The controversy began in May 2022 when a TSN investigation by Rick Westhead revealed that the governing body for ice hockey in Canada had reached a settlement with a woman who had sued them for $3.55 million after alleging that in 2018 in London, Ontario, she had been the victim of sexual assault by members of the national men's Junior hockey team. Three years later, this woman would make daily headlines as "E.M." when her case led to a second criminal investigation, charges against five players, and a sensational trial that dominated headlines that summer. (More on that case and Westhead's investigative efforts shortly.)

In response to the payout scandal, Canada's Minister for Sport froze Hockey Canada's federal funding and called for a forensic audit into whether public money was used for the London settlement. Then, one major sponsor after another bailed on Hockey Canada. Among the biggest names, Canadian Tire permanently cancelled its sponsorship while Scotiabank, General Motors Canada (via Chevrolet), Bauer, Imperial Oil (which markets the Esso brand in Canada), Telus, and Tim Hortons withdrew support for the 2023 World Juniors and the entire 2022–23 season. The 2022 World Junior Ice Hockey Championship in Edmonton had no sponsorship.

Hockey Canada president and CEO Scott Smith and the board of directors underwent several weeks of grilling by the federal Standing Committee on Canadian Heritage, which had opened an inquiry into Hockey Canada's handling of the 2018 London incident. Reeling from the daily assault of bad publicity, Hockey Canada couldn't keep up with all the revelations. They objected to the media's use of the term *slush fund* to describe Hockey Canada's National Equity Fund, from which minor hockey membership fees were partially used to settle sexual misconduct cases.* Despite the outrage of hockey parents across the country, Smith said the fund was necessary because Hockey Canada's insurance wouldn't

---

under seven to hockey and ensuring their first exposure to the game is a safe and positive experience. For more information, see https://www.hockeycanada.ca/en-ca/hockey-programs/coaching/under-7.

* In December 2022 it was revealed that the National Equity Fund was used to pay all $2.9 million in settlement fees for that fiscal year and that the only money going into the fund came from player registration fees. (Ashley Burke, "Hockey Canada Paid Out $2.9 Million in Settlements This Fiscal Year,

cover all types of claims. The payouts included $6.8 million for settlements related to Graham James, of whose victims Kennedy, Fleury, and Fleury's cousin Todd Holt were believed to be the tip of the iceberg.

"We haven't used money to protect our image," said Smith, putting his best spin on the situation. But the CEO came off sounding more like a beleaguered cleric from the Boston archdiocese during the investigation of the *Boston Globe*'s Spotlight team. "We've used money to respond [to] and support victims ... so we've used money to support families," he said.[74] Members of Parliament from all political parties called on Smith and the board to resign, condemning Hockey Canada as a "secretive and unaccountable organization" that "sweeps cases under the rug and moves on."[75] Prime Minister Justin Trudeau, sharing his fellow Canadians' disgust, accused Hockey Canada of wilful blindness and said the organization could no longer be trusted.

By October, Smith and the entire board of directors resigned. A new board was elected in December. By April 2023, Ottawa was prepared to renew funding, and Hockey Canada launched its Beyond the Boards Summit aimed at changing hockey culture by making the game a more positive experience for everyone. Three months later, they named Katherine Henderson the new CEO, the first female president in the organization's history, and appointed their first vice-president of diversity and inclusion, human rights leader Irfan Chaudhry. Bauer reinstated its sponsorship. Then, following a review by retired Supreme Court justice Thomas Cromwell, Hockey Canada agreed to open up their books and post their audited financial statements online. (Before that, the only way to obtain them was through an *Access to Information Act* request.)

Meanwhile, the Standing Committee on Canadian Heritage continued its inquiry into Hockey Canada's handling of the 2018 London incident. When it began, none of the players allegedly involved were required to participate in Hockey Canada's internal investigation. After public pressure, the organization

---

Using Player Registration Fees," CBC News, December 22, 2022, https://www.cbc.ca/news/canada/hockey-canada-audited-financial-statements-released-1.6695731.)

announced that any player who refused to participate would be banned from all Hockey Canada activities and programs immediately, and players from the 2018 World Junior men's team would be barred from competing in international competition until the investigation was complete and the legal ramifications clear. That paved the way for the final chapter in Hockey Canada's reckoning: a criminal trial for the London case in which five players (the London Five), all of whom had gone on to NHL careers, would be charged with sexual assault. Once their names were released, the NHL contracts for those players—Michael McLeod, Dillon Dubé, Alex Formenton, Cal Foote, and Carter Hart—were allowed to expire and were not renewed.

Apart from Donald Trump's daily assaults on Canadian sovereignty, the eight-week Hockey Canada trial, which ended in late July 2025 with all five players acquitted, was the summer's top news story in Canada. In determining the accountability of all parties, the trial focused on the issue of consent. On June 18, 2018, the twenty-year-old woman known as E.M. was at Jack's bar in London when she met members of Canada's World Junior men's team, who were celebrating their gold medal victory. Hitting it off with McLeod, also twenty, she agreed to accompany him back to the Delta Hotels London Armouries and have sex with him in his room. At issue was whether she consented to what happened next. E.M. said she was tired and drunk and expected to stay the night before leaving in the morning. She didn't realize that McLeod, still game for more action, was texting his teammates: "who wants to be in a 3 way quick. 209- mikey." Hart, Dubé, Formenton, Foote, and up to five other teammates showed up at his door.

E.M. told the court she was intimidated by the sudden appearance of so many towering hockey players who expected sex from her and didn't want her to leave. After telling her to lie on the floor, she said, some of them dropped their pants and demanded blow jobs while putting their dicks in her face. She said some of them slapped her, spat on her, and made jokes about inserting golf balls and a club into her vagina. She admitted that she never said no or resisted the men (whom the defence team repeatedly referred to as "boys") because she wanted to get through the experience without confrontation and feared the consequences of saying no. (Those comments about golf clubs didn't help, either.) The defence team focused on the players' recollection that E.M. had adopted a porn-star persona, as if this were a sign of consent rather than a coping mechanism. They also produced two "consent videos" which they claimed proved her eagerness to participate. Hammering away at E.M.'s reputation throughout the brutal cross-examination, they painted her as a more than willing temptress. Justice Maria Carroccia, in acquitting all five players, ruled that she did not find E.M.'s claims "credible or reliable" enough to convict. Her ruling ignored the argument that consent videos produced under duress—McLeod, recording the videos after the sex, can be heard coaching E.M. from the background, telling her to "Say it!"—do not constitute true consent.

Lost in the debate about consent was the peculiar nature of Team Canada's bonding rituals. These players, who had reached the summit of hockey success at the World Junior men's tournament several months earlier, had returned to their respective teams and finished their seasons before reuniting in London for the mid-June celebration. Having spent the day getting reacquainted before attending formal celebrations of their gold medal victory (including dinner with an open bar, where free bottles of wine were placed on each table), these young men—some below the legal drinking age—kept the party going after dinner, when they went bar-hopping. By the end of the night, apparently only one of them was sufficiently charming or sober enough to "score" with a young woman and take her back to the hotel. But, good teammate that he was, McLeod wanted to share.* As if they

* In covering the trial, Rick Westhead found it remarkable that "the players seemed to talk about EM as if she were not a person. They described her with the emotional detachment of someone recalling a set piece in a locker room. She was a prop, not a participant." (Rick Westhead, *We Breed Lions: Confronting Canada's Troubled Hockey Culture* [Toronto: Penguin Random House, 2025], 325.) Westhead also noted how E.M. told London police that McLeod had ordered chicken wings and was eating them while watching his teammates have sex with her.

hadn't already spent enough time together that day, some eight or nine players didn't hesitate to show up when McLeod offered a "three-way."

These guys hadn't exposed themselves to each other since the showers after winning the gold medal at New Year's. Now they would again. The presence of a single nude woman would absolve them of any taint of homosexual desire, any hint that they enjoyed each other's manhood while getting naked in such close proximity (but, of course, without ever touching each other). And they could slut-shame the woman by playing out S&M porn fantasies that only reinforced their hetero cred. That is why, on the eve of the verdict, I posted a satirical scenario on my Substack suggesting that the Team Canada players should have had sex with each other instead of involving a woman.[76] Of course, such a scenario could never have occurred. But there was a point to my combining the issues of homophobia and misogyny: Consent would have been easier to establish, and no woman would have been put in a vulnerable position. In any case, the trial was held, the London Five were acquitted, and the NHL reinstated the players.* Hart was the

* For fans who had grown cynical about the NHL's accountability efforts, the London Five's reinstatement came as no surprise. The previous summer, the league had reinstated former Chicago Blackhawks executives Stan Bowman and Al MacIsaac and head coach Joel Quenneville three years after their suspension for failing to adequately address allegations of sexual assault against video coach Brad Aldrich by player Kyle Beach in 2010. That spring, the Blackhawks were in the midst of a playoff run toward their first Stanley Cup win in half a century. Beach, a twenty-year-old member of the team's AHL affiliate, had been called up as a "Black Ace," an injury replacement fill-in. Although Beach reported the incident to another coach and meetings were held about it, no action was taken until after the Cup parade more than three weeks later, a celebration Aldrich was allowed to attend. Given the choice of resigning or facing investigation, Aldrich chose the former. No further action was taken until eleven years later, when commissioner Gary Bettman fined the Blackhawks $2 million USD for "inadequate internal procedures and insufficient and untimely response in the handling of matters" relating to the accusation. Quenneville was reported as having said the team's pursuit of the Cup was more important than sexual assault. By 2024, the three suspended staffers were deemed to have learned their lesson through sensitivity training and workshops and reinstated. Within weeks, Bowman landed a job with the Edmonton Oilers, and a year later, Quenneville signed with the Anaheim Ducks. MacIsaac continued to seek employment. ("Kyle Beach Comes Forward as John Doe in Blackhawks Investigation," NHL, October 28, 2021, https://www.nhl.com/news/kyle-beach-reveals-himself-as-accuser-in-blackhawks-investigation-327302872; Jason Owens, "NHL Reinstates Stan Bowman, Al MacIsaac, Joel Quenneville, Who Resigned for Lack of Response to Blackhawks Sexual Assault Scandal," Yahoo! Sports,

first to be signed, agreeing to a professional tryout with the Vegas Golden Knights. As the biggest star of the London Five, the former first-string goaltender for the Philadelphia Flyers insisted he'd done nothing wrong and should be entitled to continue his NHL career.*

If the gay orgy idea seems too frivolous for such a solemn issue, here's another thought: Instead of a yes or no answer on the legal question of criminal conduct, what if the London Five trial was really about respect and how we ought to treat each other? What if McLeod, knowing full well that E.M. had *not* consented to a gangbang when they first hooked up, had just let her sleep after their sex instead of greedily texting all his teammates for more action? (He could also have been a gentleman by taking the couch if sleeping with her seemed too intimate.) What if he'd bought her breakfast the next morning and sent her off with cab fare? Or, even if he *had* gone ahead with the "three-way" idea and sent the text, what if his teammates—seeing she was the only woman in a room about to be filled with men who could easily overpower her—had changed their minds, wished E.M. and McLeod a nice time, and turned in for the night?

Coverage of the London Five trial shed new light on several troubling aspects of hockey's bro culture and its toxic masculinity. Early in the 2022 hearings into

---

July 1, 2024, https://sports.yahoo.com/nhl-reinstates-stan-bowman-al-macisaac-joel-quenneville-who-resigned-for-lack-of-response-to-blackhawks-sexual-assault-scandal-214017363.html.)

* Hart passed the audition, signing a two-year contract with the Golden Knights and—after serving a brief conditioning stint with the team's AHL affiliate—played his way back into NHL form. After Vegas coach Bruce Cassidy was fired in late March 2026 and replaced by John Tortorella, Hart's former coach in Philadelphia, Tortorella made Hart his starting goaltender as the Golden Knights began a deep playoff run. As *Cutting Edge* went to press, Vegas was in the final and Hart in position to win a Stanley Cup—and possibly the Conn Smythe Trophy as playoff MVP—less than a year after his acquittal in the London Five trial. Before the final began, Hart gained new notoriety by appearing in a social media post wearing a "Free Alberta" T-shirt, suggesting support for the MAGA-inspired western Canadian separatist movement.

the case, Hockey Canada's doomed CEO Scott Smith—in yet more mimicry of a defensive Roman Catholic cleric—refused to use the word *systemic* to describe the repeated occurrence of sexual assault allegations against Junior hockey players. But retired NHL player and two-time Stanley Cup champion Daniel Carcillo knew otherwise. "Systemic failures," he wrote in a statement, "continue to occur in protecting the children and young people who play in the CHL [Canadian Hockey League]." A notorious goon during his professional career who led the NHL in penalty minutes for the 2007–08 season, Carcillo was best known in retirement as an advocate for mental health issues and awareness of post-concussion syndrome among players. But after reading about a hazing scandal at St. Michael's College, a private all-boys Catholic school in Toronto, details of ritualized torture such as a boy being raped with a broom handle called up buried traumatic memories of the sexual assault Carcillo had endured as a Junior hockey player from 2002 until 2005.

In the wake of news coverage of the St. Michael's scandal in November 2018, Carcillo launched a fifteen-tweet thread on Twitter in which he recalled his 2002–03 season with the Sarnia Sting Hockey Club in particular. Like Kennedy and Fleury in their respective memoirs, Carcillo used social media to demystify the usual narrative of success on the road to an NHL career. In one tweet, he described how having "teammates beat you on a daily basis with the sawed off paddle of a goaltender's hockey stick, takes both a physical & mental toll on a teenager." In another, he recalled being "stuffed inside the bus washroom with 6–7 other rookies, while veterans hurl[ed] their spit from chewing tobacco through a vent in the door at you."[77] Carcillo's Twitter thread prompted other CHL players to share their own experiences. In 2020, Carcillo and sixteen others launched a class action lawsuit against the CHL.

Three years later, the suit was dismissed as un-certifiable due to its scope. But in his ruling, Ontario Superior Court justice Paul Perell noted, "The evidence establishes that some unknown number of ... players in the WHL, OHL, or QMJHL were hazed, bullied, assaulted, threatened, stigmatized, mocked, demeaned, derided, ridiculed, slandered, and humiliated by their teammates, team staff, agents, employees, and servants of the WHL, OHL, or QMJHL."[78] With regard to specific incidents of hazing, the judge ruled that players had been

> tortured, forcibly confined, shaved, stripped, drugged, intoxicated, physically and sexually assaulted; raped, gang raped, forced to physically and sexually assault other teammates; compelled to sexually assault and gang rape young women invited to team parties, forced to eat or drink urine, saliva, semen, feces, or other noxious substances; forced to perform acts of self-injury, forced to perform acts of bestiality.[79]*

During the 2022 Hockey Canada hearings, a trio of reporters from the *New York Times*'s *The Athletic* published an investigative piece citing several examples of Junior hockey incidents involving sexual violence, misogyny, and mistreatment of women.[80] Among them:

- Former Junior B London Nationals defender Logan Mailloux, while on loan to SK Lejon in Sweden during the COVID-19 pandemic, was criminally convicted of secretly photographing and sharing with teammates explicit photos of a woman he'd had sex with, without her consent. Even after he went public, advising NHL teams not to select him in the 2021 draft, the Montreal Canadiens drafted him in the first round anyway. He played eight games for the Habs before being traded to the St. Louis Blues in 2025.
- Two members of the 1989 Memorial Cup–winning Swift Current Broncos, accepting a seventeen-year-old girl's invitation to watch TV at her parents' home, raped her in what she called a non-consensual assault that left her bleeding profusely. When sexual assault charges against the two players were stayed, their coach—future convicted pedophile Graham James—noted how

* For more details of the sadistic, homosexualized torture rituals players were subjected to, see the "encyclopedia of depravity" that comprised more than a dozen player affidavits filed in this case, recounted by Rick Westhead in *We Breed Lions*, 237–241.

difficult the ordeal had been for his team. In a Kafkaesque twist, the girl was then charged with mischief. She attempted suicide by taking sleeping pills, but she survived and was later acquitted.

- Three players from the Guelph Storm were charged with sexual assault after a sixteen-year-old girl told police they forced her to have sex with them at the team's season-ending party. The charges were dropped on the eve of their trial.
- Five members of the Saskatoon Blades were investigated for sexual assault after a sixteen-year-old girl said they'd had sex with her while she was unconscious at a house party. Both the Blades general manager and WHL president Ed Chynoweth slut-shamed the girl, saying she had a reputation.
- Three members of the Windsor Spitfires faced multiple charges after a twenty-four-year-old woman said she was sexually assaulted in her apartment and forced by the players to have anal intercourse.
- Three members of the Barrie Colts were charged with sexual assault of a sixteen-year-old girl. The charges were withdrawn several months later due to unlikely prospect of conviction.

The Athletic reporters cited a book published twenty-four years earlier to explore why incidents of sexual violence continued to plague Junior hockey despite anti-hazing policies and partnerships with advocacy groups to educate players about diversity, inclusion, and respect.[81] The book's author, Laura Robinson, told *The Athletic* that the real issue was "aggressive maleness" in high-masculinity sports such as hockey, football, and basketball. Athletes who played such contact team sports, she said, were more likely to participate in such sexual violence. Meanwhile, an independent review panel commissioned by the CHL and its member teams concluded that hazing, bullying, abuse, and harassment persisted because of the CHL's "culture of embedded behaviours," as well as "deficient incident reporting" and a "code of silence around maltreatment that helps perpetuate it."[82]

So, what's being done about all this? *The Athletic* reporters spoke with former hockey referee and player advocate Don Smith, a board chair for the Toba Centre for Children & Youth, a charitable organization that helps child abuse victims. Smith, they noted,

> laments the way young players are commodified, professionalized, and prioritized at such a young age. He says that without proper boundaries, infrastructure, and education to help cultivate normal emotional development, players' sense of the world around them becomes distorted and they become entitled.[83]

According to *The Athletic*, some Junior hockey teams with a history of abuse (such as the Sarnia Sting) have conducted training on issues such as "healthy masculinity, consent, bystander intervention, and using proper language." But these players are usually sixteen or seventeen years of age by the time they get this training. Surely they would benefit from receiving the information much earlier than that. "I would honestly say that twelve or thirteen is the right age to start this," said Trish Vanoosterom of the Sexual Assault Survivors' Centre Sarnia–Lambton.[84]

Part of this education requires extra vigilance around how the game is marketed. After the London Five trial, a *Globe and Mail* report exposed a Canadian clothing company, HockeyBenders, that produces T-shirts with slogans using veiled locker-room slang to demean women and girls as sex objects.[85] One shirt reads "Barduzz, Getting Huzz," which loosely translates to "Scoring Goals, Getting Hos (Whores)." HockeyBenders tours rinks and shopping malls across Canada, targeting teenage boys to ask how many "puck bunnies" they connect with on social media. Their answers (one who claims a hundred such girls is dubbed "lover boy") are uploaded to TikTok, boosting the brand's sales and profits. While the company owners say it's all in good fun, others would argue it's not in good taste. How can they market such T-shirts after the Hockey Canada scandals have tarnished the game's image based on this kind of mentality?

Katherine Henderson, Hockey Canada's new chief executive, expressed frustration with the language on the T-shirts, noting her disgust at seeing such slogans on kid's clothing. The company's response did not exactly suggest enlightened self-reflection. "The boys [HockeyBenders founder Cole Lequier and marketing director Aiden Dale] are two hardworking young hockey entrepreneurs and make videos for people to enjoy and laugh, that's it. And like to keep everything they do positive. They like to stay in their own lane with their fans and followers," read an email from "the HockeyBenders Team" in response to a request for comment.[86]

A quarter century ago, a popular website known as the Junior Hockey Bible included plenty of anecdotes about hockey's "bitches" and "whores" while promoting the clothing brand Gongshow Gear. The site offered a raunchy glossary of hockey terms. Women were "swamp donkeys" and "puck sluts." A "closet show" was defined as "a player letting his teammates watch as he has sex with the 'sluttiest broad in the league,' adding, 'Many true team players will let their girlfriends be watched.'"[87]

The *Globe and Mail* article noted that Gongshow's founders took down the website and issued a public apology when confronted about it in 2004. The Junior Hockey Bible has since been scrubbed from the internet. The question a quarter of a century later is whether anything has really changed, given that another hockey brand outlier is promoting itself with T-shirts, hoodies, and videos objectifying young women. Katherine Henderson hopes so. "There's a number of places," she told the *Globe*, with considerable understatement, "where dark corners can show up in hockey that maybe a good systemic look hadn't been done in a way that allowed us to say, well, here's where there's weakness."[88]

On November 4, 2025, I had just completed the writing for this chapter when Penguin Random House dropped a bombshell on the hockey lit market: *We Breed Lions: Confronting Canada's Troubled Hockey Culture* by TSN investigative reporter Rick Westhead. It was Westhead who broke the story about the 2018 Hockey Canada sex scandal and "slush fund" payouts to sexual assault victims that led to the London Five trial. Veteran hockey scribe Stephen Brunt, in his foreword to *We Breed Lions*, called it the most important hockey book since *Net Worth* by David

Cruise and Alison Griffiths.[89*] As well as expanding on his own journalism about Hockey Canada and the London Five trial, Westhead took the deepest dive possible into hockey's tradition of omertà, the cult of secrecy that has long governed bad behaviour in Canada's hockey culture. What he discovered through hundreds of interviews was that toxic masculinity is by no means confined to the past.

Misogynistic treatment of women and team hazing continue to be passed down from previous generations, and it's getting harder to educate the younger generation; players are becoming intoxicated with dreams of NHL stardom from a much younger age. "I've seen nine-year-old players walk into arenas in and around Toronto carrying $400 Bauer Vapor Hyperlite sticks, several to a player," Westhead wrote. "I've watched preteens doing on-ice drills wearing top-of-the-line $1,400 True Hockey SVH custom skates." Former NHL player Anthony Stewart, calling hockey "a place where money talks," put it more bluntly to Westhead: "Minor hockey is full of rich, entitled brats now. People don't say no to them. You see these kids in the Klevr League walking into rinks [wearing] their team track suits, their name stitched on their jerseys; they've got their paid coaches with the best training. Kids have an attitude like, 'My daddy tells me I'm the best of the best.' They're so young and they already have been put on a pedestal."[90†]

---

* In *Net Worth: Exploding the Myths of Pro Hockey* (Viking, 1991), Cruise and Griffiths blew the lid off the NHL's vault of secrecy around player salaries. This groundbreaking book was a shocking exposé of player exploitation by team owners and general managers from the league's earliest days, the struggle for players' rights, and events leading to the creation of the NHL Players' Association.

† In one of the more surreal episodes of prepubescent hockey entitlement described in *We Breed Lions*, Westhead recalled staying at the Delta Hotels London Armouries during the London Five trial and chatting with a hotel employee one day. She was recovering from the past weekend, when the hotel had hosted a youth hockey tournament called Rising Stars, which brought dozens of eleven- and twelve-year-old boys and their families to the hotel. Apart from wreaking havoc all weekend—banging on doors after midnight, crashing a wedding, ripping wallpaper off the walls, stuffing paper into the sauna stove, going into staff-only areas, littering the floor with popcorn, burgers, and fries, and turning over garbage cans—some of them asked staff to show them Room 209, as if the location of an alleged sexual assault should be a tourist attraction (Westhead, *We Breed Lions*, 252–53).

Perhaps the best way to rid Canada's national sport of toxic masculinity is to put more women in charge. Women with credibility who've earned respect for their achievements in the game. Slowly but surely, it's been happening for twenty years now. In 2006, Team Canada star Cassie Campbell became the first woman to perform colour commentary on *Hockey Night*. Since then, other women have joined her to provide TV coverage of NHL games, including four-time Olympic medallist and 2025 Hall of Fame inductee Jennifer Botterill on Sportsnet and professional broadcasters such as Kenzie Lalonde on TSN and NBC's Kate Scott.

Women have also been breaking the glass ceiling of employment with NHL teams. Within a short time of the league's November 2019 purge of toxically masculine men (see Chapter 9), more women began showing up on hockey operations staff for several NHL teams. By October 2025, about 150 women had such employment throughout the league, including one—Jessica Campbell with the Seattle Kraken—serving as a full-time assistant coach. Following the 2025–26 season, when her contract expired, Campbell parted ways with the Kraken to pursue new opportunities. This followed the exit a few weeks earlier of Ron Francis, who agreed to step down as president of hockey operations due to the team's failure to make the playoffs for a third consecutive year. Campbell's groundbreaking role is discussed in Chapter 12, as is an important gesture of allyship by Francis. Each of the league's thirty-two clubs employ women in their front offices and in hockey operations. NHL assistant general managers include Cammi Granato and Émilie Castonguay in Vancouver, Hayley Wickenheiser in Toronto, Kate Madigan in New Jersey, and Meghan Hunter in Chicago. In Anaheim, the Ducks hired former player Laura Veharanta as the team's director of player health and safety. In Washington, Emily Engel-Natzke became the first woman hired for a full-time coaching position when she was named the Capitals' video coach in 2022. With so many women turning up in NHL jobs, it's no wonder that the women's game, which got so many of them into those positions, has been on the upswing as well.

CHAPTER 8

A Woman's Place Is in the Hall of Fame

"Trailblazing is bold, it's brave, and it can be very scary and lonely. But it's worth it."

—BILLIE JEAN KING, at the first Professional Women's Hockey League amateur draft (2023)

Women's hockey has come a long way from its origins to reach the popularity and esteem it enjoys today. Given that women have been playing hockey for almost as long as men, the struggle for recognition of their game seems an injustice. As far back as 1890, there's photographic evidence of the female hockey player in the image of Isobel Stanley, keeping warm in her long winter coat while playing shinny with friends on the Rideau Canal. Lady Isobel was the daughter of Frederick Arthur Stanley, the sixteenth Earl of Derby and Lord Stanley of Preston, better known as Canada's sixth Governor General and for the trophy that bears his name. As mentioned earlier, the Stanley Cup was Lord Stanley's great gift to the game and remains hockey's holy grail. But for women, the biggest obstacle to enjoyment of hockey and success in the game has always been men.

In 1894, a Queen's University women's team in Kingston, Ontario, challenged a men's team to a match. This drew condemnation from the local archbishop, who regarded intersex competition as "the first blast of the apocalyptic trumpet."[91] The women played on anyway, calling themselves the Love-Me-Littles in witty response to such holier-than-thou clerical righteousness. (Twenty-two years later, the Church was at it again, this time in Quebec: Catholic priests warned young females from the St. Patrick's parish to avoid women's hockey because such a sport was "not for ladies."[92]) According to women's hockey historian Wayne Norton,

> Society expected many things of women in Edwardian times, but a serious inclination to play hockey was certainly not one of them. To play ice hockey, women had either to dismiss or ignore society's discouragements, roadblocks, and restrictions.[93]

And they did. Over the first three decades of the twentieth century, women who defied this orthodoxy came from all social classes, "from a governor general's daughter to a married teacher, from an unmarried bank clerk to a coal miner's daughter."[94] Until the outbreak of World War II, such women—and more across Canada—followed their bliss by playing hockey.

When I began writing this book, I knew next to nothing about the origins of the women's game in Vancouver and elsewhere in British Columbia, let alone the rest of the country. In Western Canada, I learned, two provinces boasted significant pockets of activity for women's hockey in the early days. In Alberta, there was the Banff Winter Carnival and women's teams based in Calgary and Edmonton. In BC, there were teams in the West Kootenay region, from Rossland to Nelson to Grand Forks, and in the West Coast pockets of the Lower Mainland and Victoria. It was only upon reading Wayne Norton's excellent hockey history, *Women on Ice*, that I learned about the Amazons, a group of players once heralded as the best women's team in Western Canada.

The Amazons were one of two Vancouver teams established by the famous Patrick brothers, Frank and Lester, who went on to become legendary builders of the National Hockey League. The first team was the Vancouver Millionaires. Led by offensive superstar Fred "Cyclone" Taylor, the Millionaires won the Stanley Cup on March 26, 1915, as part of the Pacific Coast Hockey Association (PCHA), two years before the NHL was established.* The other team was the Amazons. Inducted into the BC Sports Hall of Fame in 2024 in honour of their outstanding 1921–22 season, the Amazons were initially composed mostly of students from King George High School in Vancouver's West End. They first made news in 1918 when they challenged the more established Vancouver Ladies Hockey Team (VLHT), in a letter, "to come and get defeated at hockey."[95] The VLHT, affronted by the girls' audacity, accepted the challenge and defeated them, though not without some bruises courtesy of the Amazons' scrappy play. But the Amazons gained in confidence and, in the final game of the season, got their revenge by defeating the Vancouver Ladies 1–0 to win the city championship.

"Over the next decade," their BC Sports Hall of Fame citation says, "the Amazons were the most successful women's hockey team in the Lower Mainland and arguably the province."[96] Their success was all the more remarkable given that they played on the West Coast, where winters were warmer and there were few, if any, outdoor rinks. The Patrick brothers, wanting to expand hockey's reach across the continent, built indoor arenas in Vancouver and Victoria in 1911. The Denman Arena in Vancouver was the more famous; with 10,500 seats, it was the largest hockey rink in Canada and introduced artificial ice for the first time. The fact that it was the Millionaires' home rink gave the Amazons an advantage over other women's teams: They could practise there whenever they wished.

When the women's teams in Victoria and New Westminster folded, this meant the Amazons had to travel to Alberta not only to find opponents but, as Norton explained, to compete for the Western Canadian Championship held at

---

* When the Millionaires won the Stanley Cup on home ice at the Denman Arena in 1915, Robert Borden was Canada's prime minister, and the First Canadian Division was about a month away from fighting in the Second Battle of Ypres during World War I. But for long-suffering fans of the Vancouver Canucks, who have yet to win a Stanley Cup in their fifty-six-year existence, losing all three times they've been to the final, the ancient history of that single Cup victory for the city remains all we have to cling to.

the Winter Carnival in Banff. They were the only team from BC to do this, and they were up against teams from Calgary, a city with a much larger player pool and thus more teams. The Amazons first made the thirty-hour train trip to Banff in February 1921, but their initial bid for the Alpine Cup was unsuccessful. After defeating the Calgary Patricias 2–1 in a match that required five periods and two days to play, the Amazons were exhausted when they faced the defending champion, the Calgary Regents, in the final. The Regents beat them 4–1 to win their fourth Alpine Cup in five years.

But the Amazons were on the upswing. Catherine Patrick, wife of Frank, had chaperoned the Amazons to Banff and later regaled her husband and brother-in-law Lester with stories of the great reception the team received at the Winter Carnival. The brothers, seeing an opportunity for a lucrative event, decided to organize a West Coast Women's Championship with teams from Victoria and Seattle as well as the Amazons. Although the idea helped raise the Amazons' profile, the team and women's hockey in general became, quite literally, a sideshow. "Games would take place alongside already scheduled PCHA games in Vancouver, Victoria, and Seattle," the BC Sports Hall of Fame citation said, "the women taking the ice for ten minutes in both of the first and second intermissions and then for another fifteen minutes after the PCHA games had ended."[97] The Amazons, fresh off their action in Banff, dominated the series and won all four of their games without giving up a goal. When they returned to Banff for the 1922 Alpine Cup tournament, they once again met the defending champion Calgary Regents in the final, this time beating them 2–1 in overtime to cement their place in history.

The Amazons continued to play locally for the rest of the decade while making seven straight trips to the Banff Winter Carnival. But they never won the Alpine Cup again. As key players grew older and moved on from hockey to other pursuits, there was no real succession plan to develop new players, and opportunities for women's hockey in Vancouver dried up after the Denman Arena burned to the ground in 1936. Meanwhile, societal attitudes about women in sports like hockey were changing. Hockey spectators were exclusively men and boys, even for the women's games at the Banff Winter Carnival. And media coverage of women's hockey often described the game in "condescending or dismissive terms."

> The newspaper reporters could not resist references to the laughter from the spectators. The same early reports managed to link the matrimonial status of the players to the positions played—referring to married women on defence as "well settled" and to debutantes on the forward line as adventure seekers ... Their attire sometimes received as much attention from reporters as did their play. This of course is akin to a female politician's hair colour or shoes being a subject of comment while her male counterpart's policies receive attention.[98]

In this vein, women's games were described as "sweet battles" and the players as "fair ones." *Vancouver Sun* sports reporters couldn't help femming up the players, whom they referred to as "lady puck chasers." They called the Seattle Vamps the "Seattle Sweeties" and said they "looked all right, but the local Amazons had them beaten, even on looks." They were also amused by a supplementary rule that "ladies [would] also be required to deposit hatpins, hairpins, and other implements of militant feminism in their dressing room."[99]

Not even the most cynical *Sun* sports reporter could deny that the women's game defied such facile stereotypes. "The weaker sex did not appear very weak when it came to laying on the wood," went one game report in the *Sun*'s "Puck Patter" column. "Miss Kathleen Carson, Amazon left wing, uncorked a shot which should make [Vancouver Millionaires leading scorer] Smokey Harris green with envy."[100] But still, the men couldn't avoid treating these players like "ladies." At the end of one game, Nan Griffith and Edna Curry were each recognized for their excellence with a prize that the men thought would delight them: a box of Purdy's chocolates.

In central Canada, the first woman's league appeared in 1900 with teams from Montreal, Trois-Rivières, and Quebec City. The first money-making games were held in Montreal as fundraisers to assist wives of Canadian soldiers fighting in the Boer War. In the first couple of years of World War I, the women's game drew more attention as most healthy men of hockey-playing age were on the battlefields of Europe. The earliest captured moments from the women's game reveal how the players' movement was inhibited by their clothing: Women had to skate and hold their sticks while wearing formal dresses. Even while playing the sport they loved, women were still bound by societal mores and couldn't show too much leg for fear of causing offence. But for all the formality, their game could still be rough and tough. Here's a post-game report published in the *Montreal Daily Star* on January 18, 1916:

> Casualties were heavy. Miss Hill of North End Stanley received a blow with a stick across the face. Miss Allbutt of Telegraph gained a black eye. Miss May Doloro of Maisonneuve stopped the puck with her forehead and sports a fine big bump, and Miss Thompson of Telegraph hurt her arm when she fell in a mix-up with another young lady on top of her.[101]

The greatest women's team in Canada before World War II was the Preston Rivulettes. Between 1930 and 1939, the Rivulettes won ten regional championships in Ontario and Quebec and six national titles, losing only twice in 350 games. They were led by two pairs of sisters: Hilda and Nellie Ranscombe and Helen and Marm Schmuck. Hilda Ranscombe was a natural athlete who excelled in softball and tennis, but hockey made her famous. The talented right winger was noted for her speed, stickhandling, and—in an era where even women's hockey was known for rough play—keeping her cool. Reporting on the 1935 women's championship match between the Rivulettes and the Winnipeg Eatons, the *Montreal Daily Star* described how all hell broke loose when Helen Ransom of Winnipeg and Marm Schmuck of Preston "dropped their sticks and gloves and exchanged a number of full-swing blows that had the crowd gasping."

> Those lassies from the wild and woolly west, where the men are men and the women rule the roost, certainly can pick them up and set them down. [The] Rivulettes did not back up however and both teams were throwing around everything but the chairs and the box seats.[102]

Hilda, to her credit, remained out of the fray. As for those two losses? Both occurred during the same long road trip West in 1933, when Preston's flu-ridden roster arrived by train in Edmonton to play the hometown Rustlers for the first Dominion Women's Hockey Championship.

In the years before World War II, the women's game suffered from constant financial struggles. While no expense was spared for the men's game, even the elite women's teams could not meet travel or equipment expenses, especially during the Depression. Players from the dynastic Rivulettes often paid out of pocket to keep their on-ice magic going. In 1938, their coach even mortgaged his house so they could play for the women's championship in Prince Edward Island. In 1939, they were about to embark on a European tour when World War II broke out. Some players went to work in munitions factories, but there still wasn't enough cash to keep the hockey going. "Gasoline was rationed and money was tight, and a woman's hockey team—no matter how good—wasn't deemed essential to the war effort," wrote hockey historian Michael McKinley.[103] The team folded in 1941. Twenty-two years later, the Rivulettes were inducted into Canada's Hall of Fame as the greatest women's hockey team ever.

During the mid-1950s, NHL president Clarence Campbell was asked what he thought about the possibility of a major women's hockey league. His response was that hockey was "too rough for gals."[104] Apparently, he had a short memory: He had been a referee in Edmonton during the 1930s, when that city was home to champion women's hockey teams. One wonders what he would have thought had he lived to see Olympic medal status for women's hockey at Nagano in 1998.

Or the advent of the Professional Women's Hockey League in 2023. Or women behind the benches of NHL teams. Women's advancement in hockey has largely been driven by their own efforts, by their determination to break through the game's glass ceiling and push hockey's male gatekeepers to get with the times. We're at a point now in hockey history where more women are joining the stage with those gatekeepers, and on a more equal footing than ever.

In March of 1990, the International Ice Hockey Federation held the first ever Women's World Championship tournament in Ottawa. Given the historic significance of this event, the TSN sports network decided to broadcast four of Team Canada's games—including the gold medal match against the US. That game, which Canada won, drew nearly nine thousand fans to the Ottawa Civic Centre, at that time the largest crowd in history for a women's hockey game. But when the tournament began, something weird happened during the introduction of the host country's players: Team Canada was dressed in hot-pink jerseys instead of Canada's official red and white. The Canadian Amateur Hockey Association, a.k.a. Hockey Canada, was responsible. Their promotional film *Pretty in Pink* reinforced the notion of women's hockey as a quaint novelty. Ottawa restaurants, getting into the spirit, began serving pink menu items on special.

I remember my groaning reaction when I saw those jerseys: This could *not* have been the players' idea. A bunch of dudes in a boardroom must have dreamt it up. I was not alone in this reaction. Watching on TV from her parents' basement, an eleven-year-old girl who would grow up to become the greatest women's hockey player in the world was mortified. "I despised those jerseys," wrote Hayley Wickenheiser in a 2021 memoir.[105] The Olympian, multiple gold medallist, and Toronto Maple Leafs assistant general manager recalled the pink jerseys as a desperate publicity stunt aimed at getting Canada's mostly male sports journalists to notice an event they'd ignored in the lead-up. "The jerseys were a last-minute ploy to grab their attention and get fans in the stands," recalled Wickenheiser. "To me, all they said was that women's hockey wasn't a real sport. That female hockey players representing our country didn't deserve to wear our country's colours. We had a long way to go before we would be considered legit."[106]

Within eight years, Canadian women—including Wickenheiser—would be wearing Canada's colours with pride as they competed in their first Winter Olympics at Nagano, Japan. Despite Canada's crushing loss to the US in the gold medal match, Wickenheiser saw Nagano as literally a game changer for all women playing hockey. With a single tournament, stars like US forward Cammi Granato and Canadian goaltender Manon Rhéaume exposed the women's game to people around the world who before that moment didn't even know that women played hockey. That these names now appeared in Nike commercials or on cereal boxes gave young girls new heroes to replace Gretzky and Lemieux.

It had been a long road for Wickenheiser, who was partly driven by rejection in the men's game. At fifteen, she was the only girl to have played boys' Midget AAA hockey in Alberta. But partway through the season, she was cut from the team because her coach couldn't deal with having a girl on the roster. "A lot of ugly things were yelled at me and whispered behind my back," she recalled. "When I was growing up, there weren't a lot of other girls in the game. The kids could be bad. Some of the dads too. But the moms, the small-town gender police, they were the worst." They called her a "freak," told her to "go play ringette," said she didn't belong there, and warned her to keep away from their sons.

> The way they saw it, now I was taking the shine off someone's son, hogging their time, [taking] their roster spot. Some people resented the attention I drew, the talent I had. By the time I was in Bantam, it was so toxic that at age fifteen, I developed an ulcer. The constant stress and anxiety were tearing me up inside. On the ice, I was a target. Guys took runs at me. Coaches goaded their players into putting me in my place. I'd climb into my dad's car after games all banged up and bruised. It was hard for him to watch.[107]

Many years later, when she had reached the summit of hockey success with the 2002 Olympic gold medal at Salt Lake City, there was still one more challenge Wickenheiser had to meet: playing professional men's hockey. The NHL was out of the question, but Tampa Bay Lightning executive Phil Esposito did offer her a fifteen-game stint with the Cincinnati Cyclones of the East Coast Hockey League. Wickenheiser turned him down—that league was notorious for its goonish play. Instead, she signed with HC Salamat in Finland's third division, centring the team's third line. During her first practice, the coach sent the team's biggest, heaviest defender to take her out along the boards, slamming into her repeatedly. When she asked why, the coach said he needed to know whether she could take the abuse during a game. "I was suddenly one of the smaller players on the ice. I couldn't run over opponents anymore—most of them were bigger and stronger than me," she wrote. "The switch to full-contact hockey also forced me to change how I saw the ice; I needed to play with eyes in the back of my head, especially as a centre coming up the middle. Full contact means you can't just follow the puck; you have to always know what is coming at you. One bad hit could end my career."[108]

The women's game would continue to grow, with more big stars coming into prominence from Canada and the United States, the sport's two great powers. As of November 2025, fourteen women, including Wickenheiser, have been inducted into the Hockey Hall of Fame as players, with all their elite careers beginning after 1990: Cammi Granato, Angela James, Geraldine Heaney, Angela Ruggiero, Danielle Goyette, Jayna Hefford, Kim St-Pierre, Riikka Sallinen, Caroline Ouellette, Natalie Darwitz, Krissy Wendell-Pohl, Jennifer Botterill, and Brianna Decker. Other big stars are shining. For Canada, there's perhaps the greatest player in the women's game today, Marie-Philip Poulin, as well as Cassie Campbell, Meghan Agosta, Vicky Sunohara, Shannon Szabados, Nancy Drolet, Brianne Jenner, and Natalie Spooner. For the US, there are 2026 Olympic gold medallists Megan Keller, Hilary Knight, and Joy Dunne, along with three-time Olympic medallists Meghan Duggan and Tricia Dunn-Luoma, to name a few.

In the lead up to Nagano, the women's game had advanced so much that a pro league was all but inevitable. From 1999 until 2007, there was the National Women's Hockey League. That was followed in September 2007 by the Canadian Women's Hockey League (CWHL), which folded in 2019. In both cases, financial instability prevented the leagues from flourishing. But from the ashes of the CWHL, a new players' association was born when hundreds of prominent players from Canada and the US joined forces to form the Professional Women's Hockey Players Association (PWHPA). The PWHPA's first move was to boycott existing leagues in favour of establishing a financially stable pro league. The next was to establish partnerships with corporate sponsors and NHL teams while staging exhibition tournaments to attract more support.

The big break came in 2022, when the PWHPA entered a partnership with the Mark Walter Group and BJK Enterprises, respectively led by Los Angeles Dodgers owner Mark Walter and tennis legend Billie Jean King, with the intent to establish a new league. Within a few months, the two partners had purchased the assets of the Premier Hockey Federation, which ceased operations. The PWHPA then negotiated a new collective bargaining agreement that would apply once the new league was established. In August 2023, the Professional Women's Hockey League (PWHL) was born, with an Original Six group of charter franchises: Boston, Minneapolis–St. Paul, and New York City in the US and Montreal, Ottawa, and Toronto in Canada. The inaugural season was 2023–24. On April 23, 2025, the PWHL announced its first two expansion teams, Vancouver and Seattle, whose players hit the ice in 2025–26.

CBC Sports and investigative reporter Karissa Donkin explored the birth of the PWHL in a 2025 book that highlights many prominent women in today's game.[109] *Breakaway* explores the "dream gap" between aspiring male and female hockey professionals, especially when it comes to financial opportunity. One aspect of inequality the PWHL was determined to address was the lack of basics; when the CWHL was established, women's hockey still lacked exclusive access to locker rooms, health benefits, and even stick tape! Then there was the power of real estate. While NHL teams were often the exclusive tenant of major rinks seating more than 18,000 fans, wrote Donkin, CWHL games were played "at community rinks where the best female hockey players in Canada shared space with minor hockey teams and beer league grinders."

One player Donkin interviewed recalled how "one CWHL game end[ed] with two minutes left on the clock. It was 9 p.m. and the rental was up, so their game was over. Two men's beer league teams were waiting to take the ice."[110] A charmingly Canadian moment, from one point of view—a complete insult to women hockey pros, from another. In 2017–18, the CWHL addressed its revenue problem by adding two teams from China. This provided an instant boost to the league's cash assets, which went from less than $60,000 to more than $2 million in a single year. But it was brutal on the players, who had to play in China at least once that season and—to be able to travel—had to use up vacation leave to take time off from their day jobs.

Thanks to their 2017 boycott of the Women's Ice Hockey World Championship held that year in Michigan, the US National Women's Team laid much of the groundwork in the fight for equity that led to the PWHPA's creation. With only a couple of weeks before its scheduled opening, the players announced on social media that they would not play in the tournament "unless significant progress [was] made on the year-long negotiations with USA Hockey over fair wages and equitable support." This meant "equal treatment when it came to compensation, travel expenses, hotel accommodations, publicity and marketing, equipment, meals, and staffing, as well as equal support at the grassroots level for girls."[111] The campaign ended in victory for the players: On the eve of the championships, they signed a new agreement with USA Hockey.

The women who went on to form the PWHPA staged their own action two years later when they decided not to play professional hockey until they were properly paid. In addition to fair compensation, they wanted professional facilities and a guarantee that they wouldn't have to drag their equipment home every day. Their outreach over the next few years made a difference. By the time the league was up and running, the Montreal team had sponsorships from CCM (which provided player equipment), Gatorade, and Canadian Tire, which, having cancelled its funding of Hockey Canada due to the sexual assault payout settlements, needed a new home for its donations. The players' eight-year deal with the PWHL included an average salary of $55,000 in the first season with a 3 percent increase each season and a housing stipend for contracted players beginning at $1,500 a month—a drop in the bucket compared to the NHL, but the fact that no player would earn less than $35,000 when the previous salary was $2,000 meant that fewer women players needed a second job just to make ends meet.

Donkin's focus on the Montreal Victoire's development is enlightening. In a city so steeped in hockey traditions—and haunted by the ghosts of dynasties past, thanks to those twenty-four Stanley Cups—one point of pride for the Victoire is having their own rink: Centre 21.02 at the Verdun Auditorium, a centre of excellence for women's hockey named for the date (February 21, 2002) that Canada won its first Olympic gold medal in women's hockey. Women were making their own hockey history now, as revealed by a glass case in the Verdun Auditorium filled with mementoes from Montreal women's hockey. "There were pucks and sticks and jerseys featuring the Les Canadiennes team and various gold-medal-winning Olympic teams," reported Donkin. "There was a framed photo of the Les Canadiennes team that won the 2012 Clarkson Cup in a season that saw forward Caroline Ouellette put up an astounding 66 points in twenty-seven regular-season games. There was the puck that Jessie Eldridge shot into the net with less than forty-three seconds remaining in regulation to secure the PWHPA championship for Team Harvey's earlier that year."[112]

The real star of Donkin's book is Montreal Victoire captain Marie-Philip Poulin. A three-time Olympic gold medallist and four-time World Champion with Team Canada, which she has captained since 2015, Poulin was most famous for having scored the game-winning goal in three of the four Olympic gold medal games she competed in before 2026 (in the Winter Games of 2010, 2014, and 2022), a feat no other player of any gender has achieved and a distinction for which she's been dubbed Captain Clutch.* She also captained her first pro team, Les Canadiennes, with whom she won two Clarkson Cups and was named the CWHL's most valuable player three times. The first female hockey player to win the Northern Star Award as Canada's top athlete of the year, Poulin is generally

* Sadly for Canadians, Poulin was unable to make it four for four at the 2026 Olympics, where Canada made the gold medal game once again but this time lost 2–1 in overtime to the United States. A few months later, however, Poulin was able to lead her Montreal Victoire teammates to the team's first PWHL championship, defeating the Ottawa Charge in a thrilling four-game final to win Montreal's first Walter Cup.

Team Canada's "Captain Clutch," Marie-Philip Poulin, seen in action with the Montreal Victoire of the Professional Women's Hockey League regarded as one of the greatest women's hockey players of all time and one of the best Canadian hockey players of any gender.

By Donkin's account, what makes Poulin special is her humility and grace, the sincere modesty about her own achievements that allows her to centre other players instead of herself, a quality shared by many of our national sport's greatest players. As with any true leader, Poulin's greatest acts of generosity occur off-camera—particularly her insistence on taking the time to chat with young girls inspired to follow her footsteps. "She's the face of women's hockey," wrote Donkin. "She's the name on half the signs in the stands, the player who always takes an extra second to speak to a wide-eyed child, who always remembers a girl who attended her annual summer hockey camp."[113] Poulin has her own heroes too. Montreal Victoire general manager Danièle Sauvageau told Donkin how an eleven-year-old Poulin had met her at a hockey festival and addressed her respectfully as "Madame Sauvageau." The woman who would one day become Poulin's mentor asked the young girl if she played hockey ("Yes") and if she was any good ("I'm okay"). Twenty years later, after Poulin returned from the Beijing Olympics, she quietly draped her gold medal around Sauvageau's neck.

The greatest female hockey player in the world, affectionately known as "Pou" by her Victoire teammates, also happens to be a lesbian. Half of *Breakaway*'s Chapter 14 is dedicated to her relationship with Montreal (and Team Canada) teammate Laura Stacey. In Montreal's first game against Ottawa, Stacey scored the game-tying goal. A Toronto hockey journalist tweeted a photo of Stacey and Poulin embracing after the goal, saying "score a goal and celly [celebrate] with your fiance." When some guy named Marcus replied, "Her fiancee is there? Didn't see him behind the glass," another poster replied, "her fiancée is #29 Poulin. she's gay, marcus." Donkin notes how the exchange went viral, becoming the PWHL's first meme. By the time Montreal celebrated its Pride Night at Verdun Arena in April, "She's gay, Marcus" was appearing on signs, T-shirts, and friendship bracelets at games throughout the league. This good-natured dig at an obtuse fan sent a clear message about the PWHL: The league was a welcoming enough place to celebrate the loving relationship enjoyed by the greatest player in the women's game. Poulin and Stacey themselves wore "She's gay, Marcus" T-shirts in good humour at Montreal's Pride Night, and again at their bachelorette party before getting married that summer. A private soul not known to be forthcoming about her personal life, Poulin is nonetheless happy to join pride events, knowing what a difference her example can make for young queer folk.

Poulin and Stacey are hardly alone as high-profile hockey players in same-sex love. Ever since a 2022 *Sports Illustrated* feature on international relationships between players, the acceptance of queer sisterhood in the women's game has been completely normalized. The story revealed that former US captain Meghan Duggan was married to three-time Olympic champion Gillian Apps of Team Canada. So were two other pairs of former American and Canadian national team players: Julie Chu and Caroline Ouellette, and Kathleen Kauth and Jayna Hefford. Talk about centre ice diplomacy—no need for "Elbows up!" once the game is over, right? These women, the story noted, "have bridged the divide to build lives and families together away from the rink, proving once and for all that love is thicker than ice and vulcanized rubber."[114]

How do they manage? "It's not something that I would necessarily recommend, for people to compete for an Olympic gold medal against the person that you're dating," Apps told *Sports Illustrated*. "But I think it says a lot for us to respect each other enough to know that we can handle something like that and that if we can get through [it], then other challenges that come at us we can handle too." Easy for her to say. The last time Apps was in the Olympics, at Sochi, she and her teammates devastated Duggan and *her* teammates by winning the gold medal after a dramatic game-deciding goal by—remember?—Marie-Philip Poulin. "I'm not going to sugarcoat it," said Duggan. "It was an incredibly challenging time for us." But she and Apps got through it by giving each other space. Four years later, Duggan got her revenge when the US beat Canada in a shootout to win gold. These lovers' hearts would continue being put through the wringer when the two nations again switched places as gold medal winners in 2022 and 2026.

According to stereotype, women who play hockey have long been assumed to be lesbian, just as men who figure skate have been assumed to be gay. It is fair to say that hockey-playing women have a better sense of humour about their stereotype than figure-skating men do about theirs, and with good reason: Women in hockey are not stigmatized for loving each other, whereas a figure-skating man's every expression in the spotlight is deconstructed for signs of his inner self, assumed to be at odds with that of any man who plays hockey. At one time, this perception posed great difficulties for figure-skating men who happened to be straight. Having respect for their gay fellow skaters, many of these men felt that affirming their straightness would be an unforgivable lapse in solidarity. Of course, there are many straight women who play hockey, but most don't care if people mistake them for dykes. Women are generally more fluid and open about their sexuality than men, so it's a non-issue for them. That's why I have always been envious of hockey-playing women: If more men were as comfortable in their sexuality as women are in theirs, perhaps men like me would never have left the game of hockey at puberty.

I brought this up during an interview with my friend Sand Northrup, a women's recreational hockey player from East Vancouver who still plays at age sixty-eight. I told Northrup that I didn't know about the *Sports Illustrated* article on international lesbian hockey marriages until three years after it was published. Why was there no big deal about that story? If something similar happened on the men's side—like, say, if Jarome Iginla was revealed to be in love with Jeremy Roenick and the two men were shacked up with a couple of adopted kids and a Dachshund—the mainstream media would go apeshit. Northrup stopped me when I suggested that society is more accepting of lesbian love. More to the point, she said, the lack of controversy around the *Sports Illustrated* feature might simply have been a case of mainstream media indifference due to male heterosexism—the assumption that lesbians just don't count. "It's like, 'Oh yeah, they're only lesbians. It's not like they're faggots doing each other. The women, what do they do with each other, anyway?'" she said. "It's a kind of invisibility of women's sexuality generally, where women are kind of lesser than. So they're not our real heroes."

Northrup told me she didn't start playing organized hockey until she was forty. I assumed at first that she was a late bloomer. But as she recounted more of her story, it became clear that she was returning to the game after a formative childhood experience. From the age of nine or ten, over four winters in Edmonton, Northrup joined her older brother and his friends for games of shinny in an outdoor rink. She played goal while wearing figure skates. "We were always at the rink, and even though I didn't play throughout, that piece of it where you're a Canadian kid, and you love being outdoors and skating and the freedom of skating and trying to do something with your stick and all of that stuff—all of that was a part of my upbringing," she recalled. "And, of course, because I was a tomboy ... I wanted to do that. Also, my brother was a year and a half older than me, so super motivating. So we'd go down to the rink early before school, or after school we'd hang out and go until after dark ... I loved being outdoors, I loved being with my brother, and the fact that he was my best friend growing up, the fact that he advocated for me. He had my back, and he told everyone, 'Of course she can play.' For people who argued, 'Oh, girls can't play,' there was no question my brother would say, 'Yeah, *she* will.' [I loved] the fact that my brother advocated for me to do something I really enjoyed, the fact that he stuck up for me."

At the time, Northrup wished she could have had hockey skates instead of figure skates. There wasn't a lot of money, so her parents couldn't afford to buy them for her. Somewhere, there's a photo of her holding the "new" hand-me-down figure skates she received for Christmas. ("The look on my face is like, *I think I'm excited about this?* Because they weren't hockey skates.") Decades later, one winter in the late 1990s, while she was visiting Ottawa, Northrup put on hockey skates for the first time and was exhilarated by the experience of gliding through the Rideau Canal. When she returned home, she signed up for a women's learn-to-play hockey program at Britannia Rink.* "So many women have come to hockey because there was an environment that was inclusive for women to come to learn to play. You could come and not even know how to skate," she said, praising the Britannia program. "You'd do skills and drills and a little scrimmage at all levels."

* The program, offered to women and gender-diverse players aged nineteen and older, is now called Women + Gender Diverse Learn to Play Hockey.

Northrup improved her skating and started playing in women's rec leagues. At first she played centre but switched to defence because of her stockier build and height. Her larger body size also gave her the confidence to play on men's rec teams.

"I enjoyed coed because I'm big, and that was one of the issues playing women's hockey, because there's always incidental contact, even if you're careful," she said. "And because I'm bigger than many women, the fact is, to be able to play with my full strength is quite a treat. You know, to be able to really outmuscle someone for the puck in the corner. With women, you don't want to knock someone over. In women's hockey, if you have a big person like me and a small person go in the corner and the small person falls over, it's a penalty whether they ran into you or not. So I liked playing with men for that reason." Northrup played on the same men's team for three years. She enjoyed the speed of the game, the hard passes, and the challenge of upping her game to be more competitive. But there were downsides as well.

"I like learning the game, so that part of it I really liked, playing with the men," she recalled. "What I didn't like was getting moved up to forward again—they put you on the wing, because that's kind of where you can cause the least damage on a team, and we had a couple of women on defence. So I played on a line, the Asian Connection, we called them, these two small fast Asian guys who were tight friends, and they'd never pass me the puck. And of course I was slower, but I'd skate my heart out to be third man high, and I'd holler for the puck, and they'd never give it to me. And of course, they were our goal scorers. They were really good, but other teams figured that out and shut the two dudes down.

"And so I lost my shit with them one day. After the third or fourth game I played with them, I came back to the bench and said, 'What is your fucking problem? I'm not invisible, I'm taller than both of you fuckers. I'm calling for the puck, so give me the goddamned puck. I'll give it back, you know!' You should have seen their faces. I was furious because I was trying to figure out how do I fit in with these guys and make myself useful? I'm the other player on the line, for goodness' sake. This is recreational, and I'm paying my money too, so I don't want to just sprint up and down the fucking ice over and over and over again." At the end of the game, Northrup approached the two players and apologized for swearing at them.

They responded by inviting her upstairs for a beer, which surprised her because they didn't normally drink. "They had obviously talked about it, and they apologized and bought me a beer," she said. "And they wanted the whole team there so they could say that they really understood where I was coming from and that it wouldn't happen again. They would treat me like a hockey player and not a third wheel. And they did pass me the puck more, and we were much more effective as a line, of course. So that was a very positive outcome."

Returning to the theme of sexuality, a question I posed to Northrup in advance of our interview was whether she had encountered tension between lesbian and straight players in the women's game. I had asked this question for the purpose of comparison with the men's game, assuming it would be a non-issue for women. At first, Northrup confirmed that. "I don't feel there's been a lot of tension around sexuality, over being gay and straight," she told me. "Most of the teams I've been on, some of them have been 100 percent gay, most are at least half and half. Nobody cares—we're just there for hockey." But there was one exception. The one place where she did encounter that tension, ironically enough, was at Gay Games VII in Chicago.

By 2006, when she was forty-nine, Northrup had gained enough skills and confidence to achieve her goal of playing hockey at the Gay Games. As described in Chapter 4, the Gay Games movement was founded on the principles of inclusion, respect, and doing one's personal best. The inclusion part meant that straight allies were welcome to participate—nobody checked your sexuality credentials at the door, and the best allies were perfectly comfortable with being mistaken for the sexual minorities they were there to support. But in Chicago, Northrup recalled, one of the women's hockey teams made a complete mockery of the inclusion principle. The host city's team, the X-Factor, was composed mostly of University of Chicago students between eighteen and twenty-two—women half the age of many of their opponents. And if the number of boyfriends supporting them from the stands was any indication, they were mostly straight. This was not just a few allies joining their queer teammates in solidarity, noted Northrup; this was essentially a team of straight women competing against lesbians at an LGBTQ+ tournament.

By Northrup's account, the X-Factor should not have registered in the recreational division—it was too easy for them. Word soon got around about how good they were. When Games organizers asked them to move up to the competitive division, which was more appropriate to their skill level, they refused. By remaining in the recreational division, the Chicago team was sure to dominate every game and cruise their way to a goal medal. Sure enough, the X-Factor cleaned up at the tournament, demolishing every opponent by 9–0 and similar scores. This not only violated the Gay Games' principle of doing one's personal best, it was also a shitty thing to do to their opponents, who soon learned how high a priority their hosts placed on fair play.

Northrup's team, the Northern Lights, was the only Canadian team in that division, and they met Chicago in the final. "So they've kicked everybody else's ass, and we've ended up in the final with them," she said. "And their coach is yelling stuff like 'Hit her!' They're aggressive, they're mean, and they don't lay off. Even if they're killing [their opponent], they're still celebrating goals. At the Gay Games, it's supposed to be a 'friendly.' And they were not friendly. They're the home team, they've killed everybody, and they think our goalie is the weakest link. So they're taking slapshots from the centre line because they think they're going to pelt her with everything they can without a penalty. I mean, they were assholes."

Northrup recalled that she had taken a minor penalty and, after coming out of the box, was pummelled with a deliberate blindside hit by an X-Factor player. Several of her teammates were targeted as well. But despite these attempts to intimidate, the Chicago lead was only 1–0 by the halfway point of the game. All twelve of the other teams in the tournament, having been eliminated, had shown up at the rink to attend the final. "They were all cheering for us," she said, "even though they were all Americans. We were the only Canadian team in this tournament, and this is the part where I went, 'Wow.' When Chicago scored, nobody was cheering except for their fellows—they had their little group there. But the other teams watching, every time we'd block a shot, get a pass or a shot on net, the entire crowd would erupt."

While Chicago won the game and thus the gold medal, Northrup recalled feeling like it had been a victory for Vancouver; the Northern Lights had *not* been blown out of the rink like the other teams had, and every member of those defeated teams was in the stands going wild for the Canadians. As she and the rest of the Northern Lights lined up to receive their silver medals, everyone was standing and cheering, clapping, going nuts. Then, when it was the X-Factor's turn to receive their gold medals, the arena went nearly silent.

Everyone knew who the real champions were.

CHAPTER 9

De-Whitening the Game

"I've been watching hockey for about twenty-five years now and I watch more and more kids that look like me play the game, but I'm not seeing it being offered to the kids over here in America ... The kids need to know that there is an option to play hockey if you look like me."

—SNOOP DOGG*

If you're in Toronto and happen to visit the Hockey Hall of Fame, the first player tribute you'll see after passing through the entrance—before those for Gretzky, Lemieux, Lafleur, Orr, Howe, Hull, Rocket Richard, and the rest of the all-time greats in the men's game—is for a man who played only forty-five games in the NHL, scoring a grand total of 4 goals and 14 points. Willie O'Ree's hockey story was never about statistics or Stanley Cup rings; it was about uncommon courage and indefatigable perseverance. On January 18, 1958—six years before US civil rights became law—O'Ree became the first Black man to play in the NHL,

* During his failed attempt to bid on the Ottawa Senators ownership, the well-known rapper commented on the overwhelming whiteness of Canada's national sport. ("Snoop Dogg Says Sens Bid Could Boost Hockey Among Black Youth," CBC News, May 2, 2023, https://www.cbc.ca/news/canada/ottawa/snoop-dogg-ottawa-senators-espn-first-take-1.6829452.)

Willie O'Ree exhibit at the Hockey Hall of Fame in Toronto, Ontario, October 11, 2025

"hockey's Jackie Robinson," breaking the sport's colour barrier. O'Ree, with typical modesty, has said that Larry Kwong—the NHL's first player of Chinese descent—technically owns that distinction, having made it to the Show ten years before O'Ree (if only for a single shift), with the New York Rangers. But given the intensity of anti-Black racism in North America while O'Ree was carving out a hockey career, there's no doubting the significance of his achievement.

When the Boston Bruins called him up from the minor pro Quebec Aces, O'Ree had been partially blinded as the result of an injury in 1955 when he caught a slapshot in his right eye. But he never told the Bruins about it, nor anyone else he played for afterward; he feared that knowledge of his disability would derail his career. Sent back to the minors after two games, he wouldn't get another call-up from the Bruins for two more years; the 1960–61 season would see his only remaining NHL action. O'Ree would then toil in the minors for another seventeen seasons before retiring in 1979 at age forty-three. Through all those years, he endured an endless barrage of racist abuse, including violence, from opposing players and fans. But despite having good reason to fear for his life, he kept on playing for the love of the game.

One time, the Bruins were playing against Chicago when Blackhawks centre Eric Nesterenko spat out the N-word at O'Ree before butt-ending him in the face, knocking out two of his teeth and prompting a bloody brawl. The next time they met, Nesterenko slashed him on the ankles. Thirty years later, Nesterenko had an opportunity to apologize to O'Ree when the two met at an all-star game. But he didn't. In his memoir, O'Ree reflected on why he never responded to racist taunts, noting that it's part of the competitive spirit for hockey players to try to get under each other's skin—or, in his case, his skin colour.[115] "If I tell the whole league on national television that racial barbs really bother me, I can pretty much guarantee that I'll hear more of them," he wrote. "Above all, you want to be team-first. That's just hockey culture. Talking about your own unique challenges is about as far from team-first as you can get."[116]

Nearly twenty years after his retirement, the NHL finally recognized O'Ree's trail-blazing hockey career, which had inspired future Black hockey stars like Mike Marson, Grant Fuhr, Tony McKegney, Angela James, and Jarome Iginla. In 1998, the league appointed O'Ree as director of youth development for its diversity task force, which encouraged minority youths to play the game. Another twenty years later, O'Ree was inducted into the Hockey Hall of Fame in the builder category, in recognition of his outreach efforts, which had "touched countless lives, leaving a legacy of inclusivity and community-building."[117] At the same time, the NHL established a Community Hero Award in his name, honouring "the candidate who has made the most impact in their community, culture or society through hockey."[118]

The O'Ree display begins an extensive Hall of Fame exhibition called *The Changing Face of Hockey: Diversity in Our Game*. "As immigrant diversity affected the social fabric," the lead panel explains, "athletics also became more diverse, no longer the exclusive domain of white Protestant men. The game of hockey is no exception." There are multiple displays celebrating the women's game, especially on the international stage, and there are sledge hockey and other displays celebrating players with disabilities, including blind and hearing-impaired players, amputees, and wheelchair users. There are also many images for the Ethnicity in Hockey display. A panel in English and French quotes O'Ree above an image from his playing days with Boston: "Hockey is for everyone—and that standing out is a beautiful thing."

The Hall of Fame's front-facing exhibition promoting diversity is revealing in a number of ways. As Canadian society has become more culturally diverse through immigration, hockey's official gatekeepers have been eager to keep up with the times by recognizing the expanding interest in Canada's national sport across all ethnicities. But they're also eager to turn the page on some of the sorrier episodes in our collective history. Triumphant displays of hockey diversity and inclusion might seem to imply that societal problems of institutional racism, sexism, ableism, and homo/transphobia have been eliminated and thus excised from the game.* Of course, that would be wrong. But even for their own sake, the

---

* The Hockey Hall of Fame's *Changing Face* exhibition includes a few small displays related to LGBTQ+ issues. One features a rainbow-taped hockey stick once used by Edmonton Oilers forward Benoît Pouliot during the Hardest Shot event in a club skills competition in 2016. This made the Oilers the first NHL club to use Pride Tape to promote inclusiveness in sport and to support LGBTQ+ hockey players.

players' stories featured in the Hall's *Changing Face* exhibit provide insight into the actual challenges that BIPOC hockey players historically faced if they dared attempt to normalize their presence in a white male supremacist milieu—the abuse they endured for no other reason than playing while not white.

Like O'Ree, two other players who broke hockey's colour barrier—Kwong and Fred Sasakamoose, the NHL's first Indigenous player—had to be exceptionally courageous in pursuing their hockey dreams. People often forget how much harder it was for *any* hockey player to make it to the NHL, regardless of ethnicity, during the pre-expansion era, when these men played. During the Original Six era (1942–67), no more than a hundred rosters spots were available. Team owners, interested in winning above all else, knew that selling tickets for novelty reasons could only go so far. In such intensely racist times, non-white players like O'Ree, Kwong, or Sasakamoose had to be very good to draw the kind of attention from scouts that earned one an invitation to an NHL tryout or training camp. And they were that good.

Their stories have a few things in common. All three were inspired as children by Foster Hewitt's radio broadcasts of Maple Leaf games, the excitement of his live commentary filling their hearts with glee and the hope of one day playing in the NHL. This was a dream they shared with more privileged Canadian kids until the sobering realities of adulthood exposed them to the grim likelihood of their dreams remaining unfulfilled. All three were delighted to be noticed for their play and thrilled by the accolades of scouts and coaches as they made their way up to the Show. And all three felt the crushing blow of defeat when—teased with visions of glory, having finally made it to the big league—their NHL careers were cruelly snatched away before they could enjoy the satisfaction of being there, much less of making their mark on the game.

Another display features a warm-up jersey worn by Vegas Golden Knights forward Paul Cotter during the team's Pride Knight promotion in conjunction with You Can Play in 2021. The jersey features the word *LOVE* in block letters shaded in seven rainbow colours, with the team's official logo occupying the *V*.

Tellingly, the three share one other unfortunate fact of Canadian life. Despite the geographic gulf between their upbringings (Kwong's in Vernon, BC, Sasakamoose's in Debden, Saskatchewan, and O'Ree's in Fredericton, New Brunswick) and their different pathways to the NHL between 1948 and 1958, all three would at some point pass through the town of Chicoutimi, Quebec, and experience a traumatic incident of racist violence there.* O'Ree's happened while he played for the minor pro Quebec Aces. During a game in Chicoutimi, a racist spectator taunting O'Ree while he was in the penalty box tried to jump him from behind. O'Ree knocked him backward with a single punch, drawing a hostile response from the racist crowd—some of whom tried to get at him in the penalty box until teammates intervened. Kwong experienced a similar incident while playing for the minor pro Valleyfield Braves in Chicoutimi's home rink. While sitting on the bench, he tried to ignore a local fan who kept shouting racist abuse at him. At one point the fan grabbed him and tried to prevent him from going onto the ice. Three Chicoutimi players attacked Kwong until his teammates stepped in. In the case of Sasakamoose, the incident occurred off the ice while he was living in town as a member of the Chicoutimi team. Sitting in a bar one night with some English-speaking teammates, he got up to go to the washroom and was followed in by a large man who began shouting at him in French. The last thing Sasakamoose heard—and understood—before he was knocked out and left on the floor, blood pouring from his forehead, was "Sauvage!"

---

* One of the largest boroughs in Quebec's Saguenay–Lac-Saint-Jean region, Chicoutimi has a long history of white supremacist xenophobia and anti-Indigenous bigotry. More recent events range from racist signs popping up all over the community in 2014 to Indigenous people receiving indifferent or hostile health care at Chicoutimi Hospital. In fall 2020 one man shared horror stories about being ignored or ridiculed by nurses not long before he died at the hospital. (See Lela Savic, "'I'm Not Going to Let This Go': An Atikamekw Man's Last Cry for Justice Before He Died," *APTN News*, October 16, 2020, https://www.aptnnews.ca/national-news/im-not-going-to-let-this-go-an-atikamekw-mans-last-cry-for-justice-before-he-died/.

Like O'Ree's, Kwong's journey to the NHL is all the more impressive given the odds against him.* Born in 1923, he was the fourteenth of fifteen siblings from two mothers. In order to bring his second wife to Canada in 1904, his father had to pay the Chinese head tax—which by then had risen to $500, about the same as two years' wages for an immigrant worker. Two weeks after Kwong's birth, the head tax was replaced by the *Chinese Exclusion Act*, which cut off Chinese immigration and separated families through deportation. Growing up in a racist society, Kwong's ascent in the hockey world began from the moment he started playing with his brothers on a makeshift rink in a vacant lot outside the family home.

Hockey resources were scarce in Vernon; the Okanagan Valley was then best known for producing apples, not hockey players, and there were no local arenas. Like other natural athletes who picked up the game in that era, Kwong took advantage of winter weather to spend hours honing his skills on frozen ponds. From his first organized game at age twelve, when he joined players two years older than him and scored all three of his team's goals in a tied match, he was unstoppable. Moving from the Midget Hydrophones, playing at Vernon's new Civic Arena in 1938–39, to the Trail Smoke Eaters, the gifted forward became a major attraction. A beautiful skater who lifted fans from their seats with his dazzling moves, Kwong was an artful playmaker—including from behind the net, an area that became his "office," much as it later would for Wayne Gretzky.

After a New York Rangers scout discovered him, Kwong played for their farm team, the New York Rovers, who happened to share tenancy at Madison Square Garden. Told he would get his chance with the Rangers once he proved himself in the minors, Kwong excelled with the Rovers and was money in the bank: Rovers game attendance rose from 2,500 to more than 15,000 after he joined the team. But while waiting for his big break, Kwong watched helplessly as one lesser player after another got the call-up before him. When the Rangers finally brought him

---

* This account of Kwong's hockey journey is drawn from Chad Soon and George Chiang's *The Longest Shot: How Larry Kwong Changed the Face of Hockey* (Orca Book Publishers, 2024) and my review of it for *The British Columbia Review*, "Too Good for the NHL," posted on February 12, 2024, at https://thebcreview.ca/2024/02/12/2070-gawthrop-soon-chiang/.

up on March 13, 1948, for a game against the Canadiens at the Montreal Forum, he rode the bench until late in the third period, when he skated for a single not-quite-sixty-second shift. A New York minute was literally all he would get in the NHL.

The odds against an NHL career for Fred Sasakamoose might have been even greater. Born on Christmas Day in 1933 at Whitefish Lake near Debden, part of the Big River First Nation in Saskatchewan, he grew up on the Ahtahkakoop Indian Reserve on Shell Lake as one of eleven siblings, six of whom died in childhood from smallpox. Raised in traditional Cree culture until he was seven, he was then torn from his family and forcibly placed in a residential school where, at age nine, he was raped by other students. With that trauma and the punishment he suffered from school officials, his only refuge was hockey. At age eleven, he joined a team in nearby Duck Lake, where a priest serving as the school's sports director soon noticed his talent. When he left the residential school at fifteen, the priest arranged for a scout to meet him.

From there, Sasakamoose ended up on the Moose Jaw Canucks of the Western Canada Junior Hockey League. After scoring 31 goals in the 1953–54 season, he was named league MVP. That same year, he was called up by the Chicago Blackhawks for two games, then returned to Moose Jaw before getting another call-up for the Blackhawks' nine remaining games. As the NHL's bottom-feeders at the time, the Blackhawks missed the playoffs. Sasakamoose finished with no points in eleven games but was looking forward to the next season. When he got through training camp without getting cut, he thought he'd made the team for good. But he was mistaken: Sent down to the minors, he was given a choice only of where to be exiled. He chose New Westminster, BC, before ending up in Chicoutimi and on that washroom floor.

Decades later, Sasakamoose's memory of his brief NHL adventure was murky. But a few things stood out, especially the manner in which the Blackhawks promoted his Indigeneity: When his name was first announced at the Madhouse on Madison,* the organist started playing "Indian Love Call," a Broadway tune from the musical play *Rose-Marie*, made famous by the film version featuring Nelson Eddy and Jeanette MacDonald, that plays on exotic "Indian" stereotypes. Sasakamoose had gotten used to this sort of thing. When he was coming to Edmonton with the Moose Jaw Canucks to play the local Oil Kings, the team published an ad in the *Edmonton Journal* that showed the smiling Caucasian face of Oil King winger Billy McNeill with the text "Will this man be SCALPED tomorrow night? Freddy Sasakamoose, Moose Jaw's Indian 'Whiz Kid' is on the warpath ..." For the "Whiz Kid" himself, all this racism was just water off a duck's back.

"A lot of people ask me if I was offended by ["Indian Love Call"]—to be serenaded by a Broadway tune that pretended to have something to do with Indigenous traditions. Or if it bothered me to play for a team that had an Indian head as its logo," Sasakamoose wrote in his memoir.

> And my answer is always no. I didn't feel like anyone was making fun of me. I felt like they were trying to honour me, in their way. Just like in Edmonton, I felt only pride. Proud of being identified as an Indian. The fact that the white audience didn't really understand who I was or where I came from, the fact that they didn't understand the significance of the symbols they were using, well, that didn't diminish my pride one damn bit.[119]

Nor did he let it bother him when, during a game against Montreal, Habs defender Doug Harvey skated up to him and offered a "How" greeting "in that Western movie Indian-talk kind of way."[120] The casual racism of stereotypes was easy enough to disarm. "The word had barely passed his lips when I shot back, 'I'm not Howe. He plays for Detroit.' Harvey laughed out loud."[121]

---

* The Madhouse on Madison was the nickname given Chicago Stadium, the Blackhawks' legendary first arena, for its thunderous noise levels.

What did bother him was that, with a few exceptions, his teammates never made him feel welcome or as if he belonged. At the end of the season, he was thrilled to be invited on a marathon road trip to Los Angeles—by car—with Bills Gadsby and Mosienko, Jim McFadden, and Lee Fogolin. Sasakamoose thought the trip went well. He was especially entertained by a tour of a Hollywood studio that Gadsby had arranged, including a walk through elaborate outdoor sets for the Western movies that had produced so many Indian clichés. But after driving north to Seattle and then heading east, the group stopped in North Dakota, where Fogolin, the driver, told Sasakamoose they would next go straight to Winnipeg to drop off Mosienko. Sasakamoose had assumed they would go through Saskatchewan and drop him off in Moose Jaw first. But they didn't want to make the detour, Fogolin said—it was too far. So the rookie was abandoned at an empty bus station to make his own way home. Sasakamoose wondered if he had misjudged their friendship or acceptance. Apart from Mosienko, Gadsby, and two other players who had always been welcoming, he had no idea what most of his teammates thought of him.

> I sometimes wondered if some of the players resented all the attention I'd been getting. After every game on the recent road trip, reporters had been waiting for me in the dressing room. It seemed that everyone was curious about this full-blooded Indian who was playing hockey. (Interest, however, wasn't the same as acceptance. I was always aware of that.)[122]

But even if resentment was a non-issue, he added, that didn't mean his teammates saw him as one of their own.

> During my entire time with the team, not one player ever called me Fred or Freddy or even Sasakamoose. To a man, they called me Chief. Some meant it as a friendly nickname, I'm sure. But I sometimes suspected others were using it to make fun of me ... And then there

> was my experience on the ice. The fact that so few passes seemed to come my way. Was that because I was a rookie, or was something else going on? I had tried not to dwell on what others might be thinking. I tried to fit in.[123]

Sixty-five years later, BIPOC players still had grievances with a racist, white-dominated NHL.* But there were more of these players in the league now, and they were gaining the kind of power that can force change. In November of 2019, the National Hockey League's old boys' club had a moment of reckoning when three white male exemplars of "old school" hockey got cancelled within three weeks of each other. Each case involved the toxic masculinity of bullying, harassment, and/or racism.

First on the chopping block was *Hockey Night in Canada*'s Don Cherry. On the November 9 edition of "Coach's Corner," Cherry devoted part of the segment to a rant about immigrants not honouring Canada's veterans on Remembrance Day: "You people ... you love our way of life, you love our milk and honey. At least you can pay a couple bucks for a poppy or something like that." During his nearly four decades on *Hockey Night*, where he built a national platform as hockey's loud-mouthed purveyor of politically incorrect opinion, Cherry had said worse things than that. And, as some of his off-camera activities revealed, he was more

---

* So did coaches. Ted Nolan, an Ojibwe man who won the Jack Adams Award as NHL Coach of the Year in 1997, had experienced direct racial slurs, taunts, and discrimination throughout his playing and coaching career up to then. But it is also widely believed that he became the victim of institutional racism after he turned down a low-paying one-year extension of his contract with the Buffalo Sabres after winning Coach of the Year; he then failed to land another NHL coaching job for eight years. Nolan was reportedly blamed for his role in the firing of Sabres general manager John Muckler, who had won the NHL's Executive of the Year award the same season, and for a toxic dressing room environment caused by personality conflicts, including with star goaltender Dominik Hašek. Nolan and many others believed that his Indigenous heritage contributed to his limited opportunities in the NHL.

complex in real life than his clownishly right-wing public persona suggested.* But his downfall was inevitable. What had been regarded as offensive but tolerable insensitivity during the 1980s, '90s, and early 2000s—the inappropriate ravings of a drunken uncle at a wedding reception, say—was beyond the pale by the late 2010s—a wilful ignorance that could only embolden the genuine racists who were coming out of the woodwork thanks to the rise of Donald Trump.

And so, despite his popularity with working-class Canadians, Cherry's position with Canada's public broadcaster was doomed. As I wrote in the wake of his firing,

> Cherry lasted as long as he did because a large portion of his hockey-viewing audience agreed with his political views and saw him as their champion. Even Canadians who disagreed with him were willing to shrug him off as a loveable redneck, an eccentric buffoon, a good ol' boy curmudgeon whose crazy suits and colourful language made us more interesting as a country. Since his routine was money in the bank, senior executives at CBC and Sportsnet could afford to look the other way when things got racist—at least until it hurt their brand, which it finally did.[124]

Interestingly, Cherry's no less problematic glorification of fighting in hockey, which dismissed all scientific evidence of the connection between repeated hits to the head and concussion-related chronic traumatic encephalopathy (CTE), never seemed to be a concern for CBC/Sportsnet. On this issue at least, rock'em, sock'em Don was in tune with ratings-obsessed TV sports executives.

---

* This would include Cherry's interaction with the Cutting Edges in 1994, when on "Coach's Corner" he promoted our participation in that year's Gay Games, took seriously our objections to his commentary on the Royal Canadian Legion's "hats off" policy, and sent us a card wishing us good luck in New York. That's more than we could say for Ron MacLean, who produced the only homophobic moment in the Game 3 segment. Signing off with one of his usual bad puns, he pointed to Cherry's surname and said, "Nice to know there are fruits on 'Coach's Corner.'"

The next casualty, on November 20, was Toronto Maple Leafs coach Mike Babcock. There were hockey-related reasons for Babcock's firing: repeated playoff failures, a poor start to the season including a six-game losing streak, and disagreements with GM Kyle Dubas over player deployment. But the main reason was a player revolt over Babcock's manipulative coaching tactics. Most infamous was an incident during Mitch Marner's rookie season in which he asked the young player to grade the work ethic of his teammates and then shared the results with the players Marner had graded at the bottom.* Finally, on November 29, Calgary Flames coach Bill Peters walked the plank after multiple player complaints of physical abuse and racist slurs. The end for Peters came when former NHL player Akim Aliu reported on Twitter that a coach had directed a racial slur at him during the 2009–10 season while he was playing for the American Hockey League's Rockford IceHogs. It didn't take long to identify Peters as the coach who had repeatedly used a racist slur to complain about Aliu's choice of pre-game music.

One month after white toxicity's Black November, the axe appeared to be falling on Chicago Blackhawks assistant coach Marc Crawford. The team suspended him and launched an investigation after several former players—including Brent Sopel, Patrick O'Sullivan, Harold Druken, and Sean Avery—came forward with stories of his abusive treatment, which included kicking players at the bench. Sopel and Avery walked back their comments, saying that Crawford's methods had made them better players, and the Blackhawks reinstated him after concluding their investigation. But Crawford owned up to his abusive behaviour and publicly apologized to Druken and O'Sullivan, who had dreaded coming to the rink because of him.

This was Crawford's biggest crisis since 2004, when as coach of the Vancouver Canucks he was accused of encouraging his players to take revenge on Colorado's Steve Moore, who in one game had concussed Canucks captain Markus Näslund

* After four years in NHL exile, Babcock attempted a comeback when he signed with the Columbus Blue Jackets before the 2023–24 season. But he didn't even make it to training camp before pulling another dickhead move: He wanted players to give him their cellphones so he could go through their pictures (and who knows what else?) to get to know them better. He quit before an investigation took place.

with an unpenalized mid-ice hit to the head. In a later game, Todd Bertuzzi would skate up to Moore from behind and punch him in the head hard enough to knock him unconscious, then ride him into the ice, where a pile-on of players gave Moore a concussion and cracked three vertebrae in his neck. This violent assault ended Moore's career, triggering lawsuits against Bertuzzi, Crawford, and the Canucks organization that dragged on for a decade before the parties reached out-of-court settlements.

In February 2023, Crawford suddenly got into new trouble during his second stint coaching the ZSC Lions of Zurich in the Swiss league.* Late in one game, with his team losing, he was caught on video screaming at the ref and calling him a "cocksucker." Stunned by this homophobic outburst, an uncommon event in Swiss hockey, the league suspended Crawford for one game. He ended up coaching the team to a second Swiss league championship in 2023–24 and a strong start the next season. But in December 2024, with his team atop the standings, he resigned from the club citing mental health reasons, effectively cancelling himself.†

In the wake of such career-killing self-sabotage by the game's dinosaur coaches and broadcasters, there was much talk in the hockey world about how much had changed in the NHL, especially for racialized players. From barely being able to break into the league and then enduring decades of unchecked abuse by knuckle-

---

* Crawford returned to the Swiss league that season after being let go by the Blackhawks in May 2022, with a year remaining on his contract.

† Some old-school bench bosses managed to avoid cancellation altogether, thanks to good timing. "Iron Mike" Keenan, one of the most hated coaches in NHL history for his manipulative and sadistic mind games with players, was fortunate enough to wear out his NHL welcome back in 2009, a decade before social media campaigns began to target bullying coaches. After being fired by his eighth team, the Calgary Flames, he moved on to the Kontinental Hockey League and later coached the Italian men's national ice hockey team, retiring in early 2024 when he had heart surgery at age seventy-four. Russia's and Italy's traditional cultures of conservative masculinity were perhaps a better fit for Keenan's alpha male coaching style.

dragging bigots, BIPOC players now had the power—with a single well-timed social media post—to torch the career of a racist or a bully. Or, in the case of John Tortorella, to get an opinionated disciplinarian to back down from an untenable political position. In 2016, Tortorella—in his capacity as head coach of Team USA at that fall's World Cup of Hockey—threatened to bench any player who sat through the national anthem out of protest. "If any of my players sit on the bench for the national anthem, they will sit there the rest of the game," he told ESPN.[125] This was in response to San Francisco 49ers quarterback Colin Kaepernick's decision to take a knee during the anthem before NFL games in protest of racist police brutality and racial inequality in American society in general. Tortorella's stance was partly personal, as his son Nick was an Army Ranger.

But four years later, the ground had shifted. In the first few months of the global COVID-19 pandemic, racist American police violence peaked with the killing of George Floyd, a shocking video of which went viral. In the two weeks after Floyd's death, more than 110 NHL players and all thirty-two teams—including Seattle's expansion club, which would not take to the ice for another year—made statements about the killing, the protests, and racial inequality in hockey. "Torts" was no idiot. Perfectly in tune with the zeitgeist but notorious for his unfiltered contempt for certain sports reporters, the Columbus bench boss didn't bite when asked if he would still bench players for sitting out the anthem. Nope, he told *The Athletic*, his stance had changed. "I have learned over the years, listening and watching, that men and women who choose to kneel during this time mean no disrespect toward the flag," said Tortorella, adding that if a player wanted to conduct such a protest during the anthem, he hoped that player would give him and his teammates a heads-up first so they could prepare for possible reactions to it.[126]

By late August, the COVID-postponed NHL season had resumed and, for the first time ever, the conference semifinals were held in late summer. By this point, incidents of racist police behaviour in the US were out of control. The violence culminated with the attack on Jacob Blake, a Black man from Kenosha, Wisconsin, who was shot seven times in the back by a white officer and left partially paralyzed from the waist down. Social media video posts of the attack, like those of George Floyd's murder, went viral, leading to a wave of protests. The question this time was not whether professional athletes should sit or kneel during their anthems, but whether games should be played at all. While the NBA, WNBA, MLS, and MLB postponed some or all of their games, how did the NHL respond to the Blake attack? The league chose to proceed with its scheduled playoff games, making it the only major North American sports league not to hit the pause button out of respect.

This insensitive, business-as-usual stance was duly noted by the Hockey Diversity Alliance (HDA), a player-based organization founded in the wake of the George Floyd killing that aimed to eradicate hockey racism and intolerance. "The NHL is always late to the party, especially on these topics, so it's sort of sad and disheartening for me and other members of the Hockey Diversity Alliance and I'm sure other guys across the league," said Minnesota Wild defender Matt Dumba, who is of Filipino descent. "But if no one stands up and does anything, it's the same thing—it's just that silence that you're just outside looking in on actually being leaders and invoking real change when you have such an opportunity to do so."[127]

Dumba, a founding HDA member and the first NHL player to kneel during the national anthem, said the league's response to racial injustice shouldn't just fall on players of colour. He and HDA co-founder Evander Kane of the San Jose Sharks urged the league to suspend all games. The next day, all four playoff games for the next two days were postponed. "Black and brown communities continue to face real, painful experiences," the NHL and NHLPA said in a joint statement.

> [We] recognize that much work remains to be done before we can play an appropriate role in a discussion centred on diversity, inclusion, and social justice ... We understand that the tragedies involving Jacob Blake, George Floyd, Breonna Taylor, and others require us to recognize this moment. The NHLPA and NHL are committed to working to foster more inclusive and welcoming environments within our arenas, offices, and beyond.[128]

Three years later, the league and players' association put their money where their mouth was by launching the NHL Player Inclusion Coalition and putting aside $1 million USD to support its programs. Co-chaired by NHL alumni Anson Carter and P.K. Subban, the coalition was a group of twenty current and former NHL and women's professional hockey players working to advance equality and inclusion in the game, on and off the ice. This group's more action-oriented purpose represented a transformation from its 2020 focus on recommendations when it was named the NHL Player Inclusion Committee. The money would go to educational sessions for NHL on-ice officials, rookie players, and minor professionals; online platforms and networks giving voice to diversity and inclusion issues; and support for hockey events that connected with and inspired underrepresented youth. With a more practical, goal-oriented focus of improving on-the-ground realities, the coalition seemed to represent real change.

For the 2022–23 season, each coalition member selected an organization that supported diversity and inclusion to receive a $5,000 USD grant from the coalition's action fund. For example, former Team USA Olympian Julie Chu chose her partner's non-profit, the Caroline Ouellette Girls Hockey Celebration, which aimed to promote and develop female hockey via an all-girls tournament with fun and competitive games. New York Ranger Chris Kreider chose Ice Hockey in Harlem, which offered ice hockey and off-ice programming that exposed young people in Harlem to experiences that would prepare them for the future. And Zach Whitecloud of the Vegas Golden Knights chose the Dakota Nation Winterfest minor hockey tournament, an annual event that coincided with celebration of Indigenous culture. Whitecloud's grant was used to subsidize entry fees to reduce the cost for participating youth teams.

In October 2022, the NHL's first ever diversity and inclusion report revealed that 84 percent of the league's staff and teams were white. This result was not surprising, but change was coming. There were now mentoring programs for BIPOC candidates seeking NHL coaching positions, and San Jose's Mike Grier became the league's first Black general manager. More BIPOC players were showing up on team rosters. During the 2019–20 season, before the Hockey Diversity Alliance launched, the NHL had eighteen Black players and fewer than two dozen who were people of colour. Five years later, a record-setting twenty players of Black, Indigenous, Asian, or Latin descent were selected in the 2025 NHL draft. These included two first-rounders, Kashawn Aitcheson (New York Islanders) and Bill Zonnon (Pittsburgh Penguins). The previous year, a dozen racialized players were drafted, including three Black players in the first round.

"I think it's a direct correlation to organizations like us doing the real work at the grassroots level and then the NHL bearing the fruits of that labour," said HDA founder Akim Aliu.[129] But in the five years since the HDA's launch in the wake of the George Floyd killing, diversity, equity, and inclusion (DEI) initiatives had come under attack—including in the sports world, where Major League Baseball and football began dialling down their efforts. The NHL, saying it remained committed, was still working with the Player Inclusion Coalition led by P.K. Subban and Anson Carter. The coalition had so far educated more than a thousand professional hockey players on the benefits of inclusion, awarded more than $425,000 USD in grants to expand access and opportunity in the sport, and held several community events, including panels, clinics, and mentorship sessions.

But HDA's corporate sponsors were going elsewhere. While CCM, Canadian Tire, and Jumpstart remained, Scotiabank Canada, Budweiser Canada, and Kraft Heinz Canada, among others, did not renew their contracts, forcing the alliance to cut its operating budget by 70 percent over two years. Regardless of such losses, the HDA was committed to its mission; the game's environment was improving as more diverse groups were represented at hockey's highest level, so their work was too important to abandon. "We still hear stories about racism in the sport," New York Islander winger Anthony Duclair told *The Athletic*. "I think it's very important to have groups like the HDA put in the work and try to grow the game that way and try to educate kids about racism in the sport, in life, in general."[130] Aliu, the player who brought down Calgary Flames coach Bill Peters, wasn't overly optimistic that the NHL would continue to prioritize DEI initiatives, given the league's "current leadership." But he added, "Never say never ... If they show a willingness to do it in the right way, we'd be happy to take a look at it."[131]

While BIPOC players continued to make a difference in seeking change at the NHL level, other minority groups traditionally marginalized from the hockey world were coming out of the shadows and gaining more visibility at the community and minor pro levels while challenging the NHL's sense of itself as a place inclusive of everyone.

PART 4
THE FUTURE IS QUEER

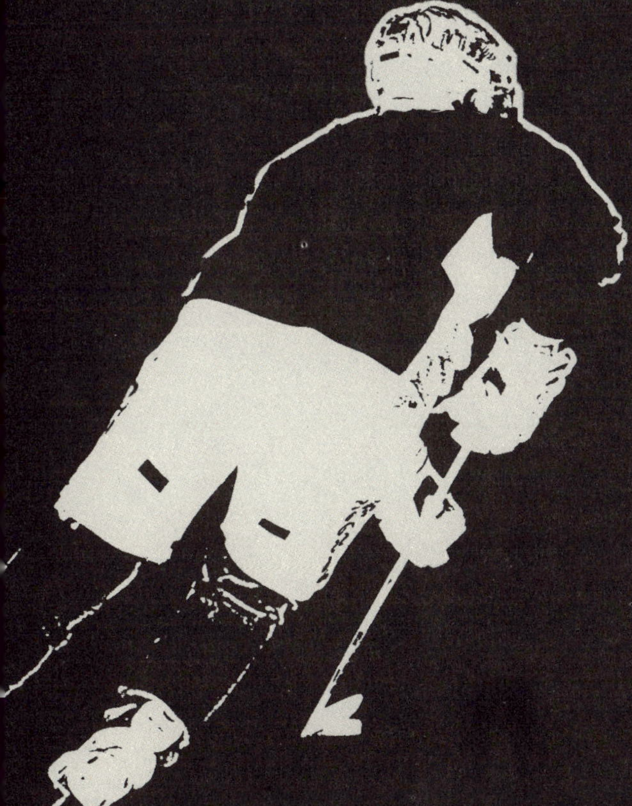

CHAPTER 10

Breaking the Hockey Binary

"We're at a crossroads: We can either continue to allow barriers against those who need sports the most, or open pathways for empathy and an expansion of sports as we know them. Choosing humanity over winning, humanity over everything else, is the way we all succeed."

—HARRISON BROWNE AND RACHEL BROWNE, *Let Us Play*

Hockey's first known transgender controversy hit the news in 1916. No, that's not a typo. In the middle of World War I, the women's game was in full swing when scandal erupted over a player considered, in the thinking of the times, too good to be a woman. The object of the fury was a precocious phenom who became the first superstar in the women's game. At eighteen, Albertine Lapensée was a natural goal scorer with a dynamic playmaking instinct. The feisty Cornwall Victorias forward could put the puck in the net whenever she felt like it. In her debut against Ottawa, she scored all three goals in her team's victory. "The gallant little lady has gained fame as the queen of all lady hockeyists," the *Ottawa Citizen* reported on March 4, 1916, noting that Lapensée had once scored 15 goals in a single game.[132] Lapensée was so good that some players whose teams she'd beaten were convinced she must have been a man. The accusation gained steam after she scored 4 goals in an 8–0 thrashing of the Montreal Westerns.

The *Montreal Daily Star* sports editor demanded proof from the newspaper's rival that Lapensée was not a man. In response, the *Cornwall Standard* dignified the request with an "investigative" article that attempted to answer the question definitively. Lapensée's masculine style of play, the article mused, could be explained by the fact she had "played more with her brothers and other boys than with her girlfriends." It concluded that she must be a "girl" because her Montreal opponents, during one of their games, had pulled off her toque "to ascertain the length of her hair and in doing so caused it to fall in long braids down over her shoulders."[133]

The Westerns' best player, Agnès Vautier, was no match for Lapensée, so Montreal promoter Len Porteous tried to find the ultimate challenger to the Cornwall superstar's reign. He thought he'd found one in seventeen-year-old scoring machine Ada Lalonde, whom newspapers described as a hockey prodigy and Lapensée's true rival. But all was not as it seemed. The only wolf in sheep's clothing, it turned out, was on the Montreal side: Lalonde was exposed as a boy. According to the *Ottawa Citizen*, the guilty lad admitted to having "dressed as a girl because he wanted to play against Lapensée ... The young boy, dressed in bloomers and a jersey top, looked like a girl and even fooled Len Porteous during the first practice."[134]

As for Lapensée? Despite scoring 80 percent of her team's goals in the 1916–17 season, she was out of hockey the following year and vanished from public view. Over the decades, her legend would build through speculation. One rumour was that she died during the 1918–1920 flu pandemic. Another was that she went to New York to have a sex change operation and then returned to Cornwall to settle down as a man, opening a gas station near town and adopting the name Albert Smythe. (An article on Lapensée in *The Canadian Encyclopedia* says that the official history of Cornwall and a profile on women's hockey by Library and Archives Canada "represent this story as fact, although it has little credibility."[135]) According to a 1940 profile in the *Cornwall Standard-Freeholder*, Lapensée married a man in New York named Albert Schmidt and was living as a woman. Her Wikipedia entry records her as having died in her native Cornwall, at age sixty-four, on January 7, 1963.

In the years since Albertine Lapensée skated circles around everyone in the women's game, similar stories are hard to find. (And the "transgender" controversy surrounding her, such as it was, did not involve an actual trans person; I share it here as a reflection on the sexism and misogyny of the times in which she played.) After women's hockey went into hiatus at the launch of World War II, the game that re-emerged decades later with the first Women's World Championship in 1990 was no longer policed by men as it had been during the first wave of women's hockey. Media interest in the new women's game, at least at the beginning, was more focused on the quality of the hockey than on the stories behind the players. So a new, more self-determined culture was able to emerge in which the players—not the outside world—decided what was acceptable in a teammate and what was allowed for public consumption.

It should come as no surprise, then, that it was the new era of the women's game, post-1990, that produced the first two openly transgender players in professional hockey. The very first was a trans man, Harrison Browne. Browne began his hockey life playing the women's game in Oakville, Ontario, where he was assigned female at birth and raised as a girl. A gifted player, he advanced quickly; in less than a decade he went from putting on his first pair of skates to leading the Hamilton Junior Hawks in scoring, then winning a silver medal with Team Canada at the 2011 Under-18 Women's World Championship in Stockholm, Sweden. After getting a scholarship to Mercyhurst University and playing his first season in the National Collegiate Athletic Association (NCAA), he transferred to the University of Maine.

While at college, Browne chose not to come out publicly as a trans man, for fear of losing his scholarship and not being allowed to play anymore. But he did come out to his coaches and teammates on the Black Bears. Browne was heartened by their support—it would later become a major factor in his decision to medically transition after retirement from professional play in 2018. However, word gets around. Sure enough, one of his well-meaning teammates outed him to the University of Maine's compliance officer, who called a meeting. There Browne was offered a private locker room if he wanted one and the option to change his name and pronouns on the roster. He declined those offers.

"I wanted to get ready for games and practices alongside my teammates; the locker room is a place of joy and camaraderie. It didn't feel like a 'women's room' to me. It's simply where I felt most comfortable," Browne wrote in the introduction to a book he co-authored with his journalist sister Rachel. "As for publicly changing my name and pronouns, I just wasn't ready yet. I was too scared of how it might be perceived by those outside my little hockey bubble, and how my parents would react as I still wasn't out even to them at this point."[136] Browne also promised the compliance officer not to go on hormone treatments as long as he played in the NCAA, where such treatments were seen as performance enhancing—a violation of anti-doping laws.

In 2015, Browne signed a one-year professional contract with the Buffalo Beauts of the newly formed National Women's Hockey League (NWHL) and then another one the following season. In October 2016, he came out publicly as a transgender man, thus becoming the first openly trans athlete in professional American hockey. "Off the ice, I felt more comfortable having my friends call me what I wanted to be called, referring to me with the pronouns that I wanted. If anything, my product on the ice was let loose and I could be myself," he told ESPN. He had intended to medically transition after college, but the possibility of going professional with the new NWHL was too good to pass up, so he decided to postpone the surgery. This would put him in "limbo" as a trans man on a women's team, but "you have to be your authentic self to be happy ... hockey makes me extremely happy."[137]

Browne's relationship to the game and the joy it brought him had an almost Zenlike aspect. Hockey was always his "happy place ... where I learned to push myself and thrive alongside other people in a team environment. It was home." But what drew him to sports, and why did he spend so many hours of the day on the ice or in the gym? "It's because that was the only time his mind would become quiet and calm," his sister Rachel explained in *Let Us Play*. "When he wasn't playing sports, he was constantly ruminating on his gender dysphoria, the future, or anything—the inner monologue was relentless and chaotic." There was more:

> He also felt out of control of his own body, especially during puberty when all these changes were happening, such as developing breasts and getting a period ... When he played sports, he could control what his body did, how it looked in terms of building muscle, and he gained a new relationship with what it was capable of doing ... While playing sports, he felt like an active participant whose actions made a tangible impact. He's truly not sure who he would be, or even if he would be here at all, without sports.[138]

The second openly transgender person in professional hockey had a similar relationship to the game; hockey made Jessica Platt happy, too. Platt, a trans woman, was assigned male at birth in Sarnia, Ontario, and first played men's hockey at the Catholic secondary school she attended. Her journey through the hockey world as a trans athlete was similar to Browne's in terms of navigating the challenges of adapting to one's body and reaching the decision to socially and medically transition. But there was one major difference to Platt's experience: The toxic masculinity and homophobia of the men's game, a constant sense of peril that was completely absent from the women's game, made Platt's journey more challenging.

Platt loved playing hockey so much that, for a time, she put aside her "horrible" feelings about the men's dressing room and delayed both her social and medical transition because the men's hockey milieu was the only one she knew. But it was completely homo/transphobic, both on the ice and in the dressing room.

> I tried to hide who I was and how I felt and suppressed it all for so long. Just because I didn't feel like I could play hockey and express who I really was. There were constantly gay jokes, people calling each other the F-word. If you did anything remotely effeminate, they called you "gay." People talked derogatorily about women, about girls' bodies, things they wanted to do to them.[139]

Platt didn't try out for the Juniors, the top-tier youth league, but instead ended up playing in a beer league, where the ubiquitous "bro attitude" made her feel that, for her own safety, she must not act any different from everyone else. ("It's almost a little worse ... than playing in my rep [representative or club] league," she told the Brownes.) In 2007, at age eighteen, she quit hockey altogether, "not because she didn't love the sport, but because the environment and locker room culture she was in didn't fully love her in return."[140]

The women's game, far more welcoming of difference, became her hockey salvation. In 2012, with the full support of her family, she began hormone replacement therapy at age twenty-three. Two years later, she put on her skates again for the first time since quitting hockey and began teaching kids how to skate, soon falling in love with hockey all over again. By 2016, now twenty-seven and comfortable in her own body, she set her sights on the professional Canadian Women's Hockey League (CWHL) as the place to make her return to the ice. After securing a spot on the Toronto Furies for the 2017–18 season, she then decided to disclose her trans status to CWHL coaches and administrators.

Platt's initial terror of possible rejection or alienation, the fear that never left her while she played on the men's side, soon turned to relief as her coach, teammates, league officials, and everyone else in the league accepted her. No longer worried about being judged, she decided in January 2018 to come out with an Instagram post, making her the first openly trans woman playing women's pro hockey. Before she went public, one report noted, "The CWHL and CWHL Players Association provided Platt with private guidance. Following the announcement, they doubled down and posted public messages of support for her."[141] At the time, Platt said Harrison Browne's coming out was a catalyst in her own decision to announce her identity. In September of that year, Platt was named one of Canada's Top 25 Women of Influence for 2018.

Harrison and Rachel Browne wrote *Let Us Play* in response to an anti-trans backlash that has turned the sports world into the latest battleground over equal rights for trans people. "What happens in sports reflects how tolerant we are as a society," they wrote in the introduction. "When we exclude trans people in one area of society, it sets a dangerous precedent to exclude trans people in other areas."[142] To indicate just how unhinged trans-exclusionary gender ideologues have become, the authors opened the book with a disturbing incident that took place in Kelowna, BC. While a nine-year-old girl with two mothers was competing in a school track and field shotput event, the grandfather of another competitor started yelling that she was a boy and shouldn't be allowed to compete. He called one of her mothers a "genital mutilator, a groomer, and a pedophile," all slanderous terms the Far Right uses against LGBTQ+ people. All that this obnoxious idiot achieved by harassing the poor girl and her parents was to make her cry and fail to perform her best on the field that day. The good news is that bystanders supported the girl, staff intervened, and the man was banned from all future public events in the school district.

The Brownes made an important point: Anti-trans mania negatively affects not only trans people but also cisgender people (especially cis women and girls), as well as the family members, friends, and communities that trans people call home. Anti-trans hysteria is disproportionate to the actual numbers of trans people in society; only a small number of trans people play sports.* "Given the miniscule number of trans athletes," the Brownes concluded, "the swath of legislative efforts and hateful campaigns targeting youth and high school students [particularly, but not only, in the United States] is absurd."[143†]

Let Us Play examines all the myths and mistaken assumptions around trans people that lead to such overblown hysteria about their participation in sports—especially trans women in women's sports. The first one is the "fairness" argument: the assumption that any athlete assigned male at birth has a physical advantage over cisgender women while playing as a trans woman. Obvious examples debunk the superiority of the male athlete. For one, most men who play tennis could not beat Serena Williams; for another, Usain Bolt's status as the world's fastest human only applied to the 100- or 200-metre race categories. Bolt famously said, "A woman could beat me" in the 800-metre sprint, and he was right: In 2018 alone, as many

---

* According to the 2021 Census, only one in three hundred Canadians aged fifteen or older identifies as trans or non-binary, though of course that number doesn't factor in younger trans kids who later confirm such identity or those unwilling to declare.

† Such hysteria is yet another reminder that those who use the term *gender ideology* to dismiss the trans rights movement tend to be the biggest gender ideologues in the debate.

as 498 women—including nearly a hundred teenage girls—ran faster than Bolt's best time in the 800-metre, which was two minutes and seven seconds.

As far as "fairness" goes, a more important factor than biological makeup, the Brownes argued, is access to resources like equipment, coaching, and good nutrition. As far back as the 1970s, trans tennis player Renée Richards excelled at her sport because her competitive advantage of white privilege gave her access to superior resources and training. "It's a lot easier to target someone's gender identity," concluded the Brownes, "than it is to discuss more complex issues regarding privilege and oppression."

Reading about the hockey experiences of Harrison Browne and Jessica Platt, the barriers they faced in a transphobic society, and the courage they gathered within themselves to rise above it all, I thank my lucky stars that I am merely an anonymous beer leaguer, a recreational hockey player who's never had to worry about the impact of public exposure on his personal safety or privacy.* As a cisgender gay male who loves the sport and plays it for fun, my journey through hockey has been a walk in the park by comparison. But that difference in perspective leads me to think back to the birth of the Cutting Edges in 1994.

From the very beginning, we were known as "Vancouver's gay men's hockey club," a mission statement formalized in 1998 when we registered as a non-profit society. We saw this specific identity as a politically important distinction; gay men were the most stigmatized players in the world's most high-masculinity and homophobic sport. But we also hoped that others who were curious about the Cutting Edges—straight allies, women, BIPOC people—would understand that it wasn't *just* a gay men's hockey club nor only a white one; that they would feel

* Certainly not for anything I've done on the ice. As a writer, my openly queer sexuality has, over thirty-six years, resulted in social shunning; missed employment, publishing, and other opportunities; the odd nasty review; and at least one death threat by mail.

confident enough to approach us if they wanted to play with us; that they knew they would be welcome if they were in solidarity with us and had enough game to keep up in a rec league.

And many did join us. We had at least one straight ally, a lesbian, and an Indigenous man on our eight-person roster in New York at the Gay Games, before our first season at UBC. Over the years, we've had a handful of cis women, along with several BIPOC men (both queer and straight) and some straight allies. But when I think back over our long history before the last say, five or six years, I can't recall an openly transgender player on any of our rosters. (And "club," by definition, is exclusive.) So, as a queer organization, how "cutting edge" were we now?

The first openly transgender man to play with the Cutting Edges (and who still does) was a small and speedy forward named Sam Punzo. Aged thirty-one when we sat down at 8 Rinks for an interview—just before our respective Edges rosters hit the ice to compete against each other—Punzo told me he'd been playing hockey since he was eight years old. Growing up in Maple Ridge, a small community nestled on the Fraser River about an hour's drive east of Vancouver, he played on girls teams until he graduated from high school. "I never played rep hockey," he said. "I was always like a bubble player, I just couldn't quite make that top team, and there wasn't really a very large girl's hockey program in Maple Ridge. If I was in a bigger city with more teams, I would probably have been able to play in Tier 2 and maybe move up a little bit. But basically it was you're either rep or you're house. Those were the only options. And that was kind of when I started to look into my gender identity."

Punzo said he always knew he wasn't really a girl. He had distinct memories of being four and five years old and telling his parents he was a boy. This was around 2000, when there was growing awareness of transgender issues, and his parents were supportive. They bought him boys' clothing and put him in different sports. While his sister danced, he played hockey. After high school graduation, Punzo played Juvenile for one year and then, when he turned nineteen, switched to the women's adult league. "I hadn't started transitioning yet, and I played adult women's hockey for a year. I found people I connected with, found a team—and that was when I decided to start to transition," he told me. "Once I started taking

Sam Punzo, a full-time player with the Cutting Edges, Team Blue, is the first trans player on the association's executive, serving as vice-president hormones, the league wouldn't let me play. Once I changed my driver's licence and my birth certificate—when I changed my gender marker on them—they were very adamant that I wasn't allowed to play."

He never got an explanation but suspects the league was worried about backlash from other teams, that they'd complain it was unfair because Punzo would have a competitive advantage. "Which was ridiculous," he recalled, "because they also had women who played college-level hockey on scholarships who were way better than I would ever be. And that also was supposed to not be allowed: If you were on a college team, you were supposed to not be allowed to play rec hockey—that was in the rules. But they wouldn't let me play, and then it kind of got to a point where I didn't really feel comfortable playing, even though I was on a team that was accepting and encouraging me to stay. It no longer felt like a comfortable place for me to stay. And so I actually just stopped playing completely."

Punzo remembered a sense of devastation, feeling lost when he stopped playing, because he didn't think there would be any other hockey space available to him as a trans man. Hockey had been a huge part of his life for more than a decade, so he didn't know what to do. He had lost community, friends, a place to play—even a sense of his own identity. So he channelled his hockey energy into other areas. At seventeen, he had begun teaching skating to younger kids but taken a couple of years off while he transitioned. Now he returned to teaching. "It kept me on my skates. I found a new passion; I was like the skate patrol for the public skating sessions, and I did that for a long time while I was at college."

He also wanted a change in his professional and intellectual life. After doing a business degree at Douglas College and working at an unsatisfying job, he went back to school and did a bachelor's degree in women's studies at Simon Fraser University, specializing in gender and sexuality. "I focused on sports and inclusion in sports, a lot of it on women's hockey," he said, "because at the time there was a lot happening with the creation of the Professional Women's Hockey Players Association—they had that walkout where the US players said, 'We're not going to play if you don't give us better conditions.' So all the papers I wrote were about the current atmosphere of hockey and about the women's game, and I wrote about trans athletes." This academic work filled a need while Punzo wasn't playing; he wanted to make hockey better for the next generation, "for the next queer kids behind me." He did this in different ways. As well as his academic research, he started working for the adult women's hockey league in Maple Ridge—the same one that wouldn't let him play—signing on as the assistant league coordinator. "I didn't really get a lot changed," he said, "but I was able to hopefully move the needle forward a bit. By the time I left, they actually did allow a trans woman to play in the female league, so I kind of felt like I indirectly had some sort of effect on that."

It was eight years before Punzo played hockey again. He heard there was hockey in Vancouver for queer folk but wasn't entirely sure he'd be welcome because the Cutting Edges were a self-described "gay men's hockey club"—other LGBTQ+ hockey organizations referred to themselves as "gay hockey associations" without adding the word *men*, and we were a "club," so that raised questions for Punzo. "I wasn't sure if I would be able to play there, but then I thought, 'If I'm going to be able to play anywhere, it would be on that team.' That's where I would feel the most comfortable, potentially, and I would probably have the most chance of being accepted on that team. But I wasn't going to drive to UBC from Maple Ridge." Then, just before the 2022–23 season, Punzo learned that the Edges were moving to the 8 Rinks hockey palace in Burnaby due to changing demographics within the club. That sealed the deal for him.

I told Punzo that I remembered when he first joined the club and we played together on Team Green. He was pretty quiet in those early days, a good communicator on the bench and on the ice, but not very demonstrative in the dressing room, where he would change quickly after the game and leave right away without showering. But ever since the Cutting Edges voted in 2024 to change our definition from "gay men's hockey club" to the more inclusive "LGBTQ+ hockey association," then adjusted our logo to include a hockey stick taped in the colours of the trans flag beside the rainbow-taped stick, he had become much more engaged with the Cutting Edges and more willing to share his opinions within the association. He had voted for the change. I told him that I'd noticed more trans players—mostly trans men, but also a couple of trans women and one or two non-binary players—joining us since the change. He said it made a big difference in how welcome trans players feel with the Edges.

"I think when you don't institutionalize [who the organization is for] and you don't have language on it, it's left to interpretation, and it kind of creates a bit of ambiguity," he explained. "'Gay men's hockey,' even though the intention behind it was to be inclusive, does send a message that's not inclusive. In order to clarify, someone would have to reach out or know somebody to be like, 'Oh, no, everyone's welcome.' Well, you'd have to know that. So, yeah, I think the [wording] change was huge, and times change. This description now, thirty years from now might not work too, right? But that's why we continue to evolve and grow."

Punzo admitted that his comfort level with the Cutting Edges took time to build, as it would for any new teammate, regardless of gender. "When I started three years ago, it was like, 'There's no way I will ever shower in this room, I will go home and do that.' And then I just realized that no one cared," he said, noting that he now showers with underwear on. "I've also noticed that it keeps people in the dressing room longer, so you're socializing more, you're bonding more ... I'm noticing that I'm talking to people more. You chat in the shower, you chat outside, but definitely the space the Edges have created is a space of respect. Like, it feels good to know that no one gives a shit. That no one's judging anybody in this room and no one cares. Shower, don't shower, shower with underwear on or don't—no one cares, right? And that's a really hard barrier for a trans person to get over, because these are extremely sensitive spaces."

I asked Punzo what the Edges could do to be even more welcoming. "From the moment I started, there has always been someone who went out of their way to say hi and talk to me, and I think if we can just keep doing that, it's going to improve the [association]," he said. "You know, it seems really small, but it does make a big difference to new people coming on to the team, especially when you don't know somebody already on there. It can be really difficult, especially when cliques are already established, friendships are already established, and you have to kind of figure people out. So one thing I have suggested to the board is something like a buddy system for new members."*

Another trans man who joined the Cutting Edges in recent years is Kade Lacasse, a thirty-eight-year-old Vancouver realtor born and raised in the Vancouver Island community of Courtenay, a ninety-minute drive north of my hometown of Nanaimo. Lacasse plays for Team Pink, the most highly skilled Cutting Edges roster. His hockey story as a trans man is unique, at least within our organization. For one thing, he's a better player than most of the cis gay men whose ranks dominate the four teams across the association. For another, unlike Punzo, he played mostly with boys when he was a child. Finally, he embraced his trans identity relatively recently, about six years ago. Before that he spent two years identifying as non-binary, and before that as lesbian.

Throughout our interview, he spoke of the importance of language to his own journey. "I was very much stuck within that, like, tomboy-esque [gender expression] until I was about twelve and just felt like I had to conform to survive," he said. "Because of the representation and education that we have today, I think I would have been given the language—or my parents would have been given the language—to know I was trans when I was very young. Because I was saving up for a sex change when I was five, so what's that? That's not a tomboy. There's something else there."

Lacasse played hockey on boys' teams until he was ten, when his family moved to Calgary. His parents couldn't afford to put him into organized hockey, so he just played three or four hours of pond hockey after school when he could, mostly with boys. When the family moved back to the Island a couple of years later, he

---

* Some months after our interview, Punzo learned just how important his influence within the Cutting Edges had become. At the association's annual general meeting on April 11, 2026, he was nominated and acclaimed as vice-president, making him the first trans player on the executive in Cutting Edges history.

returned to organized hockey, playing with boys but also joining a girls' rep team composed of players from all over the Island. But then, two years later, he moved back to Calgary when his father died. He was fourteen.

"At that point, they couldn't keep me out of hockey because I was excelling, and it was my full identity," recalled Lacasse, noting that after this move back to Alberta, he played full-time on girls' teams. "It made sense for me to play with girls because they had a competitive league there—quite competitive. I thought I would blow everyone out of the water because I was a big fish in a small pond, but that's not what happened. I didn't make the A team I wanted to the first year, but then I was in the highest league for the rest of my high school career there." During this time, Lacasse decided to conform by presenting as a girl, growing his hair long—before then, he'd always had short hair—and hanging out more with teenage girls than boys. "As much as we stayed in the [Comox] Valley," noted Lacasse, "I still moved around every two years from different schools, so I learned to be a chameleon to survive."

Lacasse was eventually recruited for the NCAA's Division 3 in the US. He didn't remember the name of the school because he was so disappointed that it wasn't a Division I team calling—all of his friends were going to DI. He turned down the offer ("My ego was too big to play there") and then tried out for the Calgary semi-pro women's team, but he didn't make the cut. He still wanted a shot at making it to DI and knew he would need to play at a high level to get there, so he called up the semi-pro BC Breakers, who had a tryout that fall. He made that team and played five years with the Western Women's Hockey League, the first year playing at Queen's Park in New Westminster. "We had our own change room. Between practices we'd leave our gear there, and you really felt professional," he said. "You didn't pay to play. I still play with the team gear I was given the first year I played that. I felt fancy." Lacasse was twenty-three the last time he played competitive hockey. That was 2010, the year his team folded.

He found out about the Cutting Edges through Google and Facebook searches for "queer hockey in Vancouver" but didn't follow up right away. Apart from a few pickup games here and there, he hadn't skated in a proper hockey game for about a decade when he finally showed up for his first summer tryout with the

Edges in 2022. Despite the competitive level he had reached as a player, his "big ego" went into retreat. "I was really fucking nervous, because I didn't know anyone, and I was pretty fresh in my transition—like, two and a half years in—and because of that, I didn't have that many men in my life. So it was kind of a scary thing to come in. I knew it would be predominantly cis men in the change room ... So I was really nervous, and [former Cutting Edges president] Peter Lipscombe was the first guy in the room that I talked to. He had been there for long enough that he was good to chat with. He was such a sweet and welcoming guy that he was the perfect person for me to have a conversation with."

I suggested to Lacasse that his being a talented player—and knowing it—should have given him more confidence that he would be accepted. He agreed but added that his distance from the cis male world meant that the Cutting Edges dressing room took some getting used to. "The first year, I was pretty quiet," he recalled. "If you ask Kyle [McCarthy, current Cutting Edges president and Team Pink teammate], he'd be like, 'Yeah, he didn't talk when he first came, and now he won't fucking shut up.' But yeah, it's been great for me, because I did have a lot of worry about how I'd fit into the male world. Without having a lot of male friends, it's a weird world ... Now that I present as a man, when you meet another guy, it's like, how do I shake hands with him? There's no code. These things that cis men grow up with, whereas I don't have that education, that pre-knowledge of it. So it's been really good to be around the guys, and yeah, I've met some friends, and because it was part of my identity for so long, hockey, it's great to have that back. It's self-esteem building."

Lacasse threw me off momentarily when he spoke of his privilege as a trans person. "I have a lot of privilege because of the way the world still sees me—a lot of [white] male privilege, despite being trans," he explained. "I'm almost six feet tall, which helps. The people we play against, I don't know that they know, so I also find that I have a lot of privilege in that, and being the age that I am. But especially [in comparison to] trans women of colour, I feel like I have tremendous privilege. We all have to look at it in that way, and I think that's what a lot of white cis gay men don't have, is awareness of their privilege. If you just look at the places where you've been put down or where you're not the top of the pecking order, it's easy not to see yourself as having privilege. But when you look at the world as it is ..."

When I asked Lacasse what the Edges could do differently, he mentioned that he'd like to see more awareness around the importance of pronoun usage, given who might be in the dressing room. "It's hard, because on the Pink team, maybe because it's a little more competitive—it's people that played when they were growing up, whereas I think a lot of gender-diverse people maybe didn't play when they were growing up—we have a lot of he/hims," he said. "It's mostly all the same pronouns, and I think there's a lot of assumption in that. But it's hard too, because what are we supposed to do—go around the room with our pronouns if everyone's a he/him? My point is just that it's inclusive to do the pronoun thing, but it is so one way that it's kind of hard to make [everyone] comfortable. I don't know what the solution is."

On the showering issue, Lacasse was blunt. Like Punzo, he showers with the team while wearing underwear. But then, he always has. "I've showered since the beginning because I've played competitive hockey—it was so ingrained in me that I'm not getting into the car without showering," he laughed. "So I just do the same thing, I shower with underwear. I was thinking the other day ... I don't want to do this, but I wondered what would happen if someone without a penis showered naked." I told him I'd like to think that no one would look, that no one would care, that there's a collective understanding that people have the right to expect not to be stared at or, in the case of sexual attraction, ogled in the shower. We're there for the hockey.

I told Lacasse that one cis male player I'd spoken with about this had agreed that not everyone feels comfortable when a cis male is standing around the dressing room with his dick hanging out. His solution? Turn to face the wall while wrapping himself in a towel. Easy peasy. Another solution, added Lacasse, might be an anonymous survey of every player just before the season starts, once the team rosters have been set. "Something like a beginning-of-the-year heads-up: 'Hey, this is what typically happens in change rooms, as you know. Is there anything we can do as an organization to make you feel more comfortable? Is there anything your team can do to make you more comfortable?' Maybe an anonymous survey just about that."

Most important, Lacasse concluded, is that inclusivity principles in hockey dressing rooms should begin at the minor hockey level so that trans kids are never made to feel as if they don't belong. "If you ask most people like me," he said, "my whole survival beyond having been a trans youth and not having the language [or] that support is that I had hockey. I had friends because I had hockey. I had development. I had whatever confidence it seemed I did because I had hockey." The hockey world needs to prioritize making the game a safe environment for all kids, he said, so they can stay in the game through age eighteen. "If you keep [safety] there, you keep community. It's beyond just making the game better—it keeps us connected to the people and the thing that potentially gives us the most self-esteem."

Another gender-divergent player in the Cutting Edges community is Kao Lawrie, a forty-one-year-old non-binary paramedic who lives on the Sunshine Coast, a several-hour drive and ferry ride away from our home ice at 8 Rinks. Lawrie had met members of the team a few years ago while playing at the Western Cup queer tournament in Calgary. After exchanging contact info, they signed up for the spares list. But they were having a hard time making it to the Lower Mainland for games, so they didn't see their first action with the Edges right away. While in Vancouver for paramedic training in 2023, they finally played in their first Edges game. "I was staying in a hotel near Kyle, and we connected to carpool to some games," they recalled. "I played for different teams—anyone who needed a body. I had a great time."

Lawrie had assumed that Vancouver had enough LGBTQ+ hockey players to have its own queer league, like Toronto does, and that the player population would be similarly diverse. So that first game was an eye-opener. "I was actually really surprised that the Cutting Edges play in a 'normie' [mainstream] league," they told me. "I guess I thought it was a queer league and didn't know it's queer teams in a larger league, so the first game I played in was against a rougher-than-I-expected

Kao Lawrie is the main organizer of This Tournament Has Everything, held annually in March in Sechelt, BC team [with] no rainbow sticks. It made me super proud to be part of the team with rainbow representation." By the time Lawrie played in that match, the Cutting Edges had already embraced our new identity as LGBTQ+, so they were surprised to find that most of the Edges were cis male. But the vibes were "super friendly." Lawrie will never forget their first time in the team dressing room, being greeted by "a huge speaker with lights on a trolly, bumping warm-up diva hits. It set a tone for sure. [Also] a very encouraging bench."

As with Punzo and Lacasse, the theme of inclusion—or its absence—runs through Lawrie's hockey journey growing up in Coquitlam. "I started playing hockey when I was fourteen on a boys' roller hockey team that I had to get permission to play in, because they didn't have girls' hockey, and at the time that's how I identified," they recalled, noting that they had to get changed in the broom closet and were never made to really feel part of the team. When they were fifteen, a hockey team was established in Coquitlam, the Predators, and they got to play one year on the girls' team. "But I came out that summer, and locker rooms got really weird for me," they said, "so I stopped playing [organized] hockey, and throughout my twenties I played late-night men's drop-in just for the cardio. I was never in the change room with them, I was always by myself—again, not part of the team—so [hockey became] just sort of a workout that I'd go to."

When they moved to the Sunshine Coast in 2021, they didn't know anyone in the community but found out there was a coed hockey league. Seeing it as a good opportunity to make friends, they signed up and started playing. "It was amazing, and I fell in love with the game again," they remembered. "But looking around the locker room, I felt a little isolated. I'm post–top surgery, nobody's body looked like my body, and there wasn't a lot of queer or gender-diverse representation, so I thought to myself, *Why don't I throw an event here and invite all my friends and see if there are more hockey players that are like me?*"

The result was an annual event called This Tournament Has Everything (TTHE), an inclusive hockey tournament for women, trans, non-binary, Two-Spirit, and other players who haven't had a chance to play the game they love.* "The point is to provide ice for otherwise marginalized groups of players, to create space for folks who haven't had much opportunity to access hockey," they explained. "It's a draft tournament, so you don't have to be part of a team, which is helpful. A lot of people don't have teams because they feel excluded in hockey. So it allows people to just self-identify with their level of play, [whether] they've gone to university or if they're just starting out. So it's skill inclusive. I balance the teams—there's no tournament championship, there's no trophy, it's literally a bunch of people getting together and playing hockey and making friends."

The tournament began with only four teams but has grown to eight. More than 125 players from all over North America registered for the fourth annual event (March 6–8, 2026). "We're limited by our rink," Lawrie said, noting that the Sunshine Coast Arena in Sechelt has only one sheet of ice. Despite that limitation, word has gotten around about this uniquely inclusive tournament in a geographical hockey outpost. Even the NHL has gotten involved, sponsoring jerseys for all the teams. "My wife actually designed the logo; it's of hockey gloves, and one side is the trans flag and the other is the pride flag," said Lawrie. The tournament has partnered with Métis Nation BC, who for the 2026 event provided grants to Indigenous players. "We run a sliding scale, so if you're in a place that you can pay more, know that those extra fees go to helping support other players," added Lawrie, noting that TTHE offers hardship funds through the Sunshine Coast Pride Society for anyone facing financial barriers to participation.

"There's a lot of rainbow representation," they said. "We have drag performers doing live commentary of the games throughout the week. We did a community mural last year—it's a four-foot-by-four-foot mural—that says, 'Hockey Is for Everyone' and is now hung up very proudly in the arena. So when you come to the arena from any other community, you can see that there is representation, and hopefully you feel included on the bench." The tournament donates 100 percent

---

* Learn more about TTHE on Instagram (@tthehockeytournament) or at https://tthe2025.mailchimpsites.com/.

of its proceeds to the Sunshine Coast Youth Outreach Program, which has a queer youth drop-in ("Which is important to me," noted Lawrie, "because I used to go to one when I was a kid because I didn't know any gay kids growing up").

The Cutting Edges have gotten involved as well. Lawrie told me the association donated a set of outdoor hockey sticks last year, which TTHE presented to the local U11 girls team for their dryland training. The Edges also shared social media posts to help connect their gender-diverse players with registration. "We have an enormous amount of support from the community, [and] it's all volunteer based," enthused Lawrie. At the 2025 tournament, 150 people signed up for a free workshop on inclusivity and diversity in sport, provided by a Toronto-based non-profit called the Get REAL Movement*: "We try to continue to create education and leadership opportunities for folks who want to be involved in this kind of change in hockey. I'm a big, big fan of representation. I think that it really, really matters."

Given their increased visibility in the game and breakthrough at the women's pro level, one might well wonder: Could a trans or non-binary player one day make it to the NHL? Perhaps it's still inconceivable for trans women, who, being women (despite their perceived advantages), would face along with transphobia a glass ceiling that ends behind the bench. As for trans male or non-binary players who can "pass" for cis male, consider this paradox within the dominant culture of transphobic society, which privileges orthodox masculine behaviour and appearance: In a choice between two exceptional hockey players of equal talent, even as socially conservative an organization as an NHL team might choose the cis-passing butch trans male over the cis gay male who makes no attempt to hide his sexuality.

* The Get REAL Movement's work is "focused on combatting 2SLGBTQ+ discrimination, racism, and bullying in schools, summer camps, and workplaces." For more info, visit https://www.thegetrealmovement.com/.

At the community level, queer hockey is now literally a coast-to-coast phenomenon in Canada. While the Cutting Edges and TTHE continue to grow in BC, along with queer associations in Alberta, Ontario, and Quebec, Atlantic Canada also has its own hockey rainbow with Queer Hockey Nova Scotia (QHNS), "a space where all folks, especially those who have been marginalized from hockey, are able to come together to play, learn, celebrate, and connect."* QHNS has a direct relationship with the Mi'kmaq people, recognizing their connection to hockey's origin story on the Atlantic coast, and with the more than fifty African Nova Scotian communities whose hockey presence in the region goes back as far as 1895. The QHNS website's photo gallery reveals a kaleidoscope of diversity across multiple teams, leagues, and tournaments, people from all sorts of backgrounds sharing their love for a game that unites us all.

* For more information about QHNS, visit https://www.qhns.ca/.

CHAPTER 11

Performative Allyship: The Tale of the Rainbow Tape

"Are you spreading awareness? Yeah. But are you actually creating allies and making athletes feel safe? I don't know. I don't see it yet. I've seen kids who think that if you use Pride Tape, it means you're gay! And that's not the point at all!"

—BROCK MCGILLIS

During the 1994 Stanley Cup finals, the *New York Daily News* called up then NHL executive vice-president Brian Burke for an interview. Having previously worked for the Vancouver Canucks, Burke was a key figure in the team's bid to secure Pavel Bure's playing rights from the Soviet Union. Did he have any thoughts about the Vancouver gay community's interest in Bure? Well, no, he didn't. But he came up with a perfect answer to make the story go away: "I'm just a hockey guy." Those five words nicely summed up the binary thinking around sexuality and hockey that had long governed NHL culture. What Burke was really saying was that he lived in one world and homosexuals in another, and those two worlds did not intersect. Well, not until December 10, 2007, the day his youngest son, Brendan, a goaltender, came out to him.

Karma couldn't have chosen a better NHL ambassador for the LGBTQ+ cause than Brian Burke. A hot-tempered, alpha male Irishman, Burke was a cigar-chomping, former American Hockey League journeyman forward who supported fighting in the game and, while GM of the Maple Leafs, counted "pugnacity, truculence, testosterone, and belligerence" as the highest values a hockey player could embrace.[144] As macho as it gets in a hockey world with no shortage of characters embracing such values, Burke was a devout Roman Catholic, to boot. But he was also a no-nonsense, heart-on-his-sleeve kind of guy who respected real courage and had no tolerance for bigotry. When Brendan came out to him, he took a good look in the mirror. "We were raised in a family where you never make a racist or a homophobic comment. But at school, we used all those slurs to describe gay people, and as a player, I called guys 'cocksuckers,' just like everyone else. That's how we talked all the time," Burke wrote in his memoir. "I was ignorant—we all were. I didn't have any gay friends. I didn't know any gay people—or at least I didn't as far as I knew. I am so ashamed of who I was then. I had to evolve."[145]

Burke's love for his son was unconditional, but he was worried about the consequences of a public coming out. By November 2009, Brendan hadn't yet come out to his team but wanted to. Brian counselled him to consult his coach first and perhaps wait until the end of the season to make the big announcement. But when Brendan's coach and teammates supported him right away, his older brother, Patrick, concluded that he should go public. If Brian Burke's son came out as gay, the thinking went, it could make a big difference in the hockey world. And so he did. Returning to his high school as a guest speaker, Brendan shared his experience of homophobia in the sports world and the positive impact of his father's support when he came out. When he went on ESPN with Brian to share his story, the response was overwhelmingly positive. "I let him do just about all the talking," Brian recalled in *Burke's Law*. "He made a lot of young men's lives easier because of what he did. I was so proud of the way he handled it."

But Brendan Burke's inspiring story would be cut short by tragedy. On February 5, 2010, he was driving with a friend through a blizzard near the Indiana–Ohio border, in a hurry to get back to his university campus for a game, when he skidded through an intersection and slammed into a reinforced pickup truck. He and his friend were killed instantly. The accident, less than three months after Brendan's triumphant coming out, came only a week before opening ceremonies for the 2010 Winter Olympics, an event Brian Burke was preparing for as general manager of the Team USA men's hockey squad. Gutted, Brian continued working through the Games in dedication to Brendan. After leaving Vancouver with a silver medal, he refused to take time off from the Leafs. Work prevented him from hitting rock bottom.

Two years later, Burke's other son, Patrick, launched You Can Play, an organization that honoured Brendan's memory by helping LGBTQ+ athletes deal with coming out in the sporting world. You Can Play's philosophy was based on a positive message of inclusion: "If you can shoot, you can shoot. If you can score, you can score. If you can play, you can play." In other words, if you were queer and "had game," there should be nothing stopping you from becoming part of the larger hockey community, enjoying your sport, and excelling at it. Brian, determined to keep his youngest son's memory alive, doubled down on his commitment to LGBTQ+ pride and inclusion: He not only joined Patrick's new organization but also showed up at pride parades and speaking engagements for queer organizations to spread You Can Play's message.

Nearly fifteen years later, it's important to emphasize that You Can Play was *not* a National Hockey League initiative; the Burke family was essentially freelancing a good idea, whether the league liked it or not. But what NHL governor, witnessing the crushing grief of one of their own for a lost son, was going to voice any kind of objection when Mr. Truculence began showing up at Toronto pride festivals with rainbow garlands around his neck, joining drag queens and leather men to spread the message of inclusion? Not a single one.

Thanks to Burke's gravitas as part of the NHL establishment, the league and its players' association wasted no time in signing on as partners. Individual players, led by Boston Bruins captain Zdeno Chára and Washington Capitals goalie Braden Holtby, also got on board. Today, You Can Play's mission statement is "We work with partners, sports, leagues, teams, and individuals to ensure LGBTQ+ belonging at every level of the game." There are education programs on how to be a good ally, policy consultations on trans and gender non-conforming athletes, resources for inclusive coaching, parenting, and fan behaviour, and much more.*

You Can Play also proved effective in monitoring homophobic incidents in NHL games. During a 2016 Stanley Cup playoff match between Chicago and St. Louis, Blackhawks player Andrew Shaw was handed an interference penalty late in the third period of a 4–3 Chicago loss. While in the penalty box, he pounded on the glass with his stick and shouted, "Fuck you, you fucking faggot!" at the ref who penalized him. You Can Play, learning of the slur on social media, reported it to the NHL. The league suspended Shaw for one game, fined him $5,000 USD, and ordered him to undergo sensitivity training.† Shaw apologized two days later, saying he was "sincerely sorry" for his "insensitive remarks." He directed his apology "to many people, including the gay and lesbian community," adding that he would learn from his mistake. After four years of working with its organization, said You Can Play, NHL players now knew they could "no longer use ignorance as an excuse for not understanding the power of their words and the effect they have on their teammates, fans, and the LGBT community."[146]

Burke, for his part, was humbled by all the support he received after Brendan's death and the You Can Play launch. His principled commitment to diversity in sport and especially to LGBTQ+ visibility in hockey was clearly heartfelt and reached many people. "When you work in hockey in Canada, there is no privacy, but people are so kind," he recalled of the public outpouring of support after Brendan's death. "People would stop me and hug me in elevators and on the street—just random strangers. Everyone knew. I got probably a thousand pieces of mail. People took the time to write these beautiful letters." These included one from a man whose son had come out to him, making him think, "If it's good

---

* For more on You Can Play, visit https://www.youcanplay.org/.

† One year later, it appeared that the NHL had double standards about who ought to be suspended for a homophobic slur in a playoff game. During Game 4 of the Western Conference final, Anaheim Ducks captain and Team Canada stalwart Ryan Getzlaf was caught on camera calling the ref a "cocksucker." He was fined $10,000 USD but not suspended. There was no explanation from the league as to why it suspended Shaw but not Getzlaf.

enough for Brian Burke, it's good enough for me." He also heard from boys he'd never met who told him they came out to their parents after Brendan came out or after his death.[147]

Without knowing him personally, my own respect for Brian Burke—grudging at best when he gave his "hockey guy" quote back in 1994—shot up a great deal after his son came out to him, and again when he embraced You Can Play after Brendan's death. It goes up every time he speaks out against homophobia, or when he calls out hypocrisy around the hockey establishment's inclusion efforts. Sadly, there's been no shortage of either since 2012. But then, Brian Burke and one inclusivity program were never going to solve the league's bigotry problems overnight. Much of what needs to happen to make the NHL environment less homophobic depends on leadership of at least one pay grade higher than Burke's.

An old friend of mine, Paul Isaacs, has been a season ticket holder with the Vancouver Canucks since 1980. Of all the unsettling episodes he has experienced as a fan over the years, one of the more revealing began with a harmless accident in the stands during a game at the Pacific Coliseum, in the second half of the 1992–93 season. Isaacs and a friend had just left their seats during intermission and were walking around the concourse, deep in conversation, when Isaacs collided with another man coming from the opposite direction, also walking briskly while deep in conversation. Isaacs at the time was something of a barrel-chested fitness buff, much larger than the man he bumped into, so the other man took the brunt of the collision; thrown to the concrete floor in a most undignified way, he was knocked flat on his ass.

The two men accompanying the stranger helped him back to his feet—a short white fellow in a dark suit, he looked to be an important businessman of some sort. Glaring at Isaacs as he dusted himself off, the man was clearly enraged, as if the collision had been Isaacs's fault or even deliberate. As if Isaacs were the only one who should have watched where he was going. Isaacs, stunned by the hostility in the man's expression, could not utter a word before the man spun around and walked away, his two companions in tow. Isaacs shrugged and moved along with his friend, soon forgetting about the incident. When the game was over, Isaacs bid farewell to his friend and then, as previously arranged, went downstairs with two members of Canucks staff to attend an event for season ticket holders. The Canucks were introducing the NHL's new commissioner, who that night was making his first visit to Vancouver in this capacity.

There were about eighty people in the room and a dozen or so microphones. The two Canucks staffers found Isaacs a seat in the middle of the room and flanked him as they sat down. Just as the event began, Isaacs looked up at the podium and was startled to see that the man everyone had come to hear, the new NHL commissioner now taking the microphone after being introduced, was the man he had bumped into. Gary Bettman was about to begin speaking when, surveying the room, he noticed Isaacs in the crowd. Recognizing him, Bettman frowned and pointed a finger at him. "You, please leave." Startled, Isaacs pointed at himself and shrugged, as if to say, *Who, me?* Bettman replied, insistent, "Yes, you. Please leave. Now!" The whole room turned to look, curious. Isaacs, facing the Canucks staffers who had brought him, shrugged again in embarrassment. His hosts were shocked and bewildered that their invitee was persona non grata with the new commish. Having no idea about the bumping incident, they asked Isaacs to stay. But Bettman, the NHL's new boss, was assuming his full authority as if he owned the place, as if his position superseded that of his hosts. Realizing that Bettman had every intention of calling security if he were disobeyed, Isaacs rose from his seat, thanked his hosts, and left.

Thirty-three years later, Gary Bettman is still at the helm of the NHL.* For those who've never had the pleasure of hearing his interviews or enduring his banter while he's hosting NHL awards night, handing over the Stanley Cup to the winning team's captain, or calling the amateur draft, the Paul Isaacs story suggests

---

* At least, he was when this book went to press. Having already written a book that criticized an unpopular authority figure—only to have that person vacate their position of power shortly before the book was published—I take nothing for granted.

that Bettman's is not exactly a warm and fuzzy personality.* Outside his comfort zone and in the public eye, he does not come off as friendly or sincere. This is likely due to his status as a corporate player unique to his corner of the capitalist universe, the Big Four of North American professional sports. Bettman is an untouchable figurehead whose power is guaranteed by expedient harmony with the team owners whose interests he represents.

He appears not to lose any sleep over the fact that he is widely loathed. On the contrary, he is stubbornly defiant, as if the criticism merely proves his superiority. You can see it in the supercilious grin, in the unconvincing expressions of true love for the sport he governs. Everything he says for public consumption is carefully crafted to ensure the smoothest possible delivery of the owners' wishes. As league commissioner (a position that replaced "president"), he is the first NHL chair to preside over a player lockout—not one, not two, but three of them, including the cancelled 2004–05 season. Many regard this as a shameful blight on his record. Not Bettman. He likely sees it as a badge of honour, having crushed the players' union as a viable force of resistance like no one else before him could do. He'd say it had to be done.

And so, in the hockey world, hating Gary Bettman has become something of a sport within a sport. Canadians hate him for his condescending indifference to our country's place in the NHL pecking order. We hate him for prioritizing the expansion of hockey markets in the American Sun Belt over any protection or expansion of Canadian franchises. We hate him for his stubborn insistence on keeping an NHL team in Phoenix, his refusal to admit error in keeping the former Winnipeg Jets franchise there long past the point of his own diminished credibility. We hate him because he did this while doing nothing to enable Quebec City's return to the league. Most of all, Canadians hate him because he earned his 2018 induction to the Hockey Hall of Fame, in the builder category, by enabling conditions that

* Some believe that the NHL amateur draft's conversion from a live event to a studio one in 2025 was partly intended to spare the commissioner the indignity of the booing that always greets him at live events.

make it next to impossible for a Canada-based team to win the Stanley Cup—an event that last occurred on his watch during his first few months on the job, when he handed the Cup to the Montreal Canadiens not long after bumping into my friend Paul Isaacs at a Canucks game. We hate him because he responded to his Hall of Fame induction not by sailing off into the sunset but by choosing to stick around indefinitely. Now aged seventy-four, he seems as up for the job as ever.

Americans hate him too. They know he came to the NHL from a lesser position in the National Basketball Association, not out of some deep reverence for the sport but with a strong instinct for self-enrichment. They hate him because they know that one reason he has managed to stay in power for so long is that he's an accomplished wind sniffer; he knows just how and when the league should respond to public pressure and social change. They hate him because he's a good lawyer—or at least a clever one. Of course, it takes one to know one, so perhaps Ken Dryden was the perfect lawyer to prosecute, through public discourse, Bettman's reluctance to address the long-term effects of concussions on players' brains.

In *Game Change*, Dryden was polished and diplomatic, avoiding any hint of ad hominem critique that would signal personal contempt for Bettman. (As with the proverbial sharks who won't eat them, professional courtesy among lawyers goes a long way.) To understand the workings of Bettman's mind, he said, you first need to know where the NHL stands in relation to the rest of the hockey world. The International Ice Hockey Federation, the Kontinental Hockey League, Hockey Canada, USA Hockey, and others? They all dance to the NHL's tune. "It is the NHL that sets the direction for the sport, and Bettman sets the direction for the NHL ... The rest of the hockey world understands that on any issue, if they disagree with the NHL, it is at their peril. They are all beholden to Bettman. They know it, and Bettman knows it," wrote Dryden. "Gary Bettman is in control of the hockey world. The league board of governors are his bosses, but since he won his salary cap in 2005, crushing the NHLPA, no one stands in his way."[148]

In 2013, the first group of what would eventually total more than three hundred former players launched a class action lawsuit against the NHL, suing the league for failing to protect them from head injuries or warn them of the risks involved in the NHL game. After the initial lawsuit, more than two dozen new cases were filed from across the US. In the five years the lawsuit took to work its way through the courts, the NHL faced the daunting possibility that more than five thousand players were lining up as co-complainants. (The National Football League, reaching a settlement on the same issue, could pay out as much as $1.5 billion USD to an estimated twenty thousand players.)

The NHL players' lawsuit was still in process when *Game Change* came out in 2017. Dryden unpacked the brick wall of resistance that Bettman put up in denying any liability for the players' long-term brain issues. Bettman's strategy, he noted, was comparable to that of other bad corporate actors in the face of potentially devastating class action lawsuits over the harmful effects of their product. "Decision makers want certainties, and decision makers who don't want to make certain decisions hide behind science. They may acknowledge what we know, but they focus on what we don't. They create doubt," wrote Dryden, nicely summarizing the Bettman playbook. "After ignorance, after denial, after counter-argument and strategic inaction, after being put into their final corner, that's what tobacco companies did. That's what lead and asbestos companies did. That's what climate change deniers do. They will wait for science to know, they say, because after all, we are all serious, modern, evidence-based people, aren't we?"[149]

The year after *Game Change* was published, the NHL scored a lopsided victory when a federal judge dismissed class action status for the retired players, citing "widespread differences" in state laws about medical monitoring that would have produced "significant case management difficulties."[150] This meant that, instead of settling with more than five thousand retired players, the NHL would only have to shell out for 318 of them. Four months later, they announced a settlement for $18.9 million USD. Defiant to the end, Bettman told the Associated Press at one point, "When it comes to focusing on concussions and trying to understand them and how to treat them, we've been leaders in the field."[151] No doubt, retirees with post-concussion syndrome—thanks to the league's refusal to ban fighting—stifled a gag reflex when they heard that one.*

Okay, so Bettman's an asshole. We knew that already. But what does all this have to do with ending homophobia in the world's most powerful hockey league? As the concussion lawsuit reminds us, the NHL is all about money and always has been. So in fairness—and without being overly cynical here—isn't league-wide adoption of diversity, equity, and inclusion (DEI) principles a small potatoes issue compared to the big money at stake in the concussion lawsuit? Well, yes and no. On the yes side, it could be argued that institutional change such as progressive DEI marketing to attract more fans should be a no-brainer because it's more of a revenue generator than an expense. And the NHL could argue that it has indeed become more inclusive, as the introduction of progressive campaigns (see below) suggests. It could point to the growing number of racialized men in the league and in broadcasting positions and of women in staff positions and broadcasting. It could even say it's making progress in welcoming queer fans to the league. On the other hand, the league's adoption of DEI principles is not without its challenges, especially when it comes to promoting LGBTQ+ inclusion and visibility.

---

* Just before *Cutting Edge* went to press, the hockey world got another sad reminder of the lower life expectancy for NHL players who fight regularly. On May 28, 2026, Montreal Canadiens legend Claude Lemieux died by suicide three days after serving as Habs torchbearer for their Game 3 Eastern Conference final match at the Bell Centre. His death was another blow for a league that has seen many well-known tough guys take their own lives. Lemieux, aged sixty, was a highly aggressive power forward and key playoff performer also known for dirty play that got under his opponents' skin and led to several fights and bench-clearing brawls. Although he enjoyed a successful post-playing career as a sports agent and occasional media commentator, he kept his mental health struggles private. On May 30, 2026, his family announced that his brain would be donated to Boston University's Chronic Traumatic Encephalopathy Center to research the long-term effects of repetitive brain injuries. (Associated Press, "Claude Lemieux's Brain Is Being Donated to Boston University's CTE Center, His Family Says," *AP News*, May 30, 2026, https://apnews.com/article/claude-lemieux-brain-donation-hockey-nhl-665b87f1e69191fce953306f0c028584.)

My portrait of Bettman above paints him as an opportunistic wind sniffer, someone who turns into a political weathervane whenever a risky decision is pending. While not the most attractive of human qualities, this is an important survival tool for any league commissioner in the Big Four. But when interests collide and the big league wants it both ways, problems arise. For example, the NHL says it wants to attract more queer fans. Great. But it also wants to keep the fans who love fighting and are opposed to banning it from the game, the kind of fans who tend to complain about "woke" culture. Needless to say, those are two very different fan bases. And so, hedging its bets, the NHL tries to please everyone by playing it safe.

In 2017, five years after the launch of You Can Play, the NHL introduced the Hockey Is for Everyone (HIFE) campaign in partnership with the former. HIFE was aimed at league-wide promotion of diversity and inclusion among those of all sexual orientations, gender identities, abilities, and socio-economic classes. Each team appointed an ambassador for the campaign. Most notably, Andrew Shaw—by then with the Montreal Canadiens following an off-season trade from Chicago after his homophobic slur incident in the playoffs—was appointed his new team's ambassador.* In addition, teams began hosting their own Pride Nights in conjunction with You Can Play to celebrate members of the local LGBTQ+ community. This produced some great moments—such as when Harrison Browne, cited earlier as the first openly trans athlete in professional American hockey, was a featured guest at a New York Rangers game. "A lot of people have said, 'Hey, just seeing you dropping the puck at Madison Square Garden really made me feel like I'd be welcome in that rink,'" Browne told the *Hockey News*. "So I think they're doing

* Shaw, having committed to dropping the offending F-word from his vocabulary, appeared earnest in his post-slur efforts to promote anti-homophobia awareness. But he struggled with at least one other toxic masculinity issue. Following his 2021 retirement due to concussions, he appeared in a May 2023 episode of the *Raw Knuckles* podcast and commented on the Kyle Beach sexual assault case. Afterward, some listeners accused Shaw of victim blaming in suggesting that Beach, as a young prospect, should not have put himself in a vulnerable position with the Chicago Blackhawks video coach who sexually assaulted him.

a really great job in making sure it's accessible for fans."[152] (He was quick to add that more needs to be done to make NHL players feel safe enough to come out.)

As mentioned in Chapter 9, the NHL in 2020 unveiled its Executive Inclusion Council, including a Player Inclusion Committee, that counted LGBTQ+ issues among its areas of focus. That entity later morphed into the NHL Player Inclusion Coalition, a group of current and former NHL players and women's professional hockey players who, as the coalition's website states, "are advisors, ambassadors, and catalysts in the growing movement for inclusion across the hockey community."* The group's work focuses on how the NHL can be more effective in supporting diverse players at the elite level, such as conducting inclusion workshops for NHL players, draftees, and on-ice officials, as well as folks in minor pro hockey.

The NHL's first-ever diversity and inclusion report (2022) found that 93 percent of NHL and team staff self-identified as heterosexual. But the league's commissioner was eager to send the message that, with the new focus on DEI initiatives, sexual minorities would not be ignored. "Diverse representation within inclusive environments is proven to advance innovation, creativity, and decision making—all of which are critically important to the growth of sport and our business," Bettman wrote in the report's introduction. "Recognizing these facts, we are working to better understand and accelerate our engagement across all layers of diversity—including nationality, race, gender identity, sexual orientation, disability, and religion—and their nuances and intersections."[153] But NHL team Pride Nights, the most visible public expression of inclusion, have revealed a few problems with those "nuances."

Gay hockey activist and educator Brock McGillis said he felt encouraged to see all teams taking part in Pride Nights.† But he also noted that some treated their

---

* For more info, visit https://www.nhl.com/community/player-inclusion-coalition.

† Since his retirement as a professional hockey player, McGillis has embarked on a public speaking career focusing on mental health awareness, breaking down barriers, and promoting inclusion in sports and other areas of life. In 2026 he launched his Shiftmakers Tour, a series of cross-Canada speaking engagements with the goal of reaching one hundred high school–aged minor hockey teams in one hundred days. At each event, McGillis uses his life story as a case study to humanize his experience as

Pride Night as a one-off, a chance to tick a box by giving the queer community one night to feel welcome at an NHL arena before it was back to regular programming. This was Performative Allyship 101, said McGillis, citing the St. Louis Blues as an example. In 2020, the Blues abandoned a previously successful Pride Night event in favour of a watered down Hockey Is for Everyone night that scrubbed "Pride" from the team website, removed rainbow flags and other explicitly LGBTQ+ symbols from the Enterprise Center arena, and turned the event into a road game viewing party.

"To me, performative allyship is a sense of acting in a way that makes you seem like you're an ally, like a tweet or putting a rainbow flag as your company logo, or just saying 'I'm not homophobic' or 'I'm not racist' but not actually doing the work to not be," said McGillis. "For a corporation or hockey league, it's not doing the work to shift the culture that you know is racist or sexist or homophobic."[154] One problem with the NHL's inclusion efforts, said McGillis, is that the hockey world doesn't understand its own heteronormative bias, intentional or otherwise. As an example, he cited the use of the kiss cam at hockey games. This is the moment when an arena camera, locating two fans sitting beside each other who look like a couple, shows them on the Jumbotron screen until they are embarrassed into kissing by public pressure. Usually the camera focuses on obviously straight couples who are hometown fans. But as McGillis noted, in conversation with sociologist Cheryl A. MacDonald, "It is not unusual for the camera operator to focus in on two members of the opposing team or two male fans of the opposing team as a way to poke fun at them. The undertone of the humour is that the two

---

someone different from the norm while sharing scenarios aimed at inspiring audience members to stand up and themselves become "shift makers": players who embrace their true selves and encourage others to do the same, thus making hockey "the best it can be." Tour sponsors include the NHL and NHLPA, Toronto Maple Leafs, Ottawa Senators, and Air Canada. For more information, visit https://www.brockmcgillis.com/tour.

are romantically involved. The crowd laughs and likely does not realize that this is understood as anti-gay behaviour."[155]*

If MacDonald's 2018 survey of a hundred male U18 AAA hockey players was any indication, there was some good news on the horizon: The younger generation of male hockey players appeared to be more queer friendly. Although more than 50 percent admitted to frequently sharing anti-gay jokes and one quarter said they would not be comfortable with having an openly gay coach, there was consensus on two significant statements: that a gay teammate would be accepted once everyone was comfortable with him, and that their own generation was more accepting of the LGBTQ+ community than their parents' (especially their fathers') had been. This suggested that a more queer-friendly hockey world might just be a matter of certain dinosaurs going extinct.

When it comes to the NHL's work on LGBTQ+ issues, 2023 will go down in history as the league's annus horribilis. At the end of it, Outsports—whose bullshit detector tends to go on full alert whenever the commissioner opens his mouth—named Gary Bettman its Asshole of the Year. Bettman earned the most lopsided "win" in the ten-year history of this dubious honour with several statements and policy announcements that undermined more than a decade of hard work by You Can Play and others trying to make the NHL more inclusive.

It all began in January, when then Philadelphia Flyers defender Ivan Provorov refused to wear a rainbow warm-up jersey with the rest of his teammates during Pride Night—not because he feared reprisal from Vladimir Putin's Russian government, one of the most repressively homophobic on the planet (though he may have), but because of his beliefs. "In the wake of one player telling an

* A more respectful use of the kiss cam in a gay context might be to locate a confirmed same-sex couple in the crowd and, after showing one or two straight couples kissing, give the queer couple their moment as well.

entire community of fans that their humanity wasn't worth acknowledging for just twenty minutes," Outsports contributor Ken Schultz wryly noted, Bettman responded with his usual corporate-speak to cut Provorov some slack: "We continue to encourage [players'] voices on social and cultural issues." Bettman was effectively encouraging homophobia, said Schultz, at the very moment "when decisive leadership was needed." Before you knew it, the New York Rangers, Minnesota Wild, and Chicago Blackhawks decided to get rid of their pride jerseys, "emboldened by Bettman to bend a knee to homophobia."[156]

Other individual players reinforced Provorov's bigotry. These included a joint statement from two of the three Staal brothers playing in the NHL, both members of the Florida Panthers. "As well as admiring their hockey skill and respecting the commitment it must have taken for the three of them to make it to the NHL," I wrote at the time, "I once considered the Staal brothers really hot—especially the prettiest one, tall and blond Eric ... [But] for a gay man, there is no greater buzzkill than the revelation of ignorance and prejudice in someone I find attractive, the realization that this person likely finds my very existence repulsive."[157] And so, any trace of desirability in Eric or Marc Staal disappeared the moment they opened their mouths to say this:

> After many thoughts, prayers, and discussions, we have chosen not to wear a Pride Night jersey tonight. We carry no judgement on how people choose to live their lives and believe that all people should be welcome in all aspects of the game of hockey. Having said that, we feel that by us wearing a pride jersey it goes against our Christian beliefs.

"For heaven's sake," I wrote,

> it's not like they were being asked to march in a pride parade stripped down to their undies or decked out in leather chaps; they were not expected to guest host drag storytime wearing their best high heels

> and a skirt. Pride Night is simply an opportunity for the hockey elite to broaden the appeal of their sport by inviting more people into it, becoming more interesting as a result.[158]

Thankfully, Brian Burke heard the Staal brothers' statement and called bullshit on it. "I was born and raised a Catholic. I don't see any conflict between my religious beliefs and the ability to say to the LGBTQ+ community, 'You're welcome here.' That's all Pride Night is: 'You're welcome in our building,'" he told *Hockey Night*'s Ron MacLean, dismissing the Staal brothers' fundamentalist cop-out. "To our friends in the LGBTQ+ community, don't be discouraged. We've had a couple of minor setbacks from a tiny number of players, but we've made steady and spectacular progress in this space. Thirty-two teams will have held, by the end of this season, a Pride Night. So even the teams where we had some dissenters, the teams still held Pride Night. It's still important, it's a very important part of what we do."[159]*

For Burke, who enjoyed a collegial relationship with Gary Bettman going back to their days working together at the league office during the nineties, the commissioner's enabling of player bigotry as part of a don't-rock-the-boat corporate strategy must have been frustrating. During the 2023 All-Star weekend, when asked about the sudden increase in homophobic resistance around the league, Bettman lectured the LGBTQ+ community about the importance of honouring anti-gay players' decision to be public in their bigotry. "We also have to respect individual choice," he told the media, "and part of being diverse and welcoming is understanding those differences."† Bettman's contortions of logic in defence

---

* By 2026, some NHL teams (Carolina, LA, and Utah) would opt out of Pride Night, instead offering Hockey Is for Everyone nights.

† In a cowardly move that same weekend, the NHL capitulated to the bullying of Florida governor Ron DeSantis, who complained that the NHL's career fair in Fort Lauderdale, aimed at recruiting a more diverse workforce, discriminated against white people. The NHL cancelled the event. See Michael Hiltzik, "A Cowardly NHL Bows Down to a Bullying DeSantis," *Los Angeles Times*, January 18, 2023, https://www.latimes.com/business/story/2023-01-18/the-cowardly-nhl-bows-down-to-a-bullying-desantis.

of the status quo are legendary, but he outdid himself with this bit of Orwellian Newspeak: Creating a more diverse and inclusive league meant embracing players who actively fought against diversity and inclusion.

And he wasn't done yet. In mid-June, during the Stanley Cup final, he announced that the NHL would cancel pride jerseys altogether because they were "a distraction." A few months later, at the beginning of the 2023–24 season—and, as it happened, one day before National Coming Out Day—the league office announced that the NHL was banning Pride Tape, the rainbow-striped tape for hockey stick blades that many players use during warm-ups on Pride Night. Bettman was banning its use on the ice at all times because, like the jerseys, Pride Tape was "a distraction." Happy National Coming Out Day! Reaction was swift. Some observers likened the ban to a Don't Say Gay policy, a reflection of how current political and legislative climates could have ripple effects.[160] You Can Play made it clear that the NHL, its long-time partner in advocating for inclusivity, had repeatedly shot wide of the net in 2023. "We are now at a point where all the progress made, and relationships established with our community, is in jeopardy," they said. "Making decisions to eradicate our visibility in hockey—by eliminating symbols like jerseys and now Pride Tape—immediately stunts the impact of bringing more diverse fans and players into the sport."[161]

The clearest indication that Bettman had misfired yet again came from the players themselves. Some planned to use the tape anyway. The first one who did, Arizona Coyotes defender Travis Dermott, drew widespread support for his principled defiance of the commish. Bettman was too smart to fine Dermott or otherwise double down on the rules this time, so be backed off on the Pride Tape ban. But the damage was done. "After all of his efforts," Outsports concluded, "the NHL's best pride event will be the day Bettman resigns."[162]

Meanwhile, in the summer of 2025, NHL fans were left wondering what it all meant when Bettman—along with Panthers captain Matthew Tkachuk and Donald Trump supporter Wayne Gretzky—was appointed to the US president's sports council. The council's responsibilities included playing an important role in "restoring tradition" to the athletics world, including a policy enacted earlier in the year aimed at "keeping men out of women's sports."[163]

The league's queer inclusion efforts haven't all been bad news. In 2025, LGBTQ+ visibility scored a significant victory when Andrew Sobotka, former president of the Chicago Gay Hockey Association (CGHA), was named a finalist for the NHL's prestigious Willie O'Ree Community Hero Award.* Sobotka, thirty-nine, didn't receive enough public or NHL and sponsor votes to win the award, but his story was shared on the NHL's website, giving queer hockey a much-needed boost. Sobotka, one of three finalists for the US award, was celebrated for his role in overseeing the growth of the non-profit CGHA's membership, teams, and activities within the queer community and beyond. During his first year as president in 2010, the CGHA made news when they invited the Chicago Blackhawks to join them at that year's Chicago Gay Pride Parade. The Blackhawks had just won their first Stanley Cup in half a century; their presence at Pride would also honour the memory of Brendan Burke, hockey's first anti-homophobia activist who had died tragically a few months earlier. The team agreed and sent defender Brent Sopel, who was a huge hit, riding on the CGHA float and hoisting the Stanley Cup to wild applause.

"It was actually the first time that any of the Big Four major sports trophies was in a pride parade," Sobotka recalled in an NHL video profile promoting the award finalists. "We forged a relationship with the Blackhawks through that and have been working with them ever since then." That relationship extends to the CGHA's annual tournament in August, which takes place at Fifth Third Arena, the Blackhawks' practice facility. The CGHA's reach beyond the LGBTQ+ community—it helps raise funds for other non-profits, including the American

* As the NHL website describes it, the Willie O'Ree Community Hero Award "is given to an individual who, through hockey, has positively impacted his or her community culture or society. The award honours O'Ree, the former NHL forward who became the first Black player to play in the NHL on Jan. 18, 1958, and has spent more than two decades as the NHL's diversity ambassador." The award goes to one winner from the United States and one from Canada. ("Willie O'Ree," NHL, accessed February 28, 2026, https://www.nhl.com/community/willie-oree/.)

Cancer Society and Chicago Cares, an organization that promotes civic engagement through voluntarism and education—has drawn more allies. About a quarter of the CGHA's approximately one hundred players are heterosexual. It's one reason the Blackhawks as an organization nominated Sobotka for the award. "It's really incredible to see how [the CGHA] think about their role as a community leader, not just for the LGBTQ+ community, but all of Chicago," said Sara Guderyahn, Blackhawks executive vice-president for social impact and civic affairs.[164]

When I talked to Robert Thompson, co-founder of the Toronto Gay Hockey Association (TGHA), he confirmed TGHA's ongoing relationship with the Maple Leafs. During the TGHA's thirtieth-anniversary celebrations, the organization's publicity drew much public interest. "The Leafs found out about us and wanted to do some interviews to celebrate that," Thompson told me. "Also at that time, they were evolving their LGBTQ+ Pride Night, and so they wanted more support in that area. It was our big anniversary, so the two collided. And it was great for us. Because out of that, that's how the league kept growing, because now there's awareness of it." The TGHA also has a relationship with the Burke family. Both Brian and Patrick Burke have shown up at TGHA practices and joined its players on the ice. "They played with us, a bit of shinny and a scrimmage, a couple of times in the past couple of years. I showed up at one of the games when Patrick was there and had a fantastic time. He was a great guy," Thompson said.

Naturally, my thoughts turn to Vancouver and the state of things between the Canucks and the Cutting Edges. Back in the summer of 2012, the first year of You Can Play, Patrick Burke came to Vancouver to join the city's pride parade on behalf of the organization. With his assistance, introductions were made, and two Canucks players—forward Manny Malhotra and defender Jason Garrison—joined the Cutting Edges' parade contingent. I attended that one and enjoyed chatting with Malhotra, Garrison, and Burke. But the Canucks stopped sending players after a couple of years. Only the team mascot, Fin the orca, would show up at Pride, along with Canucks admin staff. No players.

In more recent years, the Cutting Edges have participated in Canucks Pride Nights at Rogers Arena. For the first year, the NHL team offered a discount on tickets while giving the Edges space on the concourse for a promotion table and a welcome on the Jumbotron. It all seemed perfunctory, and the Edges communicated this to the Canucks as diplomatically as possible. The next year, the Canucks provided a corporate box with free food and made a much bigger deal of our presence. Former Cutting Edges president Reid Hearsum recalled that things began to change as soon as the board assigned someone with inter-business relations experience to communicate directly with the Canucks. "I think we were able to get a lot that year because Brennan [Roy-Bertin, a former board member] pushed so hard for it. It did feel like a thank you for representing the community, for getting out there and playing hockey," Hearsum told me in an interview. "But it didn't feel like it was altruistic on [the Canucks'] part. I thought they were trying to placate us for raising the hand signal to say we weren't happy."

Hearsum was quick to note that the LGBTQ+ community is just one of many communities the Canucks celebrate with the aim of drawing a larger fan base by being more inclusive. Diwali Night, celebrating the South Asian community, Filipino Heritage Night, and Firefighters Night are some of the more popular themed events. "I don't think we are owed anything by the Canucks," said Hearsum. "My understanding has always been, it's great, I like that they're doing these Pride Nights, and I understand that they have a lot of community nights now." Hearsum said the Canucks' community engagement staff he's met are supportive but limited in what they can offer. "They're very interested in forming bonds and learning and being the connection between us and the organization. The problem is that they don't seem to have a lot of pull with the higher-ups in terms of what they can offer back," he explained, adding that the Canucks have been proactive in seeking the Cutting Edges' assistance with furthering LGBTQ+ awareness in the hockey community. "We provided suggestions on helping us with our community skates, getting youth involved, and coaching. We were trying to do family-oriented skates, either for queer parents with kids or kids who've come out as queer," Hearsum said. "At our first family community skate [three] years ago, Fin did come out, and [former Canucks goaltender] Kirk McLean came out, so they were able to provide some player alumni. And Finn was a huge hit with the kids, so we really appreciated that."

But the Canucks could make a much bigger splash, he added, if current roster players attended events—a demonstration of allyship that should be easy in a city with such a visible queer population. "Obviously a lot of [our] members would like to see some current players come out to things, like the pride parade," he said. "The Canucks entry in the parade is mostly admin and staff. I like that they're out there and willing to be supportive, but with the hockey players themselves not showing support in a tangible way, it's not quite as eye-opening to kids, like, *Oh, maybe I can play*. Active players would send such a message. It doesn't have to be a star player, but any player. But that was something [the Canucks] were not able to provide or suggest that they could provide. I think it falls on the players who want to do that."

While the Canucks might not provide as much support as Cutting Edges players would like, Hearsum understood the limitations. "I think for some members of the organization, it's who can use who more. Do we need their reach or exposure more, or do they need us? There are two sides to that, and I think they could take us or leave us. They're donating $20,000 to [queer services organization] Qmunity every year, and I think we've been pretty good at using their platform as much as we can to get our name out there, always on their website as listed guests on the night. So I don't think you can say we have a partnership, but we do have a relationship."

By way of comparison, Hearsum pointed to the Pride Nights of the Coquitlam Express, a BC Hockey League Junior team: "In terms of how they do it on the ice, I think they're a model for what the Canucks could be." He realized how it must sound to be recommending a Junior hockey team's community outreach efforts to an NHL franchise, rather than the reverse. The Express, he explained, "have specific pride jerseys they wear the entire game, everyone on the team has Pride Tape, and there are ads on the boards. Their Pride Night feels more like they're doing it because they want to, not because they have to. They've invited us the last three years, we have a table there, and it's really a fun night. That opened my eyes to what a Pride Night can be, and they're just a Junior team ... The fans are really engaged, and the owner, whoever's driving it, you can tell they really want to do it. So it's just a different vibe."

There is one NHL team the Canucks could emulate for their LGBTQ+ community outreach. And I hate to break it to them, but it's one of their divisional rivals just down the road, across the border. According to my source, JR, whose identity I will reveal shortly (I tell his personal story in Chapter 12), the Seattle Kraken's latest contribution to the Seattle Pride hockey tournament is as top-notch as it gets for NHL teams extending allyship to the queer community. The first tournament was held in 2021, the year the Kraken entered the NHL, with only four teams. Four years later, it had about 350 registered players, drawing teams from across the US and Canada and even Australia. The tournament is held at the Kraken's practice facility, the Kraken Community Iceplex in the Northgate neighbourhood of Seattle.*

JR recalled one Thursday morning two years ago. The tournament's welcome reception was scheduled for that evening, with the games starting the next morning. JR, well acquainted with Seattle gay hockey's co-president and another board member, texted them, "Hey, do you guys know what's happening at the rink today?" They responded, "No, what are you talking about?" JR was coy: "Well, you're going to be pretty surprised when you walk in tomorrow for your first game." The surprise was that the Kraken's marketing team had come up with the idea of converting the dasher board displays in all three rinks of the Iceplex to rainbow colours.

"Somebody in our marketing department—unbeknownst to me, unbeknownst to the tournament—goes, 'We're hosting one of the biggest, most

* The Vancouver Canucks, who have been in the NHL since 1970 but never won a Stanley Cup, have never had their own practice facility—one of only two teams in the NHL so bereft. (The Calgary Flames will finally have theirs in 2027, as part of the new Scotia Place development replacing the Saddledome.) But in March 2026, reports surfaced that the Canucks were close to a deal with the City of Vancouver to build a standalone practice facility in East Vancouver that would replace the Britannia Community Centre's ice rink. Whether a second rink would be built for Britannia under this arrangement and what would happen to the rest of the centre's programs were yet to be determined as *Cutting Edge* went to press. See Karin Larsen and Justin McElroy, "Is a New Vancouver Canucks Training Facility Coming to East Vancouver?," CBC News, March 12, 2026, https://www.cbc.ca/news/canada/british-columbia/vancouver-canucks-training-facility-east-vancouver-britannia-9.7126486.

inclusive events for pride hockey. How do we make it even more inclusive?'" JR explained. "They went and contacted all the companies and then paid, as soon as they got the approval, to tear down all the board ads and put up brand new ones on all three sheets of ice. So that by Friday morning, when these 350 people walked into the rink, every single rink board ad was rainbow. That's a pretty big thing, [to say,] 'How can we make this even better so that when these people step into our ice arena from Australia or from Florida or Texas or Minnesota, they feel as welcome as possible?' So these people walk in on day one, and they're like, 'Wow. I feel included here.' They couldn't even go to the organizers and say, 'You guys did such a good job putting the rainbow ads up.' The organizers were like, 'We didn't do it—the Kraken did. They wanted to show their support for the 350 people spending the weekend in their arena."

While the Vancouver Canucks have work to do in upping their pride game to equal the Kraken's efforts, the queer hockey associations for both Vancouver and Seattle received a big boost from the National Hockey League in 2026. The Cutting Edges and the Seattle Pride Hockey Association were the fortunate beneficiaries of the third annual NHL Unites Pride Cup (February 28 to March 1), a tournament aimed at celebrating LGBTQ+ players, fans, families, and allies and increasing queer participation in hockey. Organized by the NHL's Multicultural Content, Audience Development, and Social Impact department—an entity that sounds like it was developed just for this moment—the event's sponsorship provided each association with $25,000 USD to assist with their respective community development efforts.

Hosted by the NHL and Pride Tape and held at the North Surrey Sport & Ice Complex, the Pride Cup drew enthusiastic crowds, media coverage, and dignitaries, including Surrey mayor Brenda Locke and the co-chairs of Canada's Parliamentary Pride Caucus: South Surrey–White Rock MP and White Rock Pride Society founder Ernie Klassen, and senator Kristopher Wells, a co-founder of Pride Tape.* For the lucky players selected to participate in the tournament, the biggest draws were former Canucks Dave Babych, Jyrki Lumme, and Corey Hirsch, other former NHLers Andrew Ference, Bill Ranford, and Dave Tomlinson, former minor league pro Bryan Richardson, Seattle Kraken head athletic trainer Justin Rogers, and pro hockey's first trans player, Harrison Browne, all of whom showed up as guest players or coaches. You Can Play was also in attendance, providing a seminar on inclusion for coaches and other hockey leaders. By all accounts, the event was a major success.

Sadly, I was unable to witness this milestone event in Cutting Edges history. It just happened to take place during the middle of my annual visit to Southeast Asia—making it the only time in winter that I have ever wished *not* to be in the tropics. Being unable to share that moment with fellow teammates old and new sent my FOMO into overdrive. And, quite apart from the celebration and the hockey action surrounding it, I regret missing the chance to meet all those hockey luminaries, especially Rogers, Browne, and Hirsch. (I would also have used the opportunity to apologize to Hirsch if he thought my review's criticism of his 2022 memoir, *The Save of My Life*, overshadowed my praise for it. His allyship is especially important.)

After the event, Cutting Edges president Kyle McCarthy took to Instagram to express what everyone was feeling about it. The Pride Cup was much more than a tournament (yes, the Edges won the series); it was a reminder that the hockey arena is a space that belongs to everyone. "For so many people, it meant seeing themselves reflected in a sport they grew up loving but maybe never fully felt welcome in," McCarthy wrote. "It meant walking into an arena and not having to shrink who you are ... It was powerful for the kid watching to see hockey is in fact for them. Powerful for the community members who fought to carve out safe spaces in rinks that weren't always kind. Powerful for allies who showed up loudly and

* Pride Tape is the organization, created in 2016 by Kristopher Wells and Jeff McLean, that produces the rainbow-coloured stick tape many hockey players use to support the queer community and to advocate for inclusive hockey.

proudly ... Hockey is at its best when it reflects the people who love it. And for a lot of us, this meant everything."[165]

As events like the Pride Cup demonstrate, ally support from retired NHL players is hugely appreciated and—given that most of those names have become familiar on the hockey pride circuit—anything but performative. Currently active NHL players have been genuinely supportive as well. But after more than a dozen years of education by You Can Play, it's telling that 100 percent of its NHL-star supporters are either straight allies or players who have yet to reveal their authentic selves. The fact that there are still no openly gay NHL players means that there isn't a single self-advocate who feels safe enough to step into the limelight, endorse You Can Play as an out and proud gay player, and thus change that pronoun to we.

Promotional poster for season 1 of *Heated Rivalry* featuring stars Hudson Williams and Connor Storrie

CHAPTER 12

Heated Rivalry and the NHL Closet

"I know there are gay guys in the NHL*, because I met one of my teammate's boyfriends. [But] it's impossible for a gay hockey player to come out within the next five or even ten years; the media attention would be too distracting for the whole organization, he'd never survive."*

—GEORGES LARAQUE[166]

"Are you ready?"

The sports agent is prepping his client, one of the National Hockey League's biggest stars, for a major announcement. The player shrugs. "Sure, I'm ready. Let's go. Let's do this."

The two men walk down the hall of the NHL rink the player has called home for half a decade, stopping outside the media room.

"Look," the agent says, grabbing his client's arm. "You know I support you a hundred percent. But it's been a long road, and you've made so many sacrifices to get here. So if there's any reason you want to pull the plug on this thing, any reason at all, just tell me now and we can cancel this presser in a heartbeat."

The player sighs. "No, no, we're not doing that. Listen, I've given this enough thought. All my teammates support me. So does management. And why wouldn't they? I helped get them *this*." He forms a fist and turns it around, exposing a gaudy silver ring bearing the team logo. "Besides, I'm set for life financially. I'm locked in with this group for at least three more years before the limited-trade clause kicks in. So what if I lose an endorsement deal or two? I wouldn't want to shill for a company that felt that way about me, anyway. And hey, who knows? I might even get a few new gigs just for doing this."

His agent smiles. "Can't argue with that. Let's go."

Opening the door, the agent leads his client to the podium, where the player's coach, general manager, and team owner await. The media event begins with the GM introducing the agent, who tells everyone how long and hard his client has been thinking about this day.

Then it's the player's turn.

"Good morning, everyone," the hockey star begins, his smile signalling great relief. "You're looking at the first NHL player to say these words in public: I'm a Stanley Cup champion who just happens to be gay."

The flashes go off at once. A forest of hands goes up. The first reporter's question is the most obvious: After all this time in the closet, what finally prompted him to come out?

"Well, it was a few things," the player begins. "But the final trigger was the fifth episode of *Heated Rivalry*, when Scott Hunter has just won the Cup and invites his same-sex lover down from the stands to join him on the ice with his teammates and their families. And then they kiss in front of everyone in the arena, in front of the whole world. Well, I have a partner too—he's right there at the back of the room, I'll introduce you afterward—and I just thought, life is too short. I've achieved everything in hockey there is to achieve, and I just want to be happy in every part of my life. I want to be like Scott Hunter. So here I am."

Okay, so that's just a fantasy. As of this writing, no such thing has occurred because of *Heated Rivalry* or any other factor, and the secrets of closeted gay NHL players are safe for now. But the overwhelming success of the Crave series, a Canadian production whose US rights were picked up by HBO and caught on like wildfire internationally at the end of 2025, has reignited the conversation about homosexuality in the last major professional sports league in North America without an openly gay player. It has made brand-new hockey fans out of queer folk who were never interested in the sport, and it has done so as far away as the United Kingdom, Australia, and even homophobic Russia. How did this happen?

Until *Heated Rivalry* burned its way into our minds, the most notable onscreen treatment of gay hockey players was *Breakfast with Scot*, a 2007 Canadian comedy directed by Laurie Lynd and produced by Paul Brown, Howard Rosenman, and Nadine Schiff. Adapted from a 1999 novel, the film was a big deal at the time because the Maple Leafs approved the use of their logo and uniforms in it. But it hasn't aged all that well. Given the degree of reactionary homophobia in the mainstream hockey world of 2007, a film that might have meaningfully explored the struggle to embrace one's own true self while ignoring what others think probably shouldn't have been pitched as comedy. The titular Scot is a gender-divergent adolescent who, in the wake of his mother's drug overdose, has been placed in the care of his stepfather's gay brother Sam, a sports lawyer, and his partner Eric, a retired Maple Leafs player turned TV sportscaster. Within minutes of his first scene, it's clear that the predominant schtick of the film will be Scot's flamboyance and how the sight gags around it expose Eric's hair-trigger paranoia as he tries to remain closeted at work.

In fairness, there is something potentially moving in a queer child's innocent puncturing of the self-denial of his closeted gay parental figures. But there is nary a hint of true gayness in this film, which also happens to be completely sexless. And the characters are one-dimensional. Scot's self-confidence in genderqueer expression seems unrealistic for his age and for the times, and yuppie Sam is too perfect. As for Eric? The comic appeal of his hockey bro uptightness and closetedness—even after his NHL career—fades long before the happy ending, when he embraces his more authentic self. But the Leafs—pre–Brian Burke and You Can Play—were good with it.

By contrast, *Heated Rivalry* as queer cultural hockey content blows away everything that came before it. For this we can thank the source material. Rachel Reid, a Halifax-based writer and lifelong hockey fan, invented a whole new subgenre of romance fiction: the gay hockey romance. Reid had become disheartened by the homophobia she saw ruining her favourite sport, so she came up with her Game Changers series as a way of imagining a better hockey world where gay men did not shut down their feelings but leaned into them. The second book in the series, *Heated Rivalry*, was published in 2019. Six years later, it became the centrepiece of a literally game-changing television series.

Heated Rivalry is the story of two NHL players who carry on a torrid gay love affair from the closet. For obvious legal reasons, the league is never actually named, and team names and logos are changed. But we can safely assume that the Montreal Voyageurs and the Boston Bears are stand-ins for the Habs and the Bruins. From their first meeting at the World Junior Championship when they're seventeen, the mixed-race Japanese Canadian Shane Hollander (who will be drafted by Montreal) and the Russian Ilya Rozanov (who will be drafted by Boston) have an instant physical attraction that will not be denied, despite cultural and ethnic differences and their competitive status as the two best young players on the planet.

Somehow they keep their relationship a secret for nearly eight years, discreetly meeting for passionate sessions of rough-and-ready sex whenever they can—despite the challenges, once they're in the big league, of playing on different teams. Their families, friends, teammates, and the rest of the hockey world, including their fans, don't suspect a thing because both are masculine presenting and date women, and they are presumed to hate each other as rivals (which they do when they first hook up). Inevitably, their false front collapses when they realize that their mutual attraction goes much deeper than mere lust and they are hopelessly in love.

Heated Rivalry is one of eight Rachel Reid romance novels that focus on LGBTQ+ hockey players. After selling like gangbusters, it was only a matter of time before one of those books got optioned, and it was Reid's good fortune that independent creator Jacob Tierney, the openly gay producer of *Letterkenny* (twelve seasons, ending in 2023) and its spinoff, *Shoresy* (four seasons, beginning in 2022, with a fifth confirmed as of this writing), was a fan. After buying the film rights to *Heated Rivalry*, and with the series to be produced by Accent Aigu Entertainment in association with Crave, Tierney hit gold when Hudson Williams and Connor Storrie showed up for their 2025 auditions to play Shane and Ilya, respectively.

Williams, a twenty-four-year-old Canadian of mixed British/Dutch and Korean descent, was born and raised in Kamloops, BC, and earned his acting certificate from Langara College's film arts program. Before becoming an actor, Storrie, a twenty-five-year-old American from Texas, trained in gymnastics and spent part of his high school education in France, where he learned French and developed an interest in other languages. At the time they were cast in *Heated Rivalry*, Williams and Storrie were both working as waiters. Within a few months, both would be international superstars thanks to their smoking-hot chemistry as Shane and Ilya.

The media campaign to introduce *Heated Rivalry* came in the early fall of 2025. Publicity stills showed two hot young men in their mid-twenties facing each other's sweaty, naked torsos, their foreheads touching and their eyes closed, their lips only inches apart. The player we'd soon know as Ilya had his fingers wrapped tenderly around Shane's neck, while Shane had an arm around Ilya's waist. Just below their bellies, their hockey pants were both open at the top. By the time the series launched on November 28, that image and the trailer were everywhere on social media. Broadcast rights had been sold to HBO Max in the US, and further rights would be sold to UK and Australian broadcasters, while other countries clamoured to jump aboard the Shane and Ilya train.

It wasn't hard to see why. Apart from their physically complementary attributes (both athletically built and smooth-skinned, the Eurasian Williams's musculature is softer and rounder, while the lily-white Storrie's is harder and more defined), the characters' mutual attraction is all the more believable because of the actors' obvious comfort with each other.* Later, Reid would comment on how haunted she was by the actors' convincing performances, by how perfectly

* Predictably, the obvious chemistry between the two actors became the subject of endless online speculation about their sexuality. Tierney shut down one interview when the reporter asked if they were gay, noting that such a question is against the law during the casting process. After two and a half months of relentless speculation, on Valentine's Day, Williams relieved some of the pressure by paying

matched they were for their roles—particularly Storrie's rendition of Rozanov with his note-perfect Russian language skills and accent. Reid told interviewers that when in conversation with Storrie, she felt like she was talking to the very Ilya she had created.

I knew what she meant by this. I didn't sign up for Crave to watch *Heated Rivalry* until after I'd read the book. But even as I was reading, the names Shane Hollander and Ilya Rozanov were burning into my brain like Sidney Crosby and Alex Ovechkin. Thanks to several weeks of pre-launch promotion, Shane and Ilya appeared in my mind as the actors who played them because I had seen enough of Williams's and Storrie's shirtless, sweat-dripping torsos in online memes and in the series trailer—enough images of their climax-ready faces gazing into each other's eyes—to easily recognize them if I ever happened to spot them on the street, despite never having seen or heard of them before the PR campaign began.

Social media commentary on *Heated Rivalry* exploded after the series launch, conquering my Facebook page like no other pop culture phenomenon before it. Thanks to the platform's algorithms, the *Heated Rivalry* onslaught began with dozens of posts that pushed other content off my news feed. From *ELLE Australia*: "How *Heated Rivalry* Became the Romance for Straight Women Who Need a Break from Men." From Gay Culture Geeks: "Just weeks ago, [Storrie and Williams] were both waiting tables ... Now they're ... attending industry parties at the Chateau Marmont with Baz Luhrmann." Et cetera. With its six episodes for season 1 breaking records, the series was quickly renewed for a season 2. *Heated Rivalry* became the highest-rated TV show of 2025, with episode 5 matching the final episode of *Breaking Bad* as the highest-rated TV episode of all time.[167] As January 2026 progressed, the show had drawn 600 million minutes of views in the US alone.

Its stars were award presenters at the Golden Globes, appeared on every major talk show, and served as torchbearers for the Winter Olympics in Italy. They even

---

tribute to his girlfriend on social media. Storrie, as of this writing, has revealed nothing about his private life.

served as peacemakers in the midst of actual, real-life hockey scandals. During his February 28 appearance as guest host of *Saturday Night Live*, Storrie shared the stage with Quinn and Jack Hughes, leaders of the US men's hockey team, who won Olympic gold at the Milano Cortina Games. The mere presence of these players created immediate tension in the studio audience, given the public relations disaster of their post-victory celebration, in which some players' behaviour was widely regarded as insulting to the Olympic gold medal–winning US women's hockey team.* After teasing the Hughes brothers about their lack of knowledge about *Heated Rivalry*, Storrie said, "I hope that some hockey players watched it," cueing the arrival onstage of US women's team leaders Hilary Knight and Megan Keller, which prompted wild audience applause. After assuring Storrie that they'd seen *Heated Rivalry*, Knight commented about their appearance on *SNL*: "We thought it was going to be just us, but we thought we'd invite the guys too." Keller added, "Yeah, we thought we'd give them a little moment to shine." The Hughes brothers rolled with it, the moment defusing the scandal as they once again declared their respect for the women's team.

Thanks to the appeal of its two main characters and the actors who portray them, along with great writing and direction, *Heated Rivalry* won industry-wide acclaim for its positive and nuanced portrayals of consent-based queer relationships in which men are convincingly vulnerable with each other.† Hollander and

---

* While celebrating their gold medal victory in the dressing room on February 22, 2026, members of the US men's hockey team were seen partying with FBI director Kash Patel. Then, on a phone call from Donald Trump, they were heard laughing at the president's joke that he would also have to invite the women's team to the White House too or risk another impeachment. The men's team's political obtuseness, at best (Trump's joke clearly demeaned the women's achievement), was widely condemned as disrespectful and insensitive, their ignorance raising the spectre of continuing misogyny in sport. See Jennifer Maas and Emily Longeretta, "Connor Storrie Honors Women's USA Hockey Team After Olympics in 'SNL' Monologue," *Variety*, February 28, 2026, https://variety.com/2026/tv/news/connor-storrie-snl-monologue-womens-men-olympic-hockey-1236675694/.

† This included breaking records at the Canadian Screen Awards on May 31, 2026, by winning in every category for which it was nominated, taking home sixteen awards in its inaugural season, including Best Drama Series and Best Lead Performer for Hudson Williams.

Rozanov's steamy sex scenes give way to more subtle interactions focused on emotional intimacy and the trust these two men manage to build based on their mutual struggle. It's hard not to enjoy their attraction as opposites: Shane the control queen, who's careful and deliberate about everything ("So boring!" says Ilya), versus Ilya the rebel, who, longing to break free of his oppressive upbringing, pushes boundaries all the time ("You're such an asshole," says Shane). Shane's character has added intrigue because of his half-Asian ethnicity and his autism (for which Williams drew from his own father's experience of the condition). Ilya's character is interesting because of the socio-political problem of being a gay man in Russia—a factor that pushed *Heated Rivalry* into a top-three position on Kinopoisk, Russia's largest film and television streaming platform.[168]

We also love Shane and Ilya for their sense of humour. Early in their romance, the two hockey stars come up with pseudonyms for their phone contacts to avoid suspicion while texting each other: "Jane" for Shane and "Lily" for Ilya. Later, while playing on the same line as all-stars, Ilya gets away with stealing a public kiss after they score a goal together. In episode 6, when Ilya finally visits Shane's cottage during the off-season, the Russian lets down his guard while he and Shane are sitting by the campfire: Startled by a sound he assumes to be a howling wolf, Ilya is annoyed when Shane teases him for freaking out about the call of a loon. "Stupid Canadian wolf bird," Ilya sneers. Soon that phrase—and the bird—began appearing on T-shirts, along with "I'm coming to the cottage," part of the rush to cash in on the show.

For the Cutting Edges, Vancouver's LGBTQ+ hockey association, such content was a breath of fresh air in a TV world not exactly abundant with stories of queer happiness. "One of the watershed things about *Heated Rivalry* for us is that it's not just a story about LGBTQ+ folks playing sports," the association's board secretary, Sam Jaffe, told *BCIT News*. "It's about them finding joy in all of that ... that's a really important message."[169] It's such positive messaging that the series has led to a wave of queer folk wanting to play with the Edges. "We've seen a massive surge in interest from people who want to return to playing since the show aired," president Kyle McCarthy told the *Vancouver Sun*. "Our social media account alone has grown by 44 percent."[170] That interest includes not only veterans coming back to the game but also people trying the sport for the first time. "We're seeing more people play who say they never felt hockey was for them before," added McCarthy. "It's a progression of acceptance we didn't have ten years ago, and things like *Heated Rivalry* are making a world of difference."

Some critics of *Heated Rivalry* have noted the improbability of three team captains in the big league being gay. That said, the sub-narrative of New York captain Scott Hunter and his gay relationship with a non-player, juice bar barista Kip Grady, has been a big hit with viewers. The couple's dramatic moment at the end of episode 5, when Hunter wins the Cup and beckons Kip in the stands to join him on the ice, where they kiss, was the X factor that pushed *Heated Rivalry*'s TV ratings into *Breaking Bad* territory. François Arnaud, the actor who plays Hunter, used his platform to call on the NHL to do more to welcome queer folk. "The Boston Bruins tagged us on different clips online, and it's getting incredible traction," Arnaud told *The Athletic*. "I'm just hoping that it's backed up by actual openness to diversity. If you're going to use our name, then back it up with real-life shit."[171]

While some younger gay viewers complained of appropriation—noting the series was written by a woman for a largely female audience—or that "gays don't fuck like that" (as if queer sex has a rigid how-to manual), other gay men became instant hockey fans after watching *Heated Rivalry*, to the extent of wanting to play it, as noted above. According to anecdotal evidence compiled by Outsports, viewing parties for episode 5 led to groups of gay men buying tickets to their first NHL games and others watching TV hockey despite knowing little about the sport. "*Heated Rivalry* has presented [NHL] hockey with the opportunity to fully recover from its 2023 LGBTQ nightmare," wrote Cyd Zeigler of Outsports, noting that new fans were either unaware of the league's "problematic recent history" or were willing to put the past behind them.[172] Even straight men kept watching through the sex scenes, the subtleties of emotional intimacy between men keeping their interest.

One group of viewers that struggled with *Heated Rivalry*, even as they admired it, were gay men who had once played hockey at a high level. On January 9, CBC Radio's *The Current* featured interviews with former professional Brock McGillis and Matt Kenny, a California resident who had played competitive hockey as a teenager while growing up in Ontario. (Kenny was invited on the show because of his Instagram post about watching *Heated Rivalry* on Christmas Eve, which went viral. "I knew watching @heatedrivalry was risky," it began. "I didn't expect it to crack me wide open ...") Like McGillis, whose traumatic personal journey through hockey I recounted in Chapter 7, Kenny found *Heated Rivalry* a triggering experience and said he had a panic attack while watching it. About twenty-five minutes into episode 1, he told host Matt Galloway, he was overcome by shortness of breath and had to stop watching. For the next five days, he felt a heaviness in his chest and persistent shallow breath.

What was going on?

When he pressed play to start viewing *Heated Rivalry*, Kenny explained, "I thought I'd be watching this TV show on some sexy hockey dudes, but what happened was, my eyes started watching something I thought I had survived and buried. It felt super private, and suddenly this whole experience was kind of being thrown back at me ... and it terrified me."[173] That experience was when, deep in the closet, he had sex with another hockey player. Shane and Ilya's first hookup reminded him of "this heavy feeling that hung over everything ... the fear, the joy, the secrecy of love that was never supposed to exist in daylight, internal homophobia, and shame that players like me wore like a second skin." But unlike Shane and Ilya, there was no happy ending for Kenny. The fear and shame led him to re-evaluate his life and leave hockey behind. "It just kind of felt like I was giving everything to this sport," he recalled, "and deep down inside I just knew that this sport that I loved probably wasn't able to love me back."

Kenny's and McGillis's raw, emotional responses to *Heated Rivalry* were so much different from my own reaction to the series. As a fellow gay man, and as a hockey enthusiast, if never a hockey talent, I experienced no triggers but simply enjoyed the good writing, performances, and production. This was likely because I had managed, long ago, to circumvent the horrors of the mainstream hockey world by being nowhere near good enough to contemplate a career in it, as McGillis came so close to achieving. How sadly ironic and unfair that a recreational beer leaguer—by virtue of a youthful activism that allowed me to carve out a safer hockey milieu in 1990—ended up having a happier hockey life (or, at least, longer sustained happiness with the game, through solidarity and fellowship with queer teammates) than untold legions of highly skilled gay players who had all the tools and talent to make it to the Show but instead had to suffer in silent isolation because the game they loved couldn't "love them back."

With so much instant commentary around *Heated Rivalry*, academia was bound to weigh with its own two cents' worth. Enter J.P. Catungal, assistant prof at the Institute for Gender, Race, Sexuality and Social Justice and the Asian Canadian and Asian Migration Studies program at the University of British Columbia. Himself a queer Asian Canadian immigrant, Catungal is a big fan of *Heated Rivalry*. In tribute, he created a syllabus that explores how the series engages "enduring critical issues of our time":

> the politics of racism and heteronormativity in sport and in policy; constructions of Asianness, Canadianness, Russianness, and masculinity especially as they relate to queerness; the role of friends and family—especially women—in identity and community formation; the politics of grief, joy, and mental well-being for marginalized communities; and the role of media, images, and representations in self-making.[174]

Assembled within a few weeks of *Heated Rivalry*'s launch, Catungal's syllabus includes reflections on the popular geopolitics of hockey ("a means through which ideas of identity, citizenship, borders, and geopolitical conflict come to be articulated and contested, on the ice, in policy, and via sporting media spectacle"), including "the spectre of Russia and the long Cold War in *Heated Rivalry*"; the racial, sexual, and gender politics of *Heated Rivalry*, including how Shane's Asian Canadianness positions him as a racialized model minority (and the racial politics of his sexual positioning as a bottom); and an unpacking of *Heated Rivalry*'s broad fan base.

For retired UBC sociology professor Becki Ross, the series was an invitation "to remember the anguished yearning, the giddy realization of shared passion, and the ecstasy of mutual pleasuring" in the early days of her relationship with her "soft butch girlfriend," now at the twenty-seven-year mark. In a Facebook post, Ross praised *Heated Rivalry* for its sex-positive messaging. "Entangled bodies featured in a multitude of positions affirm that sex, both urgent and gentle, can be messy, funny, complicated, and life affirming," she wrote. "That this M/M gay romance series exploits men's hockey as a strategy to elevate queer men's love in tortured times is the show's sly genius. While I won't be returning to the NHL or the Sudbury Wolves anytime soon, I predict that men's pro hockey will be forever transformed by this luminous Canadian queer miracle on ice."[175]

It seemed as though everyone was talking about *Heated Rivalry*. Hudson Williams and Connor Storrie were cashing in on their instant fame, overexposing their actorly bromance with every photo shoot, podcast, talk show interview, and awards ceremony available to them, titillating fans by enthusing about each other's hot butts. Jacob Tierney was burnishing his credentials as a progressive TV producer plugged into the zeitgeist. And Rachel Reid—when not doing interviews with the *New York Times*—was being invited to speak at the University of Cambridge. With all this talk, the last people to weigh in on *Heated Rivalry*, it seemed, were the NHL and its gatekeepers, including *Hockey Night in Canada*.* By December 22, there was only this comment to *The Hollywood Reporter* by a nameless NHL rep: "There are so many ways to get hooked on hockey and, in the NHL's 108-year history, this might be the most unique driver for creating new fans. See you all at the rink."[176] And that was it: an appeal for new fan dollars, but

* Imagine the chronically uptight Ron MacLean, no less a play-it-safe wind sniffer than Gary Bettman, unpacking Hollander and Rozanov's early sex scenes. Or any of *Hockey Night*'s panellists being able to discuss the series without blushing. As of this writing, it hasn't happened yet.

not a word about the culture of hockey or about the men who play the game at its highest level.

Gary Bettman finally went on the record in mid-January, telling reporters he had seen all of season 1 of *Heated Rivalry*, having "binged it in one night." And what was the NHL commissioner's verdict? "I thought the storyline was very compelling and a lot of fun," he said, "because I could [see] where they were picking at things that we had [done] in the past, whether it was [the Olympics] in Sochi or the All-Star Game in Tampa. It was very well done." While adding that *Heated Rivalry* presented "a wonderful story," he cautioned that "the content, particularly for young people, might be a little spicy. And so you have to balance that out in terms of how you embrace [the show]. There are a lot of things about the game that we think are driving more people to the game, and I do believe *Heated Rivalry* is one of those things."[177]

The NHL's tepid response to the biggest-ever pop culture phenomenon about its game only raised the obvious question: Could such groundbreaking television as *Heated Rivalry* actually help gay NHL players come out of the closet? Speaking for the yes side was retired NHL agitator Sean Avery, a long-time ally for the queer community. "*Heated Rivalry*'s success should open the door for the first gay NHL player, if there is one," he told *Rolling Stone*, noting that he must have had a gay closeted teammate at some point during his career.[178]

Speaking for the no side was Brock McGillis, the first openly gay professional hockey player and, as we've seen a few times in our story, a strong advocate for queer players. Despite his personal appreciation of the series, he disagreed that *Heated Rivalry* could help NHL players come out. While it might help some people around gay players to be more understanding and respectful if they were dating someone, McGillis said that years of media work by him and Luke Prokop (see below) since coming out had not led to a single NHL player following their example. So, with regard to *Heated Rivalry*, he said, "Nobody's like, 'Oh, yeah. This came out and now I'm ready [to come out].' It's not happening."[179] He went on: "It's probably more likely to have an adverse effect on a player coming out. And I hate to be negative because I really enjoy the show. But I also don't believe that many hockey bros are going to watch it. And I don't think, if they are watching it, they're talking about it positively." His only caveat was that, if someone did come out, hockey players were more likely to rally around their teammate in support than athletes from the other big team sports were.

McGillis may be right. Meanwhile, the *Heated Rivalry* buzz got surreal when Hudson Williams told a radio interviewer that closeted professional athletes—including hockey players—had reached out to him. "Hockey players, football players, basketball players," Williams confirmed with SiriusXM's Andy Cohen. He noted that these athletes had contacted him anonymously but said they were still active professionals and still in the closet. "They're reaching out to like Rachel [Reid], our author, who will then kind of relay these lovely anonymous emails," he told Cohen. "Sometimes they're just reaching out privately, through like Instagram, and those ones are the ones that really just kind of hit you and go, 'Oh, so this is a fun show and it's celebratory, but also sometimes it's just hitting people right in the nerves.'"*[180]

By the time the 2026–27 season gets under way, the National Hockey League will be into its 109th year of existence. Nowhere in all that time has a single NHL player—alive or dead—been identified as gay. We know that gay NHL players exist: Brian Burke says they do. Let's consider a variant of the Kinsey scale

* By late spring of 2026, it seemed to be hitting Gary Bettman in the nerves. The big talk around *Heated Rivalry* season 2 was that part of the storyline would focus on Shane and Ilya's difficult relationship with the Major League Hockey Commissioner, Roger Crowell. (As news gets around about their relationship, Crowell gets involved—and not in a good way.) NHL officials, including senior executive vice-president Kim Davis, confirmed that Bettman was taking this personally; he thought Crowell might be based on him and wanted everyone to know that he would not behave like Crowell if an NHL player came out. See Cyd Zeigler, "The NHL Is Already Worried About 'Heated Rivalry' Season 2," Outsports, May 21, 2026, https://www.outsports.com/2025/12/24/24124922/heated-rivalry-nhl-ticket-sales-pride-night-gay-lgbtq-fans/.

on the conservative side: say 5.3 percent of men exclusively experience same-sex attractions.* In a thirty-two-team league where each team has an active roster of twenty-three players (for a league total of 736), accounting for a less representative sample than the general population in a hypermasculine environment, at least forty players must be gay. That's more than one per team. And yet, unlike all the other major North American sport leagues where at least one player has come out, the NHL closet door remains firmly shut.

As I write, the only out-of-the-closet player whose name is associated with the National Hockey League is Luke Prokop, who was selected by the Nashville Predators as the seventy-third overall pick in the 2020 amateur draft. In 2021, Prokop became the first player under an NHL contract to come out as gay. But as of this writing five years later, he has yet to make it to the Show; his contract with Nashville expired in 2025, and he's playing for Edmonton's American Hockey League (AHL) affiliate, the Bakersfield Condors. I reached out to Prokop, hoping to talk to him for this book, but he didn't respond. I can't say I blame him. Since he came out, his sexuality has become *the* news story about him. He has done other interviews on LGBTQ+ visibility and helpfully participated in documentaries about inclusive hockey. But aged twenty-three when the 2025–26 season began, Prokop wasn't getting any younger. What he must have wanted more than anything was to be noticed and talked about for what he was doing on the ice.†

Prokop is a big, bruising defender at six foot three and 220 pounds. A few days after signing with Bakersfield, he was happy to talk hockey with sportswriter

---

* The original Kinsey report on male sexual behaviour (1948) found that 10 percent of American males were "more or less exclusively homosexual for at least three years between the ages of sixteen and fifty-five." I'm arbitrarily applying a figure here that is just over half that number to allow for a more conservative estimate in a highly masculine, heteronormative environment like hockey—even accounting for more liberal sensibilities in 2026 than in 1948. See Wikipedia, "Kinsey Scale," last modified January 12, 2026, https://en.wikipedia.org/wiki/Kinsey_scale.

† It's also possible that Prokop was saving himself for a bigger project. When I contacted him, I had no idea that he had been working with producer Taylor Prestidge, creator of the Hayley Wickenheiser documentary *WICK*, on an eighty-minute documentary about his life and career called *The Hockey Player*. It aired on OUTtv in June 2026 as a Pride Month feature.

Brian Swane. Reminded that other players who'd come to Bakersfield on AHL contracts—such as Vincent Desharnais—had ended up getting an NHL deal with the Oilers, Prokop, an Edmonton native, made his best pitch to his hometown team. "I believe I'm a very good skater, my hockey IQ is very good, I'm a good passer, I'm probably more on the defensive end, but given the opportunity, I can provide offence as well," he told Swane. Then, turning to his size advantage, he conceded that he might still add some aggression to his game while defending against the rush or in corner battles: "Adding a little bit of bite, adding a bit of grit to my game, which has been a little bit of an internal battle because that's not who I am off the ice. So being able to flip that switch when I put that gear on and be nasty to play against and maybe get in a fight or two. I think it's just showing a bit more intimidation and being able to use my size."[181]

Maybe get in a fight or two. Uh-oh. If any other player had said this, it would have come off as a perfectly valid insight from an ambitious minor leaguer. But the fact that Luke Prokop represents the hopes and dreams of every young queer hockey player in the world made his comment more significant. Was the first openly gay player signed by an NHL team really saying that his best shot at a call-up to the big league was to drop the gloves and throw a few haymakers? Was he saying, in effect, that an NHL team was more likely to give him a shot if he went against stereotype by proving he was one tough motherfucker? A more unsettling question: Could it be that Prokop—who knew what he was talking about, having played four seasons since coming out—was right? If so, could a more intimidating gay hockey player strike a blow, as it were, for queer liberation? And what would that mean, if so? For a hockey culture that struggles with irony at the best of times, this would be something to behold.

Regardless of the usual peer pressure that comes with the unwritten law of the Code, any gay NHLer who does decide to come out will be supported by written law; since 2013, the NHL Players' Association's collective bargaining agreement with the league has included a non-discriminatory clause that clearly mandates legal protection for gay players:

> 7.2 Neither the NHLPA, the NHL, nor any Club shall discriminate in the interpretation or application of this Agreement against or in favour of any Player because of religion, race, disability, colour, national origin, sex, sexual orientation, age, marital status, or membership or non-membership in or support or non-support of any labour organization.[182]

But most NHL players would scoff at that observation. As everyone knows, the Code has more weight in reality than any contract provision, and there are still major barriers preventing gay players from being visibly and vocally out of the closet. Université de Moncton sports sociologist Roger G. LeBlanc has created a conspiracy of silence model that explains some of those barriers. NHL peer pressure is so intense, LeBlanc noted, that players care more about how they are perceived and talked about by their teammates and opponents than about what anyone actually does in private. "Some gay NHL players today likely choose to adopt not only masculine behaviours but also hypermasculine behaviours to deter any notion or image of effeminacy that may be associated with their masculine character or hockey persona," he wrote. "For some players, hockey has not only helped shape their careers, but it has also helped shape how they view others as well as themselves ... Straight athletes achieve their dominant position in society by a process of power relations through sport. The silence of gay NHL players clearly shows that they cannot be their authentic selves."[183]

LeBlanc sees the conspiracy of silence model of NHL closeting as a by-product of hegemonic heterosexuality, the compulsory default culture of masculinity within the NHL. The way it works is that heterosexist and homophobic attitudes of the majority "actively limit, control, and regulate expressions of gay sexuality and therefore limit individual emancipation."[184]

Let's go back to Brian Burke for a moment. Before he was a Harvard Law School graduate and then an NHL executive and general manager for multiple NHL teams, Burke was a scrappy journeyman right winger who played his final season of hockey in the AHL with the Maine Mariners, with whom he won the Calder Cup. There he played beside future NHL coach Ron Wilson under future NHL GM Lou Lamoriello. So he was always "a hockey guy," through and through. Remember his comment about needing to evolve—that, until his son Brendan came out to him, he truly believed that he didn't know any gay people? This is why. "In the absence of any out gay NHL player, NHL fans and players may still have a narrow definition of what it is to be gay," concluded LeBlanc, who might have added NHL owners, general managers, and coaches to his list of the unenlightened. "The 'limp-wristed' gay image remains a strong catalyst for the unacceptability of gay hockey players. It is a safe way for heterosexual men to distance themselves from any implication that gays are like them in any way, shape, or form."[185]

Boiling down LeBlanc's academic model to some key principles, the conspiracy of silence around a teammate's gayness goes something like this (players affected in parentheses):

- Pretend that everyone is straight (all players).
- Maintain a straight-acting and straight-looking presence as part of identity management, overcompensating with convincingly macho behaviour (gay players).
- Do not stand out from your teammates, thus becoming a distraction (all players).
- Do not encourage difference but double down on bro culture masculinity by feminizing difference (straight players).
- Learn to compartmentalize: For survival's sake, behave in different ways in different contexts within different circles of one's life (gay players).

To demonstrate some of these behaviours—and the emotional toll they take on gay NHLers—LeBlanc created a fictional Player X who explains his rationale for remaining closeted. On the importance of the straight-acting/straight-looking facade to his survival, Player X says, "I've learned to be a very butch sort of man. To behave a certain way, you know, not to cross my legs. I've taught myself not to do certain things as part of my mask, as part of the portrayal of who I am so that I feel that people accept me."[186]

By the late 2010s, research showed that the main barrier keeping gay NHL players from coming out was the fear of becoming a distraction; an openly gay player would set himself apart from teammates—and the collective goal of winning games and Stanley Cups—by drawing public attention to his own sexuality. Sports sociologist Cheryl A. MacDonald, then associate director of outreach at the Saint Mary's University Centre for Sport, Business and Health, interviewed six heterosexual former NHL players and six openly gay players of elite hockey outside the NHL. Many compared the idea of a player coming out to a player disclosing a drug addiction or a mental health struggle. "[The players told me] it doesn't matter if you're gay, or concussed, or you've been sexually abused, or have mental health issues, none of those are okay because you are a distraction," MacDonald told a University of Alberta publication. "You don't want to risk it not being okay, because the perception is someone who is just as good at your job but isn't gay is going to take your spot."[187]

In a later interview with the *Hockey News*, MacDonald said the easiest way to become a distraction was to draw attention to yourself for any reason. "The best example I often get in my interviews is P.K. Subban," she said. "Why was P.K. Subban traded from Montreal? Well, [the narrative tells us] he was drawing too much attention to himself, his clothes were too flashy, he was on Instagram too much, he was screwing up the team dynamic. If you are calling attention to yourself in the media, whether you are gay or not, that is seen as selfish and is not adhering to the team-first attitude."[188] MacDonald's research, some of the results of which she published in *Overcoming the Neutral Zone Trap* (2021), also looked into the connection between homophobia and misogyny. A surprising number of the players she interviewed had no idea that the words they used to attack opponents personally were often homosexualizing or feminizing them. The latter, she said, is more prevalent than homophobic slurs at all levels of the game.

This suggests that another factor preventing gay NHL players from coming out is the fear of being feminized. Some NHL players still scoff at the Lady Byng Memorial Trophy, awarded annually to the player "adjudged to have exhibited the best type of sportsmanship and gentlemanly conduct combined with a high standard of playing ability."[189] Why? In a professional game where toughness is everything, a trophy named after a woman—and using the antiquated title of "Lady"—might be as much an invitation to ridicule as the reason for winning it. (For some players, hockey is no place for "gentlemanly conduct.") Even future Hall of Famers are not exempt from misogynistic ridicule. Twin brothers Daniel and Henrik Sedin—two highly talented finesse players who, throughout their careers with the Vancouver Canucks, refused to fight—were referred to online by some opponents and by bigoted fans as "the Sedin sisters."*

More encouragingly, however, MacDonald's interviews with the openly gay players revealed that there are definite advantages to coming out. Gay players who had come out to their teammates reported less homophobic language in the dressing room afterward and that teammates appreciated being taken aside and gently admonished if they had said "fag" without thinking. The gay players also said their teammates relaxed more around them after they'd come out, eventually finding ways to make light of their sexuality, whether by asking about their favourite type or about the nature of their sex. "The gay players said the acknowledgement was nice," said MacDonald. "From what I gathered, there is room for consensual humour."

The closeted NHLer might be surprised by how supportive the hockey community is getting. For what it's worth, Gary Bettman once told the *Chicago Tribune* that he hoped a gay NHL player would come out one day. "We certainly don't want a player to come out for our sake," he said in 2016. "It should be what's right for him and something that he must be comfortable with. But I think it's our job to create a culture and an environment where a gay player knows he is safe

* Always too classy to dignify it in public, Daniel and Henrik can now privately scoff at such ignorance from a great height; on May 14, 2026, as part of a front-office housecleaning, the Vancouver Canucks named the Sedins co-presidents of hockey operations, the highest management position on an NHL team.

and welcome. If and when that happens, believe me, that person will have the full support of the commissioner's office."[190] In 2017, then Boston Bruins star Brad Marchand responded to a homophobic attack against him on Twitter by declaring his support for gay players. "Guys would accept it, no question [if a gay player came out]. We're a team in the locker room and a family. It doesn't matter what different beliefs guys have, or where they come from, or whatever the case may be. Guys would accept it."[191] By 2025, more than one hundred NHL stars had signed on to You Can Play, including some of the world's best players, Sidney Crosby, Alex Ovechkin, Connor McDavid, Nathan MacKinnon, Austin Matthews, Matthew Tkachuk, and Steven Stamkos among them.

To convince NHL players to come out, it appears necessary for others in the NHL community to come out first. And that's already happening. In November 2020, at the height of the COVID-19 pandemic, thirty-three-year-old player agent Bayne Pettinger was growing tired of hiding his true self from the hockey world. At six foot four, Pettinger was a former Junior B player who had also played elite-level rugby for Canada's national U19 team—as masculine presenting as it gets. Professionally, he'd spent ten years as Hockey Canada's manager of hockey operations before turning to player agency. In that time, he'd become well acquainted with two of the NHL's biggest stars, Crosby and McDavid. Pettinger worried that, once he came out, those players—along with Tyson Barrie and Morgan Rielly, who were also clients—might shun him. Hockey Canada might turn its back on him, and then his hockey career would be toast.

Instead, the opposite happened. After coming out publicly with an interview in *The Athletic*, Pettinger's voice mail filled up with congratulatory messages of support, and the texts came flying in. From McDavid: "Doesn't change a thing, dude, honestly. Just happy ur happy." From Crosby: "We are happy for you and I am sure it feels good to get that off your shoulders and be able to be you." Similar support came from Barrie and Rielly. Former Hockey Canada president Bob Nicholson told Pettinger he had "never been prouder" of him. The lesson from all this? "It didn't change how the hockey community saw me," Pettinger recalled three years later, in an essay for Hockey Canada. "Instead, it was ... 'Hey, you're Bayne. You don't judge us on who we date or who we're attracted to. So why would we judge you?'... When I look back, I wonder why I was so anxious. And that's what I try to preach to people who have reached out that are still in the closet thinking they won't be accepted."[192] Perhaps the hockey world was changing faster than he thought.

During my research for this book in the fall of 2025, I learned of another out gay man who had been working in the NHL for more than a dozen years. Peter Lovins, who graduated from Ohio State law school, joined the Columbus Blue Jackets in 2012 as a legal assistant. He is now the club's general counsel, its lead legal mind, and a board member of You Can Play. Outsports has called him the most powerful out gay man in the NHL, placing him at number 20 on its Power 100 influencers list. "You shouldn't have to sacrifice your authentic self to work in sports," Lovins told Outsports's Cyd Zeigler. "I'd rather just lay low and do my job and do it well. But there are still too many kids who don't feel safe in sports, playing or working in it."[193]

The most sacred space for NHL players has always been the dressing room. Apart from the coach's pre-game pep talk and post-game interviews when reporters are briefly permitted inside, that room belongs to the players. As with other team sports, it's where the players bond. It's where things are said that cannot be said outside; it's where players can be themselves with each other, enjoying banter they wouldn't want a microphone to pick up. Think of it as the Las Vegas of athletic space: What happens in the dressing room stays there. But it has also been the source of the NHL's biggest taboo against gay men: the assumption that homosexual presence in a room filled with naked men is a direct threat to the masculinity of those men.

Justin Rogers (left), conferring with Seattle Kraken goaltender Philipp Grubauer, is the Kraken's head athletic trainer and the first openly gay team staffer in that position in the NHL

Well, guess what? That taboo was broken five years ago, if not by a player. Meet Justin Rogers, head athletic trainer of the Seattle Kraken.*

As Rogers will attest, athletic trainers aren't in the dressing room all the time—in fact, not much at all. Their job is to attend to the players' health care needs—everything from injury prevention, diagnosis, and treatment to rehab and overall wellness. So they literally have a hands-on relationship with players' bodies, physically touching them for everything from concussion inspection to muscle massage. Since much of their interaction with players occurs privately, it goes without saying that trust is a major factor in any athletic trainer's job security. Justin Rogers is Exhibit A in how to establish that trust as a gay man in a high-masculinity sport.

Rogers has been on the Kraken staff since the 2021–22 season, their first in the NHL. He came highly recommended, having completed internships in the National Football League (NFL), worked with football players as a grad student at the University of Nebraska, helped build Penn State University's hockey program from the ground up, and won both post-season and regular season Big Ten titles. To the Kraken he brought a solid reputation as a reliable professional who was not only attentive to his players but also proactive in helping them resolve their health and fitness issues. Friendly and easygoing, he was hard not to like and established trust from the beginning.

Meanwhile, he had been out of the closet for several years, happily sharing his personal life on social media. Since attending his first Outsports Pride event in 2016 while at Penn State, he had posted several Instagram photos showing himself with friends at pride events. But he was masculine presenting in comportment, so it took a while for other Kraken staff and the players to figure out he was gay. Once they did—usually through a casual chat about an Instagram post they had seen or his clarification when asked about a girlfriend or wife—no one treated him

* Rogers is "JR," the source for the story I told in Chapter 11 about the Kraken's exemplary support of the Seattle Pride hockey tournament, and the same Justin Rogers who joined the Cutting Edges and Seattle Pride Hockey Association for the 2026 Pride Cup.

any differently. By 2023, considering his unique position in the league, Rogers decided it was time to come out in a bigger way: by writing a letter to his younger self about his long journey toward self-acceptance and an NHL career, and posting it on ESPN.

Before he did, he gave the Kraken organization a heads-up. Wisely, he went straight to the top, approaching the one person who could have vetoed the plan: then general manager (and later president) Ron Francis. Thanking him for bringing up the subject and for having the confidence to approach him directly, Francis told him the essay was a great idea, gave him the green light, and asked if there was any way he could help. Rogers's "Letter to My Younger Self" was posted on both ESPN and the Kraken's website on November 3, 2023. "There will be days in locker rooms that you will hear derogatory terms tossed around in reference to queer individuals," he told his teenaged self. "There will be at least one time when you demonstrate a rehab exercise for an unsuspecting athlete who will tell you the exercise is the 'gayest thing they've ever seen.' There will be other times you will hear athletes discuss and debate gay and transgender rights. You will have to decide when to speak up and when to bite your tongue."[194] An accompanying profile of Rogers included supportive quotes from Francis and from Kraken players Jordan Eberle, Matty Beniers, and Philipp Grubauer. These players, and others on the Kraken roster who were interviewed about Rogers for an NHL documentary a year later, all spoke of his value to the team as a member of "the Kraken family."[195]

Rogers was an assistant athletic trainer when first hired by the Kraken. The year after his big announcement, he was promoted to head athletic trainer—proof that gay men can advance in the NHL after coming out. Two years after his "Letter to My Younger Self," Rogers agreed to an interview for this book. He had much to say on the subject of his own transparency as a gay man in the NHL and what he's learned from it. "I came to this job already living pretty authentically. I had developed a lot of connections inside and outside of hockey that made me feel secure, so I was kind of already there," he told me. In our conversation, Rogers emphasized the importance of self-confidence and comfort with one's own sexuality as critical factors in any decision to come out in the hockey world—don't do it until you know you're ready.

Rogers had done his research before applying for the job, and he was impressed by both the city and team he was going to. "Seattle is in a very progressive state, and our organization is a very progressive organization," he said. "When the Kraken started and they put out all their team pillars and what the organization was going to be about, my friends and I were like, 'This is incredible—they're about racial justice, they're about equality for everybody, and having women at the top,' so it was an organization from the very get-go that me and all my friends followed."

Once the team and staff were assembled for the Kraken's first season, it didn't take long to get to know the team, despite the practice of social distancing during the second year of the COVID-19 pandemic. "Everyone's following each other on Instagram or social media, and you're seeing pictures of me at pride, or seeing pictures of me and my friends at drag shows or wherever, out and about, or me posting enlightening stories about LGBTQ youth and stuff like that, so there was never a moment where I'm like, 'Oh, should I post this because someone will know at work?'" (The only time he took down a post, he said, was because a photo he had taken during a late-night drag show was grainy and out of focus and did not do justice to the performer.)

Apart from breaking the dressing room taboo, Rogers has also succeeded in normalizing queer relationships around an NHL team. It happened even faster than he expected: "So one of our players—we had a team function about a month before my article came out on ESPN—he pulled me aside, and he was like, 'Justin, where's your boyfriend?' And I'm like, 'My who?' Like, we literally at this point had been dating for three weeks. I'm like, 'What do you mean, where's my boyfriend?' He goes, 'We all know you have a boyfriend, and if you're writing an ESPN article, he'd better start being at every single team event.' I'm like, 'Yes, yes, noted!' I literally texted him right away. He couldn't come, he had to work that night, so it wasn't even like I was avoiding him being there. Most guys won't even bring their girlfriends, if you're dating for three weeks, to a team function with your owners and your investors. Like that's just something you don't do. But the players were like, 'No, he needs to be at every function.'"

And how did his boyfriend feel about that? Did he attend these functions? Rogers laughed. "He's at way too many. He comes to the majority of our games, he's down in the family room with all the coaches' wives and other significant partners, he's at team Christmas parties, he's at team holiday parties, he's part of the significant others group chats ... so they are in constant communication. They'll do an event for one of our first road games where they all get together and they have brunch and thank them for working with us and us being away all the time. So he's been able to establish himself, and I think that's just part of the normalizing aspect. I have a picture of him on my desk, so people come by, they see that. I've got a 'Safe Space' sign on my desk, I've got a Kraken rainbow on my desk, and I've got a picture of Lindsy McLean, the first NFL athletic trainer who came out as gay, who I got to meet this summer. So it's very just normal for me. And it's never been a problem."

When we got to the subject of NHL players coming out, I brought up Luke Prokop. I told Rogers that, no matter what happens in Prokop's hockey career—that is, regardless of whether or not the Oilers call him up one day—I hoped he never regretted the timing of his decision to come out, despite those who might argue that he should have waited until he got an NHL call-up. We all have to come out in our own time, and freeing oneself from an inauthentic life is always the right thing to do. Besides, who's to say the Predators would have called him up anyway while he was with Nashville? Being closeted while waiting for your big break is doubly excruciating, because you're looking over your shoulder all the time, worrying about who will find out.

Rogers agreed. "If you're not authentic to yourself, you're not playing your best hockey," he said, adding that the same goes for his own performance as an NHL athletic trainer. Rogers mused that, had he not come out, "I'm going to walk in the locker room and think, *Everybody here knows I'm gay*, and I'm going to be focused on a million other things, and I'm not going to be able to provide the best health care to my players. If [Prokop] would not have come out, [he] wouldn't be able to go out on the ice without being afraid of, 'All right, I've gotta walk into the facility today, who thinks I did this, or who saw me on a date last night?' That's our fear as gay men, is we're going to get outed, and then it's constantly on your mind. And you're not going to play your best hockey. [You're] going to risk injury on the ice."

The last comment reminded me of Brock McGillis's story about his many years of torment in the hockey closet, when he was injured all the time. "We have to be as clear minded as we possibly can, every single day," Rogers said. "Personal health and safety is first and foremost. You can't be at your best, and we can't expect the best of our fellow co-workers, fellow players, anybody within any organization, if they can't have a true, clear, fresh mind and you know who they are." I can't think of a better argument for an NHL player to come out than that. But what's the best way to go about it? How should a gay NHL player strategize his way out of the closet? Shouldn't there be a communications plan in place, a media strategy the player, his team, and the league can enact for best results?

The first time I considered the idea of an NHL coming-out strategy (see the appendix), I thought it should include a two-week time limit on the period a gay player allows for interviews about his sexuality. After that, everything should be about his hockey career. My thinking was that, once the story is out there, it's on the public record forever; reporters still interested in the gay angle can get source material from the saturation coverage that occurred during those two weeks. Since the object of the time limit is to help the player move on and resume his NHL career without causing a distraction for his team, the subject of his sexuality needn't come up again unless it's relevant. (Say, for example, when he and his partner are interviewed about an important cause they're supporting at a team fundraiser.) While the two-week limit might not deter certain right-wing media (Why respect a player's privacy if he's been willing to go public at all?), a good comms plan should anticipate negative response. Haters are going to hate, and ideologues will have their say. But they're on the wrong side of history. As the success of *Heated Rivalry* suggests, more people will accept queer NHLers than not.

And that's why I hope, for his sake, that Luke Prokop still gets to be the first. Whether the Oilers gave him a shot at training camp, put him on the roster for 2026–27, or called him up sometime after that, he wouldn't need my advice;

he's already a role model, having done great media work, public awareness education, and now a documentary about his journey. (I would only suggest that he limit his media availability on the subject of his sexuality to a brief statement about its historic significance. The messaging would go something like this: "Like any other player who's been working hard to achieve his NHL dream and finally gets the call-up, I am ecstatic to be here and hope to contribute to the Oilers' success in any way I can. My being in the NHL finally proves, once and for all, that if you can play, you can play.") But even if it never happens, Prokop can rest assured: No matter how he finishes his pro hockey career, he has already made a huge difference for queer hockey players everywhere. And that makes him a champion in any league.

As for everyone else, Justin Rogers liked my idea of a comms plan for gay or bisexual players, especially the two-week window for interviews. "I think the Kraken probably have the closest thing to a blueprint, for two reasons: me and Jessica [Campbell]," he told me. "The media storm that followed the first female coach last year was wild. We'd go to Montreal and Toronto, and we would have TV cameras following her on the ice for practice all day. They didn't even realize who the team was they were playing—all they cared about was Jessica. If you watched one of our Kraken games, like every single broadcast, all they did was talk about Jessica the whole game. I think after about a couple of weeks, our PR people finally had to tell our TV people, 'Okay, Jessica's not here playing. Let her focus so she can do her best job or she's going to not keep her job because you're going to be distracting her.' So I think what you said about a two-week [limit] is phenomenal."

In terms of his own coming out, Rogers did something similar. After he posted his letter to his younger self in his own words, there were follow-up media interviews with him, Ron Francis, and the three Kraken players. "And then we said flat out, 'We're not doing another interview for the rest of the year. It's done.' Our PR people here probably had a hundred people that reached out to them that said, 'Hey, can we do a podcast? Can we do an interview?' I said, 'There's nothing left besides my letter to my younger self. You're just going to ask the same questions everyone's asking.' So I think the PR department has to be very thorough and answer as many questions as you can, and then you're right: You have to protect that player so they're not distracted, and they can go out there and continue playing a really good game. The last thing we want is for someone to *not* get a contract extension because they did too many interviews."

Rogers also had some sobering advice about fan interest after an NHL player comes out. "If they came out today and they played Toronto in three weeks, it's going to be a firestorm, man," he said. "It's going to be tough to keep fans away on the road. The media's one part, but you're going to get fans coming out of the woodwork." When Carl Nassib came out in football, noted Rogers, he had the highest-selling jersey in the NFL. Same thing when Michael Sam came out. "There will not be a queer person—including myself—that is not going to own that person's jersey when it finally happens. Everybody will want that jersey."

Then there's personal protection. "Our players already get mile-long lines when they drive out of practice. Well, this person [the first out NHL player] is going to have a seven-hour autograph session outside. If you do it, hey, you know what? We need someone to protect this person from signing too many autographs, we need to protect this person from the media, we need to protect this person personally. They're going to have some good stalkers and some bad stalkers. So there's a lot of aspects of personal security that are going to go into this first person that many other organizations and teams haven't had to think about and do."

The NHL player's comms plan cannot be a one-size-fits-all strategy. There are different categories of player to consider. When I began this project, I'd thought there were only two. The first category is players already established as NHL regulars on a team's roster, from the anonymous journeyman to the bona fide superstar; the second is someone like Prokop, who is already drafted and may be under contract but has yet to play in the big league. But Rogers reminded me of a third category of player who would benefit from a comms plan. "Is there a young player that's already out there that, maybe at sixteen, is gay on his Junior team, and he just works his way up like it's normal, and all of a sudden now he does make it to opening night?" wondered Rogers. "Are we asking someone that's thirty years old coming out, or are we asking someone that's twenty and about to play their first game? Those two people have a very different strategy; It's lived experience versus a flip-of-a-switch experience."* That third category, Rogers believes—and I'm inclined to agree—is the most likely to produce the NHL's first openly gay player. But we shall see.

* It has also been suggested that a fourth category is worthy of consideration: the sexually fluid hockey player who self-identifies as bisexual (or pansexual or simply queer) because his sexual attraction is not limited to one gender. Because of the specific nature of closeted NHL gayness applying to men, my advice to those players would be to follow whichever aspects of the comms plan outlined in the appendix apply to their queer experience in particular.

A new game: Sand Northrup (far right) and friends attend a regular season home game of the Vancouver Goldeneyes during the PWHL expansion team's inaugural season in 2025–26

CONCLUSION

As the global response to *Heated Rivalry* indicates, there is a huge appetite for queer hockey cultural product, and not just in traditional Canadian markets. But who knew that the queer hockey romance would become its own literary subgenre? *Heated Rivalry* author Rachel Reid hit such a motherlode with the TV series for just one novel that the Halifax-based author will never again have to worry about access to medical services for the Parkinson's disease she's been dealing with since she began writing gay hockey love stories.* *Heated Rivalry* has also turned out to

* And she's got competition: A new hockey romance featuring gay characters and based on Elle Kennedy's novel series *Off Campus* began streaming on Amazon Prime Video in spring 2026. With all the hype over *Heated Rivalry*, even bestselling American novelist Don DeLillo, best known for serious, big-theme works like *White Noise* and *Underworld*, is finally willing to take ownership of *Amazons*, a campy, satirical novel he published in 1980 under the pseudonym Cleo Birdwell that features queer themes, women NHLers, and sex with male hockey players.

be a smart career move for producer Jacob Tierney, and not just for the obvious financial reasons. The chirping, bro culture humour of Tierney's earlier series, *Letterkenny*, was edgy when it launched in 2016. But that show's spinoff, *Shoresy*, might not age quite as well.

Letterkenny followed the residents of a small rural Ontario community named after a town in Ireland's County Donegal. The series subverted the small-town trope of narrow-minded, mostly white residents by having its characters share sophisticated views of social issues while speaking in poetic, rapid-fire phrases punctuated by great one-liners. Two *Letterkenny* characters, Reilly and Jonesy, serve as camp exemplars of hockey bro culture with their peculiar rituals, their chirping, and their preoccupation with fitness. Reilly and Jonesy are never seen apart, which serves to homoeroticize their presence. In one scene, the friendly duo want to make a good impression on their five older teammates at the first day of men's league, so they suggest a few ideas for hanging out together after practice. First is partying. (Reilly: "You boys wanna go wheel some snipes after praccy?" First response: "I'm married, you little bitch.") When they suggest going out for sandwiches, they get a thumbs-down because everyone else is gluten intolerant. Reilly: "So what do you guys like to do?" Response: "Winning, you little bitch."

The spinoff series' lead character, Shoresy, is more profane and offensive. His cameo appearances in *Letterkenny* were mostly verbal attacks on anyone who challenged him. ("Your lives are so fucking pathetic, I ran a charity 15K to raise awareness for it." "Your breath is an existential crisis—made me question my whole fucking life." Et cetera.) There's more than a hint of *Slap Shot* in *Shoresy*, which focuses on the Sudbury Bulldogs, a team on the verge of collapse that recruits a handful of finesse players and ruffians to help turn things around. But *Slap Shot* was made in the 1970s. To some viewers, the humour in *Shoresy* might feel uncomfortably close to reality at a time when the game has been forced into self-reckoning. While Hockey Canada was subjected to daily grilling about its payouts for sexual assault victims, each episode of *Shoresy* presented never-ending "discussions of sexual conquests, substance use, [and] fights both on and off the ice" while romancing the viewer with "an endearing hockey underdog story."[196] In this light, a new series about two gay hockey players who can't keep their hands off each other can only represent progress. Yes indeed, we have come a long way since *The Mighty Ducks* trilogy and the *Goon* sequel.*

Queer hockey is also making its way into the visual art scene. Thirty-five years after Daniel Collins's *Gay Athletes* photo exhibition for Gay Games III (plus *High Sticking*, plus multiple shoots for some risqué promotion of Cutting Edges fund-raising events), a Calgary photographer in early 2025 held an exhibition that turned hockey dressing rooms and jockstraps into a whimsical takedown of toxic masculinity in the sport. Sebastian Buzzalino's *I Am Emotionally Attached to These Men* satirized the unintended homoeroticism of colour commentary during NHL broadcasts by reframing those phrases onto twenty fictional trading cards featuring partly nude male athletes. The idea was to encourage viewers to reimagine how masculinity is portrayed in sport. For each card,

> male models of diverse sexual identities and body types are posed in various states of undress, both on the rink and in the locker room ... They wear traditional hockey attire imbued with queer elements. The accompanying broadcast quotes, severed from their original context, range from tongue-in-cheek to sexually suggestive, like that of a card featuring a model in a jockstrap that reads, "A young guy just trying to find the time to show off his hands."[197]

---

* We've come so far, in fact, that gay influencers are now populating their social media pages with mock fashion commentary on their favourite hockey hotties. During the Habs' deep playoff run in 2026, Mike Chaar, a well-known radio host and pop culture reporter for 95.9 Virgin Radio in Montreal, posted his "Montreal Canadiens Fashion Roundup," a compilation video that treats the routine arrival of the team at the rink before every game like a catwalk for runway models, complete with diva-like commentary as each player's image appears: "Looking like a snack-and-a-half: Alex Carrier, coming in with a double-breasted moment—traditional, signature. I love that he paired it with a white shirt instead of a button-up. The do, the facial hair. I am jealous of whoever got to put a ring on that." See Mike Chaar, "Montreal Canadiens Fashion Roundup," Instagram, May 23, 2026, https://www.instagram.com/reel/DYsxDpAOnPn/.

Interdisciplinary artist and curator Lucas Morneau was up to something a little different in his 2024 solo exhibition, *Queer Newfoundland Hockey League* (QNHL). Born and raised in Newfoundland and now living in Sackville, New Brunswick, Morneau conceived of the QNHL as a fictional hockey league comprising fourteen teams, all of which reclaim the pejoratives used against the queer community as their team names. The logos are fabulous creations, presented on Morneau's crocheted and rug-hooked hockey jerseys. I snicker to imagine some of the looks I'd get if I walked around my New Westminster neighbourhood representing the St. John's Sissies, the Fogo Island Fag Hags, the Dildo Dykes, the Pasadena Pansies, or the Bonavista Buggers. "QNHL, by reclaiming these pejoratives, aims to deconstruct homophobia in sports and sports culture and critique the existing hegemonic masculinity in sports culture," says the exhibition's brochure. "By bringing awareness to the toxic elements of the current hegemonic masculinity, QNHL aims to create a new, positive, and accepting masculinity for sports enthusiasts."[198]

The best sign that queer hockey culture is here to stay can be found in the very spaces where hockey is played. As the NHL continues stumbling its way toward a truly inclusive product, I hope they're paying close attention to the Professional Women's Hockey League (PWHL). As far as the on-ice product goes, the PWHL offers fast, high-finesse hockey that doesn't shy away from aggressive contact. But unlike the Code in the NHL, the strong sense of mutual respect that PWHL players share includes a much healthier regard for opponents. The league has also introduced a rule or two that the NHL ought to consider. The best example is the jailbreak rule: If a team serving a minor penalty scores a short-handed goal while killing it, the rest of the penalty is cancelled. This gives the penalized team a break while punishing their opponent for screwing up on the power play, a good incentive for teams who feel they were unjustly penalized and a warning to their opponent that the privilege of a power play has its limits.

As I witnessed during my first PWHL game as a Vancouver Goldeneyes fan in December 2025, the new women's game has also attracted a different kind of fan base from the average NHL crowd: mostly women, lots of openly queer folk, and a minority of male fans whose behaviour is noticeably more respectful toward everyone in the rink. It took most of the season for unfortunate chants of "Ref, you suck!" to finally be heard at a Goldeneyes game, but there were no obscenities thrown toward opposing players. And there was more fun and laughter—some of it due to cheap beer prices and far cheaper seats, to be sure, but mostly from a shared sense that the league truly welcomes everyone, regardless of sexuality or gender expression.

"When the PWHL came onto the scene at the start of last year, it was a time when we as queer people, and queer sports fans in particular, needed someone to show up for us," wrote Montreal Victoire fan Mel Brown in an essay posted on the CBC News website. "The league, led by some of the most powerful queer women in sports history, came through in a big way."[199] On her way to the rink for her first PWHL game during the league's inaugural season, Brown recalled being struck by the difference in atmosphere from the NHL games she had attended. "The venue was packed with women and female-presenting people, many of them holding hands with each other or carrying signs like 'Future PWHL WAG [wives and girlfriends],'" she wrote. "Everyone looked as excited as we felt. For the first time in my life, I felt at home at a professional sporting event. Beyond that, even—I felt wanted." The hockey was some of the best she had seen. Watching it with her queer chosen family in a completely supportive environment was exhilarating. "That feeling is at its heart such a big part of queerness—belonging is never implicit, it is consciously known and celebrated," wrote Brown.

I couldn't agree more. As a cisgender gay man, I also can't help being a little envious; professional women's hockey players have been upping their game for the past thirty-five years. As with so many other things, it's time for the men to catch up.

Cutting Edges players from four teams rest after a late-summer skate before the 2025–26 season

EPILOGUE

Forever a Cutting Edge

In the thirty-two years since Vancouver's Cutting Edges first took to the ice, I have taken two lengthy leaves of absence from the organization. The first was halfway through the 1999–2000 season, when I travelled to Thailand for what was supposed to be a three-month tour of Southeast Asia but turned into a three-year expatriate sojourn. After my first year in Bangkok, I resumed playing hockey—this time with the Flying Farangs, a group of expat rink rats and a handful of Thai locals. Every Sunday afternoon at a shopping mall in Lat Phrao, we gathered to play hockey in an air-conditioned rink on the fourth floor, causing no end of amusement for curious Thai shoppers who wondered what on earth we were up to. My two years playing with the Flying Farangs were loads of fun. But the best of those times was when we travelled north to Chiang Mai to play a three-game exhibition series against Thailand's national men's team.

Yes, you read that right. Coached by Aaron Story, a grandson of legendary Toronto Maple Leafs forward and Hall of Fame broadcaster Howie Meeker, the

Thai national men's team was preparing for the Asian Winter Games in Aomori, Japan (February 1–8, 2003) and needed some warm-up action. When we first played against them at Lat Phrao, the Thai players were still learning the basics. Much younger and faster than the Flying Farangs, they typically dominated us for the first few minutes of a game. "But then," I wrote in an essay at the time, "their game would fall apart as they neglected all the little things that aging Canadian expats knew by instinct after decades of playing: things like winning face-offs, using the boards, blocking shots, pinching and forcing turnovers."[200]

After six months of training with Story, the Thais had serious game. When we arrived in Chiang Mai for the mini-series, also held at a shopping mall rink, we found out that Story had spent the last six weeks putting them through a rigorous daily regime worthy of his granddad's famous hockey school in Parksville: two hours of power skating drills starting at 8:30 a.m., followed by two and a half hours of swimming and dryland fitness that included weightlifting, jogging, and running up and down the shopping mall stairs. They finished their day at 9:30 p.m. after another two-hour skating session. This time, our games weren't even close; the Thais clobbered us 10–0, 7–1, and 12–3. We tried not to feel too bummed out. They were youngsters, after all. We were in our late thirties or older. And there was some consolation in the fact that they went to Japan and managed to beat Mongolia, a country that actually has winters, 4–2. At least I can say, in all honesty, that I have played against a country's national men's team—my sole claim to such international hockey experience. Kop khun krub, Thailand!

When I returned home to Canada in the autumn of 2003, I landed more than a month and a half into the hockey season, too late to rejoin the Cutting Edges. I returned for the 2004–05 season and then played every season until the end of 2012–13. A few months later, during a year's unpaid leave of absence from my job to promote my latest book and start a new one, I flew back to Southeast Asia—this time to spend more than seven months living and working in my husband's native land of Myanmar. When I returned to Canada shortly after the 2013–14 hockey season, my hubby convinced me to stay off the ice for another season. I don't recall why I agreed to this, but we had just moved to New Westminster—yet another eastward migration from our first apartment in Vancouver—so the commute to UBC would now be even longer. But that shouldn't have stopped me from playing *somewhere*. Even after age fifty.

Before the 2015–16 season began, I was determined to play hockey again and to find a closer rink. Queen's Park Arena, literally across the road from our home near McBride Street, was the most attractive option. Queen's Park was built in 1930 and was home to the big bad Bruins teams of the late 1970s, the Memorial Cup champs coached by Ernie "Punch" McLean and led by future NHL stars such as Stan Smyl, Barry Beck, Brad Maxwell, and John Ogrodnick. The rink not only had a rich history but also a great sheet of ice, one of the best in the Lower Mainland. But the hockey was mostly drop-in or retired old-timers doing day rentals. There was no league play at Queen's Park, at least not for my level of rec hockey. (I was no Kade Lacasse.)

My best option would be the Adult Safe Hockey League at Burnaby's 8 Rinks, where divisions were organized by skill levels and age groups. I was most comfortable playing in an intermediate division for a 50-plus team. Committing to this plan meant that, for the first time in thirty-eight years, I would be playing in a mainstream league, re-entering the "straight" Canadian hockey world I had left behind before puberty. This was a big deal, but I shrugged it off as a self-actualized adult who'd been out of the closet for more than a quarter century. Besides, I was no longer using hockey to change the world; I just wanted to play my favourite sport and get as much ice time as possible without having to drive for more than an hour to get there. With the Cutting Edges I had played against straight teams since 1994 and lived to tell the tale. Surely I could join a straight team without drama. Surely things had changed in four decades, and I would not be entering the same dressing room I'd left in my teens, right?

Well, not quite. Joining the Beavers (so named for predictably vulgar reasons) was like going back in time. Within seconds of arriving in the dressing room, I felt a totally different vibe from the Cutting Edges dressing room. Here's what I learned: All it takes for a group of straight men in their fifties to revert to crude juvenilia is to get them in a room with no women present. Within minutes, these men—all married with children, some with grandchildren—were talking titties and pussy. Telling jokes about women and sex. Referring to their opponents as "cocksuckers."

One of my new Beavers teammates was so fond of this latter term that I often wondered if he had experimented in his youth. Or more recently.

Suddenly self-conscious, it occurred to me that by failing to call out this behaviour, I was closeting myself again, for the first time since those lonely days in Hope during 1988–89. So the next time I was out for beers with the manager, a city worker from the local Italian community who wore his heart on his sleeve, I came out to him after spending an hour listening to his marital woes. I'd like to stay with the Beavers, I told him, but I hoped the guys could tone it down with the sexist jokes and homophobic slurs. Sympathetic, he later had a few discreet chats with some of the players. They didn't treat me differently after that—and I was glad they didn't—but there was much less of the offensive language when I was around.

One of my linemates, however, had a momentary lapse. After getting pitchforked one night during a struggle along the boards, he wasn't satisfied when the offender was penalized for the infraction. Standing up at our bench, he leaned over the boards and shouted across the rink at the penalty box: "Why'd you do that, you faggot?" I spun around and let him know he had crossed the line. "Oh sorry, I forgot," he said, making it clear that our manager had spoken with him about me. He seemed to regret his outburst, though possibly only because he was caught. "Look," I explained, "it doesn't matter if I'm in the room or not—you shouldn't be using that word about anybody, anywhere. Ever."

After that, there were no similar incidents in the Beavers dressing room or on the bench, and I spent four seasons with the team. These were not bad men—just regular, plain-talking guys who enjoyed each other's company and, away from the wives and kids, a lack of inhibition in their humour. They knew about me but didn't say anything, preferring to accept or silently respect me for the hustle, hard work, and occasional goals I brought them. At the end of the 2018–19 season, I missed our final playoff game due to work obligations. This meant missing my first chance since the 1998–99 season with the Cutting Edges to play for a championship. Like the Edges that year, the Beavers won it all in 2019. The manager, meeting me for coffee over the summer, gave me the little silver trophy they'd won without me. Sweet.

I was looking forward to the 2019–20 season and trying for a repeat with the Beavers, but just before the season began, we learned that our best player had bailed on us, bolting to another team in a better division and taking five other players with him. The rest of us were at loose ends. The other teams in our division were fully registered, so we had to be absorbed into another division. My team manager and three other Beavers, including me, got assigned to a team composed mostly of retired RCMP officers. This was a tight-knit group of ex-Mounties who had played together since they were still in the service. They were good, but they had lost a few players to retirement. Another couldn't afford to play a full season. So they took us in.

While my Beavers mates made a smooth transition to our new team, I found it more challenging. This division was of a slightly higher calibre than our own and, within a few games, the team's manager and captain—let's call him Top Cop—started getting on my case about positioning. This man, an Anglo Quebecer who had moved to BC and become a realtor after retiring from the RCMP, took himself very seriously. When he wasn't drawing up line combinations like a chess game and waxing like Scotty Bowman, Top Cop was pacing around the dressing room talking into a Bluetooth earpiece that seemed permanently fixed to his head. In fairness, he was a solid blueliner who had kept in shape since retiring from the force. But he treated beer league play like something more important than recreation, so I knew we were not going to get along.

When I announced that I would be missing all our January games because I'd be overseas on vacation, Top Cop saw an opportunity to get rid of me. "Wait for an email in the next few days," he told me in the dressing room, in front of everyone. A few days later, the email arrived. In it, he said that I was off the team because I wasn't good enough. Teammates had complained that I'd been out of position too often. I would, of course, be refunded the league fees I'd paid for the remainder of the season. I could collect the refund when I returned the team jerseys and socks. So there I was, cut from a hockey team for the first time in my life—fired from a beer league roster, no less—in mid-December. Merry fucking Christmas.

When I called up my former manager from the Beavers to tell him what had happened, including the part about my teammates complaining about my play, he said it was bullshit and that he'd be glad for me to stay on the team. He'd heard no one raise any issues, so he concluded that this must have been coming from Top Cop and no one else. Further investigation revealed that the player who couldn't afford to play the whole season was a friend of Top Cop and could afford a half season starting in January. So Top Cop had simply transferred my place on the team to him, a member of his RCMP fraternity. But he didn't have the guts to just tell me so.

I didn't know this yet when Top Cop and I met, appropriately enough, at a Tim Hortons for the refund and team gear exchange. When we sat down for coffee, he tried his best to be nice but couldn't help himself, happening to mention that he didn't like unions—a reference to my job with the Canadian Union of Public Employees. Knowing that my Beavers mates must have talked to him at some point, I didn't ask him what else he didn't like about me and stifled the urge to tell him I wasn't the biggest fan of the RCMP. Later, I had to ask him to remove me from the team's email list, as I kept receiving messages for a couple of weeks after he dumped me.

For the first time in my adult hockey life, I was cut adrift, kicked off a recreational team at age fifty-six. After returning from vacation, I mulled over what to do. I still wanted to play—my love for hockey was undiminished—but didn't know where, nor who would take me. It was midseason and rosters were set. Seeking a second opinion, I called up my friend James Oakes, whom I'd coaxed into joining the Cutting Edges back in the late 1990s. (At the time, he had thought himself already too old for the game. But after joining the Edges, he went on to play for a decade and a half before a blood clot issue forced his retirement.) Oakes told me to stop moping and call up the Edges. "Go back to them," he said. He had bumped into the new board president, a younger player named Peter Lipscombe, and said he was approachable. I brought up the long-distance issue with UBC again, but Oakes shushed me. I'd started the Edges, he said, so I belonged with them. This might be the only chance to slip in as a spare for the rest of the 2020 spring schedule. And it would be good to see some of my old teammates again, wouldn't it?

Oakes knew me well, and he was right. When I contacted Lipscombe, all I got was green lights. Sure I could spare, he said. Here's the schedule. Let us know which dates you're available. When I showed up for my first game, it was like a class reunion with some of my older teammates. "Hey, bitch, where you been?" Big hugs all around. "Welcome back, stranger!" I found out that one of my new teammates, a scrappy forward nicknamed Wrecking Ball, lived in Maple Ridge—a forty-minute drive east of New Westminster. UBC wasn't too far for *him* to drive, he said cattily, so what was *my* problem? Busted! Thanks, Wrecking Ball—this was just the kind of chirping I needed. Every game I was available to play, I did. My Edges team, one of three in the organization at the time, slotted me in at left wing as if I'd never been gone. And what do you know? I even got my number 10 back.

I felt like I'd come home. This was the first time in five years that I'd put on a Cutting Edges jersey, and it felt perfect. I was back with the team I'd started, back with my queer folk, where I belonged. I hadn't had this feeling since 2002 when I flew from Bangkok to Sydney, Australia, for a most unlikely reunion—joining my Edges mates to play at Gay Games VI, sliding easily into one of our two tournament rosters as if I hadn't been gone for two and a half years. Just thinking about it now, I get a bit misty. Somewhere along the way, I had taken the Edges for granted; I had failed to appreciate the hard work so many had put into the club over the years to keep my "baby" going and make a difference for so many others. After spending four seasons with a straight team just out of geographical convenience and then, after that team broke up, having a shitty experience with a team that didn't want me, I finally came to realize how much I missed the Cutting Edges. That shared sense of awareness about our place in the world. Our ironic humour in solidarity and support for each other and from our straight ally teammates.

Now that I was back, there was also the added bonus of getting to play with a new generation of teammates. Now and then, I even got to share the ice with talented young dangler hotties like Ryan Cheong and Dexter Dusseault. (Why the fuck had I ever left?) Suddenly, I was back in a dressing room where all the jokes were better. No more pussy and titties talk. No more "cocksucker" as opposition insult. No more being tap danced around because I might get offended. And best of all, no self-important former-Mountie-cum-realtor asshole gaslighting me about my play. Instead, I was back in a dressing room where every new player was excited to be there because they'd been looking for a team like ours. I felt the enthusiasm of younger queer players who appreciated what the Cutting Edges represented and were aware of our long history of providing that space for players just like them, an all-important safety zone where we could all just be ourselves.

I could also share my fellow veterans' smiling recognition of how lucky we all were just to still be playing our favourite sport after all these years. As my Team Green manager and long-time linemate Trevor MacNeil likes to say, "It's a great day, because we get to play HOCKEY!" For all of this, I suddenly realized, I would drive all the way to UBC in a heartbeat. And so I did. But only a few games into my return, the global COVID-19 lockdown began, and the season was suspended. Play eventually resumed months later with strict safety measures in place at the UBC Thunderbird Arena. And then, a season or two after I rejoined, the Cutting Edges membership held a vote and decided to move to 8 Rinks. Burnaby was seen as a more central location, given the club's evolving demographics. So in the end, I got to have my cake and eat it too.

"Hey, sorry I abandoned you all," I said in the dressing room at one point. "It's really good to be back. I promise never to leave again."

Well, at least until I can't skate anymore. A full-time player again since 2020–21, I will turn sixty-three shortly after the 2026–27 season begins. As of this writing, I am still skating up and down the left wing with my queer teammates, the youngest of whom weren't even born when the Cutting Edges first hit the ice in 1994.

If you come to one of our games now and I happen to be playing, you will probably hear me on the bench between shifts, screaming at the top of my lungs, "Let's go, Edges!"

APPENDIX

COMING OUT IN THE NHL

A STRATEGIC COMMUNICATIONS PLAN FOR PLAYERS AND TEAMS

By Daniel Gawthrop

Introduction

This plan, which applies to gay and bisexual players, is intended to harmonize the intentions of the National Hockey League's Hockey Is for Everyone campaign and the principles of You Can Play with the spirit of Clause 7.2 of the NHLPA collective agreement, which prohibits discrimination based on sexual orientation. This plan recognizes the desire of all NHL players to achieve their personal best as players and as members of their community. If adopted by players in coordination with their respective NHL teams, it will be to both parties' mutual benefit. If executed properly, it will enhance fan engagement and increase revenues for merchandise related to the players concerned while netting other positive results, including but not limited to a reduction in use of the league's player assistance program.

This plan recognizes that NHL hockey is a team game first. The league and NHLPA place the highest priority on fostering an environment that allows teams to achieve excellence without placing any one player above his teammates. Players can be celebrated for individual achievements, but all players strive for their personal lives and activities not to become a distraction to the team's goals of winning games, making the playoffs, and competing for the Stanley Cup. At the same time, an increasing focus on improving mental health outcomes has shown that on-ice performance in the NHL has seen significant improvement when the player is able to pursue his goals unencumbered by mental health challenges. Such challenges can include struggles for self-expression caused by heterosexism and homophobia in hockey culture.

This plan is aimed at assisting gay and bisexual hockey players in three different categories of career development to harmonize their personal and professional lives by coming out of the closet (by revealing, declaring, or allowing disclosure of their sexual orientation) while minimizing that disclosure's potentially distracting effects on their respective teams. The player categories are as follows:

1. **Players under contract who have played and continue to play in the NHL (Veterans):** As regular roster players, these players are well known to their fan base in varying degrees but are not yet out of the closet.
2. **Players who have been drafted by NHL teams but have yet to play an NHL game (Next Ones):** Such players may or may not be under contract, but they are not yet out of the closet either.
3. **Players who are still playing at Junior or College level and are highly touted (Prospects):** Such players are teenagers who are already out of the closet. They are projected to go high in the NHL draft within a couple of years and do not wish to hide their sexual orientation in order to get drafted

Stages of Coming Out

This section forms the entire plan, from beginning to end. (Details vary according to player category.)

Stage One

Who to Tell and What to Tell Them

1. **Veterans:** After you've informed your partner/spouse (if you have one) and your family and friends of your intention to come out, talk to your teammates, your coach, and your general manager, as well as your agent. Tell the team and your agent that you have waited too long to be transparent about your personal life and that your play has suffered as a result. The best argument for coming out is that it will make you a better player and teammate.
2. **Next Ones:** Tell your partner/spouse (if you have one), your family, friends, and agent that you plan to come out. Contact the general manager of the team that drafted you and tell them that you want to start your NHL career with complete transparency so that your teammates will know who it is they're getting.
3. **Prospects:** If you are under eighteen, tell only your parents and your partner (if you have one) of your coming-out intentions. If you're eighteen or above, also tell your agent. Your message is simple: You've never been in the closet and don't plan to be as you move up in the hockey world. This is a newer, freer generation of hockey players, and you want to be a leader off the ice as well as on it. You are talented enough to show such leadership, even at this early stage of your hockey life, and you should be commended for it.

Stage Two

Deciding When to Actually Come Out

1. **Veterans:** Do *not* come out during the Stanley Cup playoffs, or in the lead up to post-season play after the trade deadline. This will be a major distraction for your team as it's preparing for the playoffs, turning off the very people you are trying to enlist as allies. The optimum time for a veteran to come out is during the off-season, during training camp, or mid-season, depending on how your team is doing. (Of course, if you win the Cup, you could pull a move like Scott Hunter of *Heated Rivalry* by inviting your partner/spouse onto the ice to celebrate with you after your team has received the Cup—ideally if the win is on home ice. No one but a troglodyte is going to deny you ultimate happiness after all you have done for their favourite team.) If you're in a contract year, it is best to come out privately to your general manager before your agent gets into negotiations. You will know from the reaction whether or not you will want to sign with the team again, never mind whether to come out publicly while a member of that team.
2. **Next Ones:** After speaking with your agent, ask for a meeting with your general manager before your agent begins negotiations for your first contract. The team will appreciate your transparency in giving them a heads-up and will be better prepared to work with you on the rest of your strategy. (Making this decision on your own without consulting them sends the message that you're a freelancer, not a team-first kind of guy. A big mistake.)
3. **Prospects:** You've never really been "in," but you can send certain signals at various times through your social media channels—as you begin your first year with your Junior or College team, for example. During the pre-draft combine, when teams are kicking your tires to assess your personality and your values to decide whether you'd be a good draft pick, would be an ideal time to come out. The scouts' reaction will tell you everything you need to know about their organization, just as your

transparency tells them what they need to know about you. Remember, if you're a good enough player to make it this far, someone is going to draft you, regardless of your sexual orientation.

Stage Three

Going Public: Tools, Media, and Support for Coming Out

1. **Veterans:** If you are a well-established regular (a top-six forward or first pairing defender) or a superstar, hold a media conference. You will attract massive media attention—even more so if you know of other gay or bisexual players, either on your team or playing for rival teams, whom you can convince to join you at the press conference for a collective coming-out announcement (presuming that those other players have also followed Stages One and Two). There is power and solidarity in numbers, and you could make a major impact with two or more players saying, "Me too." If you would prefer a less media-intensive coming out, choose a strategic occasion (National Coming Out Day in October, a post-playoffs pride event, etc.) to post photos of yourself and your partner/spouse on Instagram. This will start discussion; then it's up to individual reporters to decide whether or not to ask you about it directly. Someone will.
2. **Next Ones:** Use social media to post a photo of yourself with gay friends or with your partner/spouse at an obviously gay event, such as Pride, a fundraiser, etc. Then share it across your networks and get your friends and supporters to share it as well, with encouraging comments. (Don't bother with a media conference. Unless you're a top-three draft pick, you're not well known enough to draw that level of media attention and don't want to come off as a prima donna. That only feeds into stereotype.)
3. **Prospects:** Do as the Next Ones do, and with as many social media posts as you think appropriate. This way, any team interested in you will know from the outset that this is who you are and it's part of the overall package they're getting if they draft you. (One caveat: Don't post too often,

as you don't want to send the message that you spend too much time on social media and are thus easily distracted. It might be a deal breaker for your potential employer.)

Stage Four

Follow-Up

1. **Veterans:** After the media conference, offer individual interviews to reporters for more information about your life as a gay or bisexual man. Make it clear that you will only be available for the next two weeks to discuss your sexual orientation. After that, the subject will be closed, and you will only discuss your hockey performance and other hockey-related issues. Anyone seeking more information on your sexuality can refer to what's already on the record. Make sure you are clear on this so that, after those two weeks, reporters contacting you will know they can only ask about hockey issues. Follow up the media conference with social media posts on Instagram, TikTok, and/or Facebook showing yourself in pride contexts, with or without loved ones. But no more interviews.
2. **Next Ones:** Unless you are pursued by reporters (unlikely, unless you're one of those top picks or an otherwise highly touted player), do nothing. Just let the chips fall where they may. If you haven't been sent back to your Junior team or have aged out of it, simply resume your focus on doing your best in the minors so that you can get a call-up to the Show ASAP. If you are pursued by reporters, keep your agent and general manager informed as you do follow-up work similar to that of the Veterans. And observe the same caveat about doing no more interviews about sexual orientation after two weeks.
3. **Prospects:** No follow-up necessary, other than to continue normalizing your sexual orientation with occasional social media posts about your gay social life and community. You're headed for a big draft day, and nothing will derail it. Remember: Of all three categories, you're the one who's most in the driver's seat with this comms plan because you are already out of the closet. It's up to the rest of the world to catch up with you.

Stage Five (A)

What to Do If Your Coming-Out Strategy Backfires (i.e., you draw hostile fan reaction or right-wing homophobic backlash)

1. **Veterans:** Since the blowback is hitting you personally, stay out of the fray and have allies, such as You Can Play, speak up for you. You need to preserve your dignity and the integrity of your announcement. Your GM, coach, teammates, and even league officials—if it comes to that—will expose the bigotry against you for what it is. You have already established your reputation in the league as a respected player. That's not going to change because of a few knuckle-dragging homophobes. For fans who don't understand what all the fuss is about but don't otherwise object, have your allies do brief interviews to explain why defending human rights is important.
2. **Next Ones:** Same advice: Don't dignify the bigots by engaging with them. Your agent and GM can put them in their place.
3. **Prospects:** Get your friends to go on all social media and shame the bigots with as many damningly critical posts as possible.

Stage Five (B)

How to Deal With a Sudden Surge in Fan Support (for Veterans only)

As well as media interest, your coming-out announcement will draw a great deal of fan interest. There will be a major lift in merchandise orders for your jersey, autograph-hunters, and other fans just wanting to see you, talk to you, and touch you. Consult with your agent, GM, and coach on the best way to respond to this more positive result that allows you to deal with high-volume fan feedback in a healthy way. Once the media cycle has ended and your coming-out announcement has run its course, don't forget to give yourself a pat on the back. As well as relieving yourself of a lifelong burden, you have just made the NHL—and the hockey community at large—a better and more interesting place to be. Congratulations!

ACKNOWLEDGMENTS

Every Canadian writer who loves the game thinks about writing a hockey book someday. But *Cutting Edge* was only possible because a personal dream that became reality—finding a safer space for gay men to play hockey—led to something more significant. The phenomenal growth of the Cutting Edges as a hockey association has only been possible because, over the decades, so many outstanding individuals have stepped up to handle day-to-day operations while ensuring the community presence that all such organizations need to be successful. So, my first thanks go to a couple of players to whom this book is dedicated: Kevin Griffin, for the organizing and outreach that got us off the ground and kept us running, and Trevor MacNeil, whose spirit of voluntarism and dedication to the Edges has been constant since he arrived in season two.

Thanks as well to everyone else who has served on our board of directors since 1998. A few deserve thanks for their assistance while I produced *Cutting Edge*. Then vice-president and community outreach director Dave Wodchis, when not inspiring me with his tireless dedication to the Edges or his on-ice improvement as a fellow player over sixty, kept me abreast of team developments while weighing in on hockey politics and suggesting source material. Former president Reid Hearsum shared his thoughtful insights about hockey, community, and changes in the organization over many conversations. And current president Kyle McCarthy lined up player interviews and accommodated other requests while handling media calls during the busiest period of news interest in Cutting Edges history. And thanks to webmaster Trevor Luu, for stickhandling my edit of the Edges' origin story for the association's website.

I am also much obliged to Cutting Edges Michael Neilands and Colin Ratushniak for providing valuable contacts and to those Edges who graciously agreed to formal interviews: Kevin Griffin, Reid Hearsum, Kade Lacasse, Kao Lawrie, and Sam Punzo. Thanks as well to Sand Northrup, Justin Rogers, Peter Thomas, and Robert Thompson for their interviews, and to Cutting Edges alumni Paul Isaacs for sharing his story and Russ Neely for correcting assumptions about his. I am very grateful to You Can Play's Ren Dawe, former Olympic athlete and *Outspoken* author Betty Baxter, and fellow writer pals Carellin Brooks and Brett Josef Grubisic for their effusive blurbs, and to Daniel Collins for providing his fabulous *Gay Athletes* portrait of me from 1990. I'm also grateful to my extended Gawthrop clan, and to friends and colleagues who've cheered on this project, provided source material, and shared opinions on all things hockey and/or queer: Steven Beasley, Ryan Boyce, Greg Burkitt, Steve Campeau, James Chai, Leo Cooper, David Fleming, Rod Germaine, Trevor Marc Hughes, Douglas Victor Janoff, Don Larventz, Trevor Loke, Chris Losito, Lisa Lowe, Rolf Maurer, Leo McGrady, Ian McLean, Roseanne Moran, Erin Mullan, Troy Myers, James Oakes, Marc Piché, Walter Quan, Michel Ritchie, Luke Sandford, Bernard von Schulmann, Nik Sheehan, George Stanley, Janet Szliske, Richard Theriault, Colin Welch, Rob Wiltzen, and Matt Yun. (Sorry to anyone I have missed.)

It's been great working with Arsenal Pulp Press again. I am especially indebted to publisher Brian Lam and associate publisher Robert Ballantyne for believing in this book before anyone had heard of Shane Hollander or Ilya Rozanov. And kudos to the Arsenal team for their fabulous work getting *Cutting Edge* ready for puck drop. Editor Catharine Chen worked through multiple drafts, even as *Heated Rivalry* kept moving the goalposts of queer hockey culture in real time. And thanks to associate editor JC Cham, proofreader Alison Strobel, production manager Jazmin Welch, designer Rebecca Poulin, marketing and publicity director Cynara Geissler, marketing assistant Erin Chan, and media coordinators Rachel Sentes (Canada) and Beth Parker (US).

Finally, I am most indebted to my husband, Saw Aung Htwe Nyunt Lay (Lune). As if two decades of putting up with my stinky equipment drying off in the living room after games and all my swearing at the Canucks on TV while they lose again weren't enough, Lune also had to endure the 24-7 obsession this sport became while I was writing this book. Kop khun kha, Sweetie!

NOTES

Prologue: Hockey's First Gay Superstar

1 Michael McKinley, *Putting a Roof on Winter: Hockey's Rise from Sport to Spectacle* (Greystone Books, 2000), 89–90.

2 McKinley, *Putting a Roof on Winter*, 90.

3 John Davies, *The Legend of Hobey Baker* (Little, Brown & Co., 1966).

4 Spyboy1, "1911–12 Princeton Tigers Hobey Baker Jersey," *Third String Goalie* (blog), January 15, 2015, https://thirdstringgoalie.blogspot.com/2015/01/1911-12-princeton-tigers-hobey-baker.html.

5 Lance Simmens, "Hobey Baker: An Incredible Story of Sportsmanship," *HuffPost*, April 9, 2014, https://www.huffpost.com/entry/hobey-baker-an-incredible_b_5117791.

6 Arthur Mizener, "F. Scott Fitzgerald: A Biography," *The Atlantic*, December 1950, https://www.theatlantic.com/magazine/archive/1950/12/f-scott-fitzgerald-a-biography/640064/.

7 Wikipedia, "Percy Rivington Pyne 2nd," last modified February 6, 2026, https://en.wikipedia.org/wiki/Percy_Rivington_Pyne_2nd.

8 David Duchovny, host, *Searching for Hobey Baker*, podcast, episode 3, "Going West," 30 for 30 Podcasts, ESPN, July 3, 2024, https://www.espn.com.au/radio/play/_/id/40332504.

9 David Duchovny, host, *Searching for Hobey Baker*, podcast, episode 2, "The Lost Generation," 30 for 30 Podcasts, ESPN, July 3, 2024, https://www.espn.com/radio/play/_/id/40332502.

Chapter 1: The Whitest Game You Can Name

10 Morley Callaghan, "The Game That Makes a Nation," *New World* 3, no. 12 (February 1943), quoted in Michael McKinley, *Hockey: A People's History* (McClelland & Stewart, 2006), 129.

11 Callaghan, "The Game That Makes a Nation," quoted in McKinley, *Hockey*, 129.

12 Michael McKinley, *Etched in Ice: A Tribute to Hockey's Defining Moments* (Greystone Books, 1998), 29.

13 McKinley, *Etched in Ice*, 29.

14 Ken Dryden, *The Game*, 20th anniversary ed. (Wiley, 2005), 276.

15 Marc Dumont, "Guy Lafleur's Undeniable Legacy as a Superstar," Canadiens, April 24, 2022, https://www.nhl.com/canadiens/news/guy-lafleur-s-undeniable-legacy-as-a-superstar-333303632.

16 "Guy Lafleur Won Cup Five Times in Montreal," video, posted March 22, 2017, by NHL, YouTube, 4:04, https://www.youtube.com/watch?v=99KITUbCIFk.

17 Dryden, *The Game*, 162.

Chapter 2: Elbows Up—and Gloves Off

18 "Brian Pronger," University of Toronto, accessed February 19, 2026, https://sds.utoronto.ca/brian-pronger/.

19 Brian Pronger, *The Arena of Masculinity: Sports, Homosexuality, and the Meaning of Sex* (Summerhill Press, 1990), 19–20.

20 Pronger, *Arena of Masculinity*, 22.

21 Pronger, *Arena of Masculinity*, 22.

22 Pronger, *Arena of Masculinity*, 22.

23 Pronger, *Arena of Masculinity*, 22.

24 Martin O'Malley, *Gross Misconduct: The Life of Spinner Spencer* (Penguin, 1988), 16.

25 O'Malley, *Gross Misconduct*, 81.

26 O'Malley, *Gross Misconduct*, 81.

27 "Bobby Clarke's Dirty Slash—The Most Controversial Play of the 1972 Summit Series!" video, posted March 1, 2022, by Sport Story, YouTube, 2:53, https://www.youtube.com/watch?v=ehvzTvsnFoM.

28 Dave Redekop, "Cold War on Ice—Remembering the 1972 Summit Series: Part II," *Niagara Independent*, September 20, 2022, https://niagaraindependent.ca/cold-war-on-ice-remembering-the-1972-summit-series-part-ii/.

29 Andrew Podnieks, *Team Canada 1972: The Official 40th Anniversary Celebration of the Summit Series* (Fenn / McClelland & Stewart, 2012), 221, 225.

30 "Summit on Ice," video, posted March 1, 2022, by Ugazzovision, YouTube, 2:03:16, https://www.youtube.com/watch?v=S37ROgIp3vo. This is the full 1992 *CBC Family Hour* documentary on the historic 1972 Canada–Russia hockey series.

31 Ken Dryden, *Game Change: The Life and Death of Steve Montador and the Future of Hockey* (Signal / McClelland & Stewart, 2017), 31.

32 Dave Bidini, *The Best Game You Can Name* (McClelland & Stewart, 2005), 221.

33 Bidini, *Best Game*, 246–47.

34 Dryden, *Game Change*, 56.

35 Dryden, *Game Change*, 57.

36 Dryden, *Game Change*, 57.

37 Pierre Saint-Arnaud, "NHL Enforcers Die 10 Years Younger Than Their Fellow Players, Study Finds," CBC Sports, May 10, 2023, https://www.cbc.ca/sports/hockey/nhl/nhl-enforcers-study-1.6838788.

Chapter 3: Adult Survivors of *Hockey Night in Canada*

38 William Bridel, in "'What Do You Mean You Don't Play Hockey ... You a Queer or Somethin'?': Reflections on Life as a Non-Hockey Playing Canadian Boy," in *Overcoming the Neutral Zone Trap: Hockey's Agents of Change*, edited by Cheryl A. MacDonald and Jonathon R.J. Edwards (University of Alberta Press, 2021), 229, 232.

Chapter 4: A Gay Games Sport

39 Brian Pronger, *The Arena of Masculinity: Sports, Homosexuality, and the Meaning of Sex* (Summerhill Press, 1990), 270.

40 Pronger, *Arena of Masculinity*, 270.

41 Stan Persky, "Talking Gay Without Saying a Word," *Vancouver Sun*, June 2, 1990.

Chapter 5: The Cutting Edges

42 "Thirty Years of the Cutting Edges," produced and directed by Joy Warburton for History 400 (Oral History), University of British Columbia, Fall 2024.

Chapter 6: Pavel Bure and Me

43 Paul Feinberg, "Rocket in Whose Pocket?," *LA Weekly*, June 17–23, 1994.

44 Mike Ulmer, "Purring over Bure, Panthers," *National Post*, February 10, 1999.

Chapter 7: Toxic Masculinity

45 Rick Westhead, *We Breed Lions: Confronting Canada's Troubled Hockey Culture* (Toronto: Penguin Random House, 2025), 97.

46 Robert McG. Thomas Jr., "Warning on AIDS Surprises NHL," *New York Times*, December 4, 1991.

47 Rosie DiManno, *Coach* (Doubleday, 2012), 91.

48 DiManno, *Coach*, 90–91.

49 DiManno, *Coach*, 90–91.

50 Brenda Bouw, "A Bad Choice Not to Answer: Roch Voisine and Why His Sexuality Was Kept Under Wraps," *National Post*, December 6, 2000.

51 Cheryl A. MacDonald and Brock McGillis, "'I Never Thought I'd Get Here, I Thought I'd Be Dead'": An In-Depth Interview with an Openly Gay Former Professional Ice Hockey Player," in *Overcoming the Neutral Zone Trap: Hockey's Agents of Change*, edited by Cheryl A. MacDonald and Jonathon R.J. Edwards (University of Alberta Press, 2021), 215.

52 MacDonald and McGillis, "'I Never Thought I'd Get Here,'" 215.

53 Richard M. Lapp and Silas White, *Local Heroes: A History of the Western Hockey League* (Harbour Publishing, 1993).

54 Lapp and White, *Local Heroes*, 199–200.

55 Daniel Gawthrop, "Sheldon Kennedy's Long, Dark Road," *Xtra! West*, September 18, 1998.

56 Sheldon Kennedy with James Grainger, *Why I Didn't Say Anything: The Sheldon Kennedy Story* (Insomniac Press, 2006).

57 Kennedy, *Why I Didn't Say Anything*, 81.

58 Kennedy, *Why I Didn't Say Anything*, 82.

59 Kennedy, *Why I Didn't Say Anything*, 89.

60 Kennedy, *Why I Didn't Say Anything*, 145.

61 Kennedy, *Why I Didn't Say Anything*, 203.

62 Theo Fleury with Kirstie McLellan Day, *Playing with Fire* (HarperCollins, 2009).

63 Fleury, *Playing with Fire*, 152.

64 Fleury, *Playing with Fire*, 152–53.

65 Fleury, *Playing with Fire*, 152, 330–31.

66 Corey Hirsch with Sean Patrick Conboy, *The Save of My Life: My Journey Out of the Dark* (HarperCollins, 2022).

67 Daniel Gawthrop, "Goaltender, Heal Thyself," *The British Columbia Review*, November 11, 2022, https://thebcreview.ca/2022/11/11/1618-gawthrop-hirsch/.

68 Hirsch, *Save of My Life*, 10.

69 Hirsch, *Save of My Life*, 13.

70 Hirsch, *Save of My Life*, 14–15.

71 Hirsch, *Save of My Life*, 15.

72 Gawthrop, "Goaltender, Heal Thyself."

73 Andrea Werhun, "Porn Isn't to Blame for Sexual Assault," *Globe and Mail*, June 13, 2005.

74 Richard Raycraft, "Hockey Canada Paid Out $8.9 Million in Sexual Abuse Settlements Since 1989," CBC News, July 27, 2022, https://www.cbc.ca/news/politics/hockey-canada-house-of-commons-committee-1.6533439.

75 Raycraft, "Hockey Canada Paid Out $8.9 Million."

76 Daniel Gawthrop, "Hockey's Homo-Conflicted Bro Culture," Substack, July 23, 2025, https://danielgawthrop.substack.com/p/hockeys-homo-conflicted-bro-culture.

77 Catherine Houston et al., "'I Want Justice and More': Loreto, Carcillo, and Dominant Narratives of Hockey Culture on Twitter," in *Overcoming the Neutral Zone Trap: Hockey's Agents of Change*, edited by Cheryl A. MacDonald and Jonathon R.J. Edwards (University of Alberta Press, 2021), 60.

78 *Carcillo v. Canadian Hockey League, ONSC 886* (Ontario Superior Court, 2023) at 21, https://assets.kmlaw.ca/wp-content/uploads/2023/04/Carcillo_v_Canadian_Hockey_League_Reasons_for_Decision_Certification_Perell_J_03_Feb_2023.pdf.

79 *Carcillo v. Canadian Hockey League*, at 21.

80 Dan Robson, Katie Strang, and Ian Mendes, "'We Haven't Learned a Damned Thing': Sexual Violence Is Embedded in Junior Hockey Culture," *The Athletic*, June 20, 2022, https://www.nytimes.com/athletic/3373130/2022/06/20/sexual-violence-junior-hockey/.

81 Laura Robinson, *Crossing the Line: Violence and Sexual Assault in Canada's National Sport* (McClelland & Stewart, 1998).

82 Robson et al., "'We Haven't Learned a Damned Thing.'"

83 Robson et al., "'We Haven't Learned a Damned Thing.'"

84 Robson et al., "'We Haven't Learned a Damned Thing.'"

85 Grant Robertson, "The Hockey Canada Sexual-Assault Trial Is Over, but Conversations About the Sport's Culture Continue," *Globe and Mail*, July 31, 2025.

86 Robertson, "The Hockey Canada Sexual-Assault Trial Is Over."

87 Robertson, "Hockey Canada Sexual-Assault Trial Is Over."

88 Robertson, "Hockey Canada Sexual-Assault Trial Is Over."

89 Westhead, *We Breed Lions*, xii.

90 Westhead, *We Breed Lions*, 20, 154.

Chapter 8: A Woman's Place Is in the Hall of Fame

91 Michael McKinley, *Etched in Ice: A Tribute to Hockey's Defining Moments* (Greystone, 1998), 45.

92 Michael McKinley, *Hockey: A People's History* (McClelland & Stewart, 2006), 80.

93 Wayne Norton, *Women on Ice: The Early Years of Women's Hockey in Western Canada* (Ronsdale Press, 2009), 11.

94 Norton, *Women on Ice*, 11.

95 "1921–22 Vancouver Amazons Women's Hockey Team," BC Sports Hall of Fame, accessed February 26, 2026, https://bcsportshall.com/honoured_member/1921-22-vancouver-amazons-womens-hockey-team/.

96 "1921–22 Vancouver Amazons."

97 "1921–22 Vancouver Amazons."

98 Norton, *Women on Ice*, 22.

99 Norton, *Women on Ice*, 67–68.

100 Norton, *Women on Ice*, 68.

101 McKinley, *Hockey*, 78.

102 McKinley, *Hockey*, 126.

103 McKinley, *Etched in Ice*, 45.

104 Norton, *Women on Ice*, 9.

105 Hayley Wickenheiser, *Over the Boards: Lessons from the Ice* (Viking, 2021), 13.

106 Wickenheiser, *Over the Boards*, 13.

107 Wickenheiser, *Over the Boards*, 29–30.

108 Wickenheiser, *Over the Boards*, 82–83.

109 Karissa Donkin, *Breakaway: The PWHL and the Women Who Changed the Game* (Goose Lane Editions, 2025).

110 Donkin, *Breakaway*, 38.

111 Donkin, *Breakaway*, 43.

112 Donkin, *Breakaway*, 119.

113 Donkin, Breakaway, 15.

114 Alex Prewitt, "For Married Pairs of Ex-Players, the U.S.–Canada Women's Hockey Rivalry Is Uniquely Complicated," *Sports Illustrated*, February 7, 2022, https://www.si.com/olympics/2022/02/07/us-canada-rivalry-womens-hockey-married-couples-former-players-beijing.

Chapter 9: De-Whitening the Game

115 Willie O'Ree with Michael McKinley, *Willie: The Game-Changing Story of the NHL's First Black Player* (Penguin Random House, 2020).

116 David Giddens, "Willie O'Ree Looked Past and Fought Racism to Become NHL's 1st Black Player," CBC Sports, February 21, 2021, https://www.cbc.ca/sports/hockey/book-review-willie-oree-1.5914547.

117 *The Changing Face of Hockey: Diversity in Our Game*, exhibit description at the Hockey Hall of Fame, Toronto, ON, October 11, 2025.

118 *The Changing Face of Hockey* exhibit description.

119 Fred Sasakamoose, *Call Me Indian: From the Trauma of Residential School to Becoming the NHL's First Treaty Indigenous Player* (Penguin Random House, 2022), 118.

120 Sasakamoose, *Call Me Indian*, 127.

121 Sasakamoose, *Call Me Indian*, 127.

122 Sasakamoose, *Call Me Indian*, 131.

123 Sasakamoose, *Call Me Indian*, 131.

124 Daniel Gawthrop, "So Long, Grapes," Daniel Gawthrop, November 12, 2019, https://www.danielgawthrop.com/so-long-grapes/.

125 "John Tortorella Would Bench Players Who Sit During National Anthem," *Sports Illustrated*, September 6, 2016, https://www.si.com/nhl/2016/09/07/john-tortorella-national-anthem-players-bench-sitting.

126 Greg Wyshnyski, "John Tortorella Reverses Hardline Stance on Kneeling," ESPN, June 10, 2020, https://www.espn.com/nhl/story/_/id/29293541/john-tortorella-reverses-hardline-stance-kneeling.

127 Pete Blackburn and Shanna McCarriston, "Matt Dumba, Evander Kane Criticize NHL's Lack of Meaningful Response to Jacob Blake Shooting," CBS Sports, August 27, 2020, https://www.cbssports.com/nhl/news/matt-dumba-evander-kane-criticize-nhls-lack-of-meaningful-response-to-jacob-blake-shooting/.

128 Joshua Clipperton, "NHL Postpones Remainder of Weekday Games in Support of Protests Against Police Shootings," CBC Sports, August 28, 2020, https://www.cbc.ca/sports/hockey/nhl/nhl-news-aug-27-1.5701982.

129 Julian McKenzie, "Amid DEI Attacks and Dwindling Sponsors, Hockey Diversity Alliance Skates On," *The Athletic*, August 22, 2025, https://www.nytimes.com/athletic/6549367/2025/08/22/hockey-diversity-alliance-nhl-dei-inclusion/.

130 McKenzie, "DEI Attacks and Dwindling Sponsors."

131 McKenzie, "DEI Attacks and Dwindling Sponsors."

Chapter 10: Breaking the Hockey Binary

132 Michael McKinley, *Hockey: A People's History* (McClelland & Stewart, 2006), 78.

133 McKinley, *Hockey*, 79.

134 McKinley, *Hockey*, 79.

135 See Bruce Yaccato, "Albertine Lapensée," *The Canadian Encyclopedia*, December 9, 2013, https://thecanadianencyclopedia.ca/en/article/albertine-lapensee.

136 Harrison Browne and Rachel Browne, *Let Us Play: Winning the Battle for Gender Diverse Athletes* (Beacon Press, 2025), xii.

137 Michele Steele, "NWHL Player Harrison Browne Comes Out as a Transgender Man," ESPN, October 6, 2016, https://www.espn.com/espnw/sports/story/_/id/17727834/nwhl-player-harrison-browne-comes-transgender-man.

138 Browne and Browne, *Let Us Play*, 114–115.

139 Browne and Browne, *Let Us Play*, 124.

140 Browne and Browne, *Let Us Play*, 124.

141 Donnovan Bennett, "Hockey Is for Everyone: The Jessica Platt Story," Sportsnet, February 6, 2018, https://www.sportsnet.ca/hockey/nhl/hockey-everyone-jessica-platt-story/.

142 Browne and Browne, *Let Us Play*, xvii–xviii.

143 Browne and Browne, *Let Us Play*, 3.

Chapter 11: Performative Allyship

144 Alin Mateescu, "Fan Fuel: Brian Burke's 10 Defining Moments as Maple Leafs GM," Sportsnet, January 10, 2013, https://www.sportsnet.ca/fan-fuel/brian-burke-fired-dave-nonis-gm-10-defining-moments/.

145 Brian Burke with Stephen Brunt, *Burke's Law: A Life in Hockey* (Penguin, 2020), 167.

146 "Blackhawks' Andrew Shaw Suspended One Game for Slur," ESPN, April 20, 2016, https://www.espn.com/nhl/story/_/id/15281995/blackhawks-forward-andrew-shaw-suspended-one-game-anti-gay-slur.

147 Burke, *Burke's Law*, 247.

148 Ken Dryden, *Game Change: The Life and Death of Steve Montador and the Future of Hockey* (Signal / McClelland & Stewart, 2017), 330–331.

149 Dryden, *Game Change*, 329.

150 "Judge Denies Class-Action Status for NHL Concussion Lawsuit," ESPN, July 13, 2018, https://www.espn.com/nhl/story/_/id/24088993/judge-denies-class-action-status-former-players-suing-nhl-concussions.

151 Stephen Whyno, "NHL, Retired Players Reach $19M Concussion Settlement," Associated Press, November 13, 2018, https://apnews.com/nhl-retired-players-reach-19m-concussions-settlement-27e7392bf42a41e598054b3f0c52730a.

152 Matt Larkin, "LGBTQ+ Inclusivity in Hockey: What's Wrong, and What Must Change?," *Hockey News*, March 10, 2021, https://thehockeynews.com/news/news/lgbtq-inclusivity-in-hockey-whats-wrong-and-what-must-change.

153 National Hockey League, *Accelerating Diversity & Inclusion: NHL Report on Strategies, Initiatives, and Progress* (NHL, October 2022), introduction by the commissioner, 5–6, https://media.d3.nhle.com/image/private/t_document/prd/s9u6r1ghs5g5hoz8ucbo.pdf.

154 Larkin, "LGBTQ+ Inclusivity in Hockey."

155 Cheryl A. MacDonald and Brock McGillis, "'I Never Thought I'd Get Here, I Thought I'd Be Dead': An In-Depth Interview with an Openly Gay Former Professional Ice Hockey Player," in *Overcoming the Neutral Zone Trap: Hockey's Agents of Change*, edited by Cheryl A. MacDonald and Jonathon R.J. Edwards (University of Alberta Press, 2021), 220.

156 Ken Schultz, "NHL Commissioner Gary Bettman Is Outsports 2023 Asshole of the Year," Outsports, December 18, 2023, https://www.outsports.com/2023/12/18/23997577/gary-bettman-nhl-gay-pride-tape-outsports-award-jerseys-nhl-homophobia-hockey/.

157 Daniel Gawthrop, "National Hockey League Pride Nights: Not Everyone on the Ice Is a Dinosaur," Dooneyscafe.com, March 28, 2023, https://dooneyscafe.com/national-hockey-league-pride-nights-not-everyone-on-the-ice-is-a-dinosaur/.

158 Gawthrop, "National Hockey League Pride Nights."

159 "Burke Reassures LGBTQ+ Community to Not Get Discouraged by NHL Pride Night Dissenters," Sportsnet, March 25, 2023, https://www.sportsnet.ca/nhl/video/burke-reassures-lgbtq-community-to-not-get-discouraged-by-nhl-pride-night-dissenters/.

160 Frankie de la Cretaz, "Opinion: The NHL Shows Why There Are So Few Openly Gay Athletes in Men's Sports," CNN, October 11, 2023, https://www.cnn.com/2023/10/11/opinions/nhl-pride-tape-ban-coming-out-day-de-la-cretaz.

161 You Can Play (@youcanplayteam), "If hockey is for everyone, this is not the way forward," Instagram, October 10, 2023, https://www.instagram.com/p/CyOrtj2A9s3/.

162 Schultz, "NHL Commissioner Gary Bettman Is Outsports 2023 Asshole of the Year."

163 "Keeping Men Out of Women's Sports," The White House, February 5, 2025, https://www.whitehouse.gov/presidential-actions/2025/02/keeping-men-out-of-womens-sports/.

164 William Douglas, "O'Ree Finalist Spotlight: Andrew Sobotka," NHL, May 13, 2025, https://www.nhl.com/news/willie-oree-community-hero-award-finalist-spotlight-andrew-sobotka.

165 The Cutting Edges (@cuttingedgeshockey), "The NHL Unites Pride Cup was more than just hockey," Instagram, March 4, 2026, https://www.instagram.com/p/DVdCvcsleHj.

Chapter 12: *Heated Rivalry* and the NHL Closet

166 Marie-Eve Tremblay, host, *Corde Sensible*, podcast, "Homosexualité au Hockey: Un Tabou," interview with Georges Laraque, Radio-Canada, October 26, 2018, https://ici.radio-canada.ca/ohdio/balados/5687/corde-sensible-radical-marie-eve-tremblay/418857/homosexualite-hockey-tabou-george-laraque/transcription.

167 Jacques Peterson, "How HBO's Steamy Gay Romance Heated Rivalry Tied Breaking Bad for Highest-Rated TV Episode of All Time," *Daily Mail*, December 22, 2025, https://www.dailymail.co.uk/tv/article-15406979/hbo-heated-rivalry-breaking-bad.html.

168 Angelina Trefilova, "'Heated Rivalry' Catches Fire in Russia Despite Kremlin's Anti-LGBTQ+ Repressions," *Moscow Times*, January 15, 2026, https://www.themoscowtimes.com/2026/01/15/heated-rivalry-catches-fire-in-russia-despite-kremlins-anti-lgbtq-repressions-a91681.

169 Eden Chipperfield, "*Heated Rivalry*'s Hot Hockey Romance Sparks Conversations Around Inclusivity," *BCIT News*, January 12, 2026, https://bcitnews.com/heated-rivalrys-hot-hockey-romance-sparks-conversations-around-inclusivity/.

170 Sarah Grochowski, "No One Should Have to Choose: Heated Rivalry Inspires LGBTQ+ Players to Reclaim Hockey in Vancouver," *Vancouver Sun*, January 17, 2026, https://vancouversun.com/news/heated-rivalry-inspires-lgbtq-players-reclaim-hockey-vancouver.

171 Julian McKenzie, "'Heated Rivalry' Star François Arnaud Calls on NHL to Improve LGBTQ+ Inclusion," *The Athletic*, January 17, 2026, https://www.nytimes.com/athletic/6977587/2026/01/16/heated-rivalry-francois-arnaud-nhl-hockey/.

172 Cyd Zeigler, "'Heated Rivalry' Is Driving Huge NHL Ticket Sales Among New Gay Fans, Outsports Finds," Outsports, December 24, 2025, https://www.outsports.com/2025/12/24/24124922/heated-rivalry-nhl-ticket-sales-pride-night-gay-lgbtq-fans/.

173 "Heated Rivalry Is a Hit. Can It Change Hockey Culture?" | The Current, video, posted January 9, 2026, by CBC News, YouTube, 24:41, https://www.youtube.com/watch?v=bt7aigmR_FI.

174 J.P. Catungal, *Heated Rivalry: A Syllabus* (University of British Columbia, 2025), https://www.canva.com/design/DAG9Oc2pxZo/xHjUfIHMAMM7j6lo2_QPFQ/view.

175 Becki Ross, "Heated Rivalry: A Lesbian Love Story," Facebook, February 5, 2026, https://www.facebook.com/groups/1947574676171514/posts/1990469145215400/.

176 Seth Abramovitch, "Down to Puck: Why Women Are Going Wild for 'Heated Rivalry,' *The Hollywood Reporter*, December 22, 2025, https://www.hollywoodreporter.com/tv/tv-features/heated-rivalry-hbo-max-gay-drama-hockey-players-hit-women-1236456083/.

177 Sean Gentille, "'Heated Rivalry' Has a Fan in NHL Commissioner Gary Bettman: 'I Binged It in One Night,'" *The Athletic*, January 16, 2026, https://www.nytimes.com/athletic/6975677/2026/01/15/heated-rivalry-nhl-gary-bettman-hockey/.

178 Tim Chan, "This Former NHL Player Says 'Heated Rivalry's' Hockey Romance Could Happen in Real Life," *Rolling Stone*, December 7, 2025, https://www.rollingstone.com/product-recommendations/books/is-heated-rivarly-show-book-based-on-true-story-1235479361/.

179 Alastair James, "Hockey's First Out Gay Pro Says Heated Rivalry Won't Help Players Come Out," *Pink News*, December 15, 2025, https://www.thepinknews.com/2025/12/15/brock-mcgillis-says-heated-rivalry-wont-help-players-come-out/.

180 Jim Buzinski, "'Heated Rivalry' Star Says Closeted Gay Pro Athletes Have Reached Out to Him," Outsports, January 8, 2026, https://www.outsports.com/2026/1/8/24125556/heated-rivalry-hudson-williams-shane-hollander-andy-cohen-gay-interview/.

181 Brian Swane, "New Condors Defenceman Luke Prokop Says It's Time to 'Get in a Fight or Two,'" *The Hockey Writers*, August 16, 2025, https://thehockeywriters.com/new-condors-defenceman-luke-prokop-says-time-get-fight-two/.

182 *Collective Bargaining Agreement Between National Hockey League and National Hockey League Players Association: September 16, 2012–September 15, 2022* (NHL / NHLPA, February 15, 2013), 15, https://www.nhl.com/nhl/en/v3/ext/CBA2012/NHL_NHLPA_2013_CBA.pdf.

183 Roger G. LeBlanc, "Uncovering the Conspiracy of Silence of Gay Hockey Players in the NHL," in *Overcoming the Neutral Zone Trap: Hockey's Agents of Change*, edited by Cheryl A. MacDonald and Jonathon R.J. Edwards (University of Alberta Press, 2021), 179–210.

184 LeBlanc, "Uncovering the Conspiracy of Silence," 188.

185 LeBlanc, "Uncovering the Conspiracy of Silence," 189.

186 LeBlanc, "Uncovering the Conspiracy of Silence," 196.

187 Michael Brown, "New Research Offers Insights Into What Keeps Gay Hockey Players from Coming Out," Folio, University of Alberta, February 13, 2019, https://www.ualberta.ca/en/folio/2019/02/new-research-offers-insights-into-what-keeps-gay-hockey-players-from-coming-out.html.

188 Matt Larkin, "LGBTQ+ Inclusivity in Hockey: What's Wrong, and What Must Change?," *Hockey News*, March 10, 2021, https://thehockeynews.com/news/news/lgbtq-inclusivity-in-hockey-whats-wrong-and-what-must-change.

189 "NHL Lady Byng Memorial Trophy Winners," NHL, June 12, 2025, https://www.nhl.com/news/nhl-lady-byng-memorial-trophy-winners-complete-list-287910994.

190 Harry Lyles Jr., "NHL Commissioner Gary Bettman Says League Ready for Openly Gay Player," The Comeback, June 30, 2016, https://thecomeback.com/nhl/nhl-commissioner-gary-bettman-says-league-ready-for-openly-gay-player.html.

191 "Brad Marchand Says Gay Teammate Would Be Accepted," NHL, January 19, 2017, https://www.nhl.com/news/brad-marchand-says-gay-teammate-would-be-accepted-285840476.

192 Bayne Pettinger, "In My Own Words: Bayne Pettinger," Hockey Canada, June 28, 2023, https://www.hockeycanada.ca/en-ca/news/in-my-own-words-bayne-pettinger-2023-pride.

193 Cyd Zeigler, "NHL's Most Powerful Out Gay Man Rose from Law School to General Counsel in a Decade," Outsports, October 9, 2025, https://www.outsports.com/2025/10/9/24119984/columbus-blue-jackets-peter-lovins-gay-general-counsel-nhl/.

194 Justin Rogers, "A Letter to My Younger Self," NHL, November 3, 2023, https://www.nhl.com/kraken/news/seattle-kraken-assistant-athletic-trainer-a-letter-to-my-younger-self-justin-rogers.

195 "Culture Shift | Breaking Barriers | S2, E5," video, NHL, December 23, 2024, 22:17, https://www.nhl.com/video/culture-shift-breaking-down-barriers-s2-e5-6365224934112.

Conclusion

196 Ian Kennedy, "'Shoresy' Is Not the Hockey Story We Need," Substack, November 14, 2022, https://iankennedyck.substack.com/p/shoresy-is-not-the-hockey-story-we.

197 Emma Johnston-Wheeler, "Inside Sebastian Buzzalino's Queer Reimagining of Hockey Culture," *RANGE*, March 12, 2025, https://readrange.com/sebastian-buzzalino-interview/.

198 Lucas Morneau, "Queer Newfoundland Hockey League (QNHL)," Gallery 1C03, University of Winnipeg, Manitoba, exhibit brochure (November 13, 2025–January 28, 2026), https://www.uwinnipeg.ca/art-gallery/docs/qnhl-brochure-with-links-web.pdf.

199 Mel Brown, "The PWHL Is a Gift for Queer Hockey Fans Like Me," CBC News, November 20, 2024, https://www.cbc.ca/news/canada/montreal/pwhl-queer-hockey-fans-first-person-1.7386620.

Epilogue: Forever a Cutting Edge

200 Daniel Gawthrop, "Hockey Night in Chiang Mai," *Vancouver Sun*, March 15, 2003.

IMAGE CREDITS

pp. 5 & 25 Graphics created by Rebecca Poulin with modified photos by Gerhard Crous on Unsplash
p. 18 Photo from Bettmann Archive / Getty Images
p. 45 Photo courtesy of Daniel Gawthrop
p. 81 Photo by Daniel Gawthrop
p. 91 Graphic created by Rebecca Poulin with a modified photo by Jenn G on Wikimedia Commons (CC BY-SA 2.0, https://creativecommons.org/licenses/by-sa/2.0/deed.en), https://commons.wikimedia.org/wiki/File:Yanni_Gourde_and_linesman_Travis_Gawryletz.jpg
p. 103 Photo by Daniel Collins
p. 117 Photo by Doug Shanks / *The WestEnder*
p. 142 Photo by Håkan Dahlström on Wikimedia Commons (CC BY-SA 2.0, https://creativecommons.org/licenses/by-sa/2.0/deed.en), https://commons.wikimedia.org/wiki/File:Pavel_Bure_in_Canucks_uniform.jpg
p. 147 Graphic created by Rebecca Poulin with a modified photo by Sandro Halank on Wikimedia Commons (CC BY-SA 4.0, https://creativecommons.org/licenses/by-sa/4.0/deed.en), https://commons.wikimedia.org/wiki/File:2024-10-26_Eisb%C3%A4ren_Juniors_Berlin_Frauen_gegen_Mad_Dogs_Mannheim_(Deutsche_FraueneishockeyBundesliga_2024_25)_by_Sandro_Halank%E2%80%93075.jpg
p. 190 Photo by Rh723 on Wikimedia Commons (CC BY-SA 4.0, https://creativecommons.org/licenses/by-sa/4.0/deed.en), https://commons.wikimedia.org/wiki/File:Marie-Philip_Poulin_Montreal_Victoire_2026_Takeover_Tour_(cropped).jpg
p. 200 Photo by Daniel Gawthrop
p. 219 Graphic created by Rebecca Poulin with a modified photo by Nathanaël Desmeules on Unsplash
p. 230 Photo courtesy of Sam Punzo
p. 239 Photo by Alley Rutzel
p. 270 Photo courtesy of Bell Media Inc. and Crave
p. 293 Photo by Zack Peggins / Seattle Kraken
p. 302 Photo courtesy of Sand Northrup
p. 308 Photo courtesy of Kyle McCarthy

INDEX

Photographs indicated by page numbers in italics.

Index

Photo Credit: Trevor MacNeil

DANIEL GAWTHROP is the author of six non-fiction books, including *Cutting Edge*, *The Trial of Pope Benedict*, and *The Rice Queen Diaries* (all with Arsenal Pulp Press), and one novel, *Double Karma* (Cormorant Books). A co-founder of the Cutting Edges, Vancouver's LGBTQ+ hockey association, he has written extensively about hockey for numerous publications. He lives in New Westminster, BC. ***danielgawthrop.com***